APPLIED INDUSTRIAL ORGANIZATION

APPLIED INDUSTRIAL ORGANIZATION

Towards A Theory Based Empirical Industrial Organization

Edited by

KARL AIGINGER and JORG FINSINGER

University of Linz, Institute of Economic Research, Vienna, Austria
University of Vienna, Business Economics Institute, Vienna, Austria

KLUWER ACADEMIC PUBLISHERS
DORDRECHT / BOSTON / LONDON

Library of Congress Cataloging-in-Publication Data

Applied industrial organization : towards a theory based empirical industrial organization / edited by Karl Aiginger and Jorg Finsinger.
p. cm.
ISBN 0-7923-3050-1
1. Industrial organization (Economic theory) I. Aiginger, Karl. II. Finsinger, Jörg.
HD2326.A66 1994
338.6--dc20 94-29539

ISBN 0-7923-3050-1

Published by Kluwer Academic Publishers,
P.O. Box 17, 3300 AA Dordrecht, The Netherlands.

Kluwer Academic Publishers incorporates
the publishing programmes of
D. Reidel, Martinus Nijhoff, Dr W. Junk and MTP Press.

Sold and distributed in the U.S.A. and Canada
by Kluwer Academic Publishers,
101 Philip Drive, Norwell, MA 02061, U.S.A.

In all other countries, sold and distributed
by Kluwer Academic Publishers Group,
P.O. Box 322, 3300 AH Dordrecht, The Netherlands.

Printed on acid-free paper

Printed in the Netherlands

Table of Contents

K. Aiginger and J. Finsinger (eds.), Applied Industrial Organization, 1–11.

Introduction

KARL AIGINGER and JÖRG FINSINGER

The Status of Industrial Organization and the Aim of this Book

Industrial Organization is one of the economic fields most subjected to the torrents of professional and methodological modes. The origins of IO have been marked by the conflict between the deductive and the inductive approaches. During the 1950s and 1960s, empirical research was dominant; the hypotheses under investigation were derived in a rather loose way from microeconomic theory, or from casual or even anecdotical evidence. If a theory existed, it was the socalled Structure-Conduct-Performance Paradigma, which suggested in its purest form that structure determines conduct, which itself determines performance.

Chicago versus Harvard, cross section versus time series and ultra micro versus broad aggregates are battlefields which have been well known to IO-scholars, from the beginning of IO through the present. Such dichotomies will continue to persist and are probably fruitful in a science, which simultaneously seeks to be logically stringent and of potential applicability. Looking back over history, we see that sophisticated equilibrium concepts (Nash, Bayesian, subgame-perfectness, evolutionary stability) have been developed, refined or applied for over a century. At the same time, rough rules of thumb for market delineation or "acceptable" degrees of concentration have been used for antitrust jurisdictions (merger guidelines). Industrial Organization is famous for this split; rare is the scholar able to build a bridge between these strands.

The current trend in Industrial Organization is more towards theory. Non cooperative game theory has emerged as the predominant method of analyzing the behavior of firms. Industrial organization has, in the course of this process, become to some degree the master of Economics; model classes, concepts and code words are first investigated and propagated by IO scholars and then spill over into regulation, innovative decisions, environmental economics, employment decisions, business cycle analyses, etc. Theoretical models nowadays dominate empirical applications. Within the theoretical camp, the careful study of the existence, the stability, the uniqueness and the perfection of equilibria in simplified and therefore rigid models are more popular than the modelling of a fuzzy evolution of market structure in an uncertain and constantly changing environment. Within the empirical camp the ultra micro approach dominates over industry studies, time series or panel studies are considered superior to cross sectional evidence.

The applicability of theoretical Industrial Organization to policy questions is limited by its "double embarrassment of riches", namely the multiplicity of models and the multiplicity of equilibria. This has led to the "Sutton postulate", that research should concentrate on robust predictions and on what is excluded as impossible by theory (Sutton, 1990, 1991). Robust predictions which can be derived from a relatively broad class of models are necessarily weak predictions. "Ruling out" implies that theory cannot predict which outcome will occur, but rather generates some "bound" between feasible and unfeasible results. Note that the "Sutton postulate" has a relative in empirical industrial organization: the "Schmalensee postulate" requires the robustness of empirical findings (Schmalensee, 1989). The impact of a variable should be tested under different specifications and many statistical tests ought to be carried out and reported. Robustness and significance must be checked before an author claims to have found a stylized fact.

The current book is an effort to counter this dominance of theory, by offering a perspective on the richness of the empirical frontier. The book emphasizes Industrial Organization as an empirical science. One borderline was that the more theoretical papers must at least spell out their potential empirical implications. A minority of models comes from game theory, the majority from traditional oligopoly or innovation theory. In some papers – *horribile dictu* – the starting point is a stylized fact or an empirical observation which is "recycled" into a new hypothesis. This process of moving from evidence back to theory is what P.W.S. Andrews recommended when he founded the first IO journal more than four decades ago: "If we wish to theorize fruitfully about invidivual businesses we must find out what are the facts of their behaviour and then construct a general theory especially in order to take account of those facts" (Andrews, 1952, p. 75).

Purely theoretical papers which further would add some small modification to specific theoretical models are not included in this volume. The papers focus on three seminal topics in Applied Industrial Organization. Their order of presentation has been revised in order to demonstrate current shifts in emphasis, which hopefully will continue. We begin with the *role of innovation*, proceed to the *evolution of market structure and firms*, and conclude with studies on the *determinants of performance*. Although innovation is thought to be the driving force in modern firms and industries, IO books usually deal with this topic in some later chapter. We intentionally placed it at the beginning of our book, since we believe that innovation is a factor crucial in determining the behavior of firms and economies; their behavior is not just the result of size, competition and other structural variables. We then present a collection of papers dealing with the evolution of markets and firms and their rapid change. This is in contrast to models defining a very specific and rigid environment, which is held constant up to the emergence of a sophisticated equilibrium. Such a set of equilibria marks the end of the story in the models, while in the real world, equilibria are rare phenomenona. The third part encompasses a collection of papers on the determinants of profitability (or success), which is a topic traditionally presented at the beginning of a textbook dominated by the structure conduct performance paradigma. We extend the notion of performance to include goals such as price flexibility, successful tenders and monopoly regulation.

The fifteen papers use more than a dozen very different data sets. Regionally they refer to the US European countries and Australia (none refers to developing countries or economies in transition). A few contain cross section data, some include time series. Panel data provide the most popular source for empirical research. Some data are on the firm level, some refer to aggregates of 2 or 3 digit industries. The data come not only from published statistics, but also from surveys, and in one case from experiments. We are glad to see that the multiplicity of models in theoretical research is paralleled by a new richness of data bases for empirical research. The excuse that theories cannot be tested due to a lack of data no longer seems justified. However, the data never exactly fit to the concepts, the aggregation level, and the institutional conditions necessary to test the theories rigorously. Similar problems did not prevent empirical researchers from estimating cost and production functions, applying duality theorems and estimating sophisticated consumption expenditure systems. The gap between the theoretical assumptions and concepts and the empirical world should be kept in mind and bridged as far as possible in IO as well as in other economic fields. But it is more a difference in degree than in kind.

The Role of Innovation

Scherer investigates whether the productivity slowdown in western countries and specifically in the US is due to a diminishing impact of innovation on growth.

Scherer shows that the productivity slowdown appears more severe when we carefully study problems arising from the rapidly declining prices in the computer industry. Declining prices imply severe problems not only for the supplier of durable goods, but also for the statistician. Scherer shows that outside the computer industry, the productivity decline was much faster than and that there was no revival of productivity during the eighties.

Scherer then uses two disaggregated data sets to study the impact of innovation on productivity growth. The results are good news insofar as the impact on productivity of innovation increased during the eighties, as compared to the seventies. The implied rate of return is quite substantial for product innovation, less for process innovation and innovation embodied in capital goods or material purchased from other firms.

Geroski & Machin also focus on the impact of innovation on performance. Performance here means firm growth and firm profitability, rather than aggregate productivity growth. Instead of measuring innovation as an expenditure sales ratio, innovation is defined as a discrete event of some "major innovation". Geroski and Machin use the SPRU data set, which counts the major innovations produced and used in the UK, specifically a subsample for 441 firms over the period 1972 to 1983. The authors model two effects of innovations with two different empirical approaches to test them. An innovation's first effect is a *temporary increase* in performance. This effect could be tested by introducing an innovation variable into some performance equation. The other effect is the *permanent change* in the internal capabilities of a firm. This effect could be tested by running different equations for innovating firms and non innovating firms. The paper addresses the second question and splits the sample into 98 firms which achieved a major innovation between 1972 and 1983, and 441 firms which did not. Although the data show that performance is slightly better (higher growth, higher profits) for innovating firms, the most important result is that the equations for innovating and noninnovating firms are significantly different. Innovation changes firms' behavior by making them more flexible. Therefore, profitability does not plunge during recession, and shocks can more easily be absorbed. Whereas concentration is important for the profits of the non innovating firms, the subsample of innovating firms can overcome the effects of (de)concentration. A parallel result is that reported (below) by Audretsch and Mahmood, which indicates that small innovating firms can overcome the problems arising from their suboptimal size.

Hutschenreiter & Leo investigate the Schumpeter Hypothesis that innovation increases more than proportionately with firm size. Using a new data base ("Innovation Survey") the authors cannot conform the hypothesis for the relationship between expenditures and size. The relationship between research personell and size even looks regressive. Disaggregation into industrial sectors and different types of innovation highlights interesting features of the innovation process. However, a cross section approach can be only provide a starting point into investigations of the innovation process, which is dynamic and evolutionary in nature.

The relation between theory and empirical research in modern Industrial Organization is addressed in Hey's paper. The starting point is a patent race model by Fudenberg *et al.* (1983), in which a firm that is falling behind has the potential to overtake the leading firm in a model with finite and known length. While Hey finds that the participants in his experiments did not behave inconsistently with the model, the hypothesis that the individuals were using the relevant probability distributions (for the mixed strategies) was rejected at virtually every significance level.

The following methodological critique applies to innovation models, and more generally to the multiplicity of models in Industrial Organization (on "every page of Tirole's book"). Hey fears that the theory may be on the wrong track, and experiments aggrevate the problem, when they try to mirror *extremely simple problems which have extremely complicated solutions*. Hey proposes that experiments should model complicated problems ("ill defined experiments"), the experiment should monitor actual behavior, and then provide potential explanations. *Experiments should be theory suggesting rather than theory testing.* A two stage game with a pre selection of capacity and suboptimally large number of agents is one of Hey's proposals for an "ill defined experiment". Preliminary results show that some rules of thumb and even cycles come up. This could sooner or later lead to a new theory of behavior, which explains real behavior in a complicated real world.

The Evolution of Markets and Firms

Hey's methodological critique is the bridge to this chapter. Industrial organization should not concentrate on extremely simplistic models with complicated solutions, but rather acknowledge that the real world is characterized by a complicated and rapidly changing environment.

Audretsch & Mahmood begin with the observations that the bulk of firms in each industry is small and therefore operating at a suboptimal scale, and that entry is not deterred by existing economies of scale. They use a dynamic model, in which entry is a subjective, evolutionary process, during which firms weigh their scale disadvantage against their innovation potential. Using a data set for small US firms, with biannual reports gathered between 1976 and 1986, they employ a hazard model to show that the probability of exit is larger in industries with large scale economies and smaller for firms with a larger start up size. The innovation outlays do not seem significant at the first glance. Splitting the sample into one subsample of firms investing more than 5 percent of sales into R&D and another subsample with lower innovation expenses reveals that survival in low tech industries is determined by size and economies of scale, while in the high tech sector MES (Minimum efficient scale) and start up size play no role. The greater subjectivity of knowledge in this sector spurs the start up of new firms even in the presence of scale economies.

Blonski's paper contrasts the maximizing approach ("neoclassical") with the evolutionary hypothesis, which postulates time constant routine decisions. This paper can be seen as another link between the innovation and the evolution block in this book.

Blonski models an innovation strategy in a dynamic game for an oligopolistic industry. He finds that under certain assumptions the firm's optimal strategy is constant, long term R&D investment is independent of short term innovations and the opponent's behavior. This is interpreted as a compromise between the maximizing approach and the evolutionary hypothesis.

The paper is remarkable in several respects. While it is theoretical in nature, it carefully presents four empirically testable hypotheses: (i) a constant R&D rate, (ii) the independence of profits from R&D over time, (iii) the dependence of the routine strategy on industry parameters and the value of own state change (independence of degree of interaction) and (iv) increasing R&D with the velocity of change in industry and for firms with increasing value of own state change. Secondly the paper does not seek to present a robust result, but rather specifies the conditions under which a specific result (the bridge between neoclassical and the evolutionary approach) may be achieved. It is therefore to some extent in line with Hey, who suggests that we should observe behavior in rather ill defined situations, and also with Nelson and Winter, who propose using evolutionary hypotheses when analyzing the innovation process. It contrasts however with Sutton's postulate to watch for robust results. Thirdly, Blonsky's results are in discrepancy to nearly all the empirical papers in this volume, which explain or exploit some time variance of innovations and find a significant relation between profits and innovation. But this point should not be seen as a major problem, since the regressions usually explain only a small part of the variance, and perhaps many negative results may have been suppressed, since there was no theory available capable of explaining constant innovations or random profits.

Weizsäcker addresses in a highly innovative note, a puzzle presented by two stylized facts of real world production, which cannot be explained in a static maximizing model but may stem from evolutionary processes.

The first observation is that reliance on a very small number of suppliers is a characteristic shared by most industries. The second is that the price cost margin is substantial (maybe up to 30 percent), while the profit sales ratios are rather small, thus implying that marginal costs are lower than average costs, and existing economies of scale are not exhausted.

Several balancing forces explain this situation, which can not be in static equilibrium. On the one hand, consumers incur search costs and therefore tend to purchase from a small number of suppliers. When intermediaries reduce their search costs, the product differentiation advantage is reduced, and the increased competition leads to a shake-out of suppliers. On the other hand, imitation induces the entry of new firms and thereby deconcentration. However, deconcentration creates incentives to split the market (product differentiation). Constant unexhausted economies of scale and high profits at the margin are the result of these forces and are claimed to describe an evolutionary equilibrium. Weizsäcker calls this phenomenon the law of small numbers.

The format characteristics of this equilibrium have to be worked out. The stylized facts with which the note starts may also not be entirely innocent. Managers, who claim they would like to increase sales at the existing price may disregard certain costs; empirically reported price cost margins are calculated with a large arbitrariness as to which cost component is variable and which is fixed. But markets, as defined by firms, are quite small indeed and have very few suppliers (Aiginger, 1987). Furthermore, a rapidly changing environment and unexhausted economies of scale are characteristics which were also addressed in Audretsch and Mahmood's paper on entry. The potential of economies of scale, as well as the empirical fact that concentration, size and sometimes even market share have lost their positive coefficient and, as in the papers by Aiginger, Mooslechner & Schnitzer etc. are even negative, encourages thinking along innovative lines, as proposed by Weizsäcker.

The evolution of firm structure and vertical integration is examined by *Windsperger*. He develops a concept of coordination efficiency, which is defined as the sum of transaction, risk and set up costs of the coordinated design. The first of these cost components is positively related to uncertainty. This could be a bridge to empirical results showing that profitability declines with variance of demand (Aiginger, below). Transaction specificity, transaction frequency and transaction volume are the other determinants. Windsperger then applies the concept to the evolution of the vertically integrated firm, showing that the evolution of vertically integrated firms is less likely, the more symmetric the interfirm transactions are. In comparison to Williamson's approach, there is less likelihood that vertically integrated firms will evolve.

Determinants of Performance

Performance has always been an ambiguous term in Industrial Organization. What is good for General Motors may not be good for the USA. High profitability is the goal of each firm, which may, however, decrease consumer or total surplus. Haskel addresses the question as to why profitability rose in the United Kingdom during the eighties. Aiginger and Mooslechner & Schnitzer focus on profitability differences between industries and firms in Austria. Weiss investigates the price flexibility of industries. Neumann investigates the impact of demand and market structure on the assets and leverage of firms. Domberger investigates criteria necessary for successful versus unsuccessful tenders. Dröttboom & Leininger study the success of a regulatory scheme to restrict firms from monopoly profits. To some degree, structure determines performance in all these papers, though the intervening impact of conduct, regulation and institutions destroy much of this relationship. And the feedback from performance to structure should at least be kept in mind, although it is not explicitly modelled in the following papers.

The first two papers investigate the determinants of profitability and try to bridge the gap between game theoretical hypotheses and empirical research.

Haskel addresses the question as to why profitability rose during the eighties in the United Kingdom (using a panel of 53 3-digit industries). He starts with the Cowling-Waterson-model and adds elements of varying degrees of collusion, capacity constraints and union power, thus including elements of the game theoretic models from Kreps & Scheinkman, Porter & Green and Rotemberg & Saloner. The main empirical result is that the profit decline in the early eighties was due to demand reduction, while the following increase was caused by declining union power. Collusion is procyclical and the data are therefore more in line with the Porter Green model.

Aiginger begins with the Bain story of a positive profit concentration relationship with a collusion background. He then screens the model class of supergames for potential determinants of differences in the capability of industries to collude. The empirical part employs cross section data on 91 3-digit industries and a panel of 900 firms.

The main empirical result is that profitability differences depend negatively on time variability, and positively on the predictability of demand. This is in line with the prediction of supergames that exit risk, unobservability of demand and a higher time discount limit the possibility to collude. The result is not trivial, insofar as the portfolio theory implies that profits should increase with (undiversifiable) risk.

In both papers, purists could well criticize the loose connection between the theoretical models and the empirical investigation. The models determine the behavior of individual firms, they explain results in equilibria, they relate ideally measured profits to hardly observable variables, such as coefficients of conjectural variation, time discounts, exit profitabilities, capacity limits and utility functions of unions. Much trust in the results depends upon whether the variables used in the empirical test really mirror the theoretical concepts. But both papers show that *game theoretical models may be useful for empirical research* insofar as they indicate potential determinants of profits. Both authors are careful not to claim that they tested game theoretical models. Instead, the variables used in the empirical work are related to determinants which game theoretical models claim are important. The empirical results are more or less in line with either one model or another. That this can be considered progress comes from the fact that the old concentration-performance relationship has lost its relevance: in Haskel's paper, profits rise during a period of declining concentration; Aiginger has a difficult job getting rid of the incorrect negative sign of concentration in his "plain vanilla" (term by Salinger, 1990) regression of profits on concentration.

The paper by *Mooslechner & Schnitzer* shows that it may be too early to dismiss the cross section structure performance approach. The paper addresses one sector (banking), carefully creates a new micro data base (956 observations), demonstrates specific knowledge of the institutions and bookkeeping practice in the construction of the dependent variables and the structural variables, and adds a pooled time series cross section database.

The paper thus comes up with many objections usually voiced against the cross section approach. The authors look for robust relations and provisional stylized facts as proposed by Schmalensee. A positive impact of market shares and concentration is not among these facts. If anything there is a slight indication that concentration reduces profitability, market shares are a bit more helpful but still not robust. The overall explanatory power of the variables used in the paper is satisfactory and readers must admit having learned a lot about the structure and performance of the industry (besides the concentration profitability issue), which may help to build better theories.

Weiss investigates the sensitivity of prices to demand and cost changes, and provides an interesting link between a topic investigated in Industrial Organization and the macro economic question of price rigidity. He uses a multiple leader follower model to show that cost changes are less fully transmitted into prices in concentrated industries, while the opposite should prove true for demand changes. The effect of concentration on prices is therefore not direct, but is rather an indirect influence on the sensitivity of the price equation on cost and prices. This leads to a complex relationship between prices and concentration, and may explain why the impact of concentration on profitability has become so disappointing during the last decade (as reflected in the papers in this volume). In a world of increasing domestic concentration and growing internationalization, there is not hope for a simple relationship between profits (or prices) and concentration. Weiss uses a panel of 19 2-digit industries to test the hypotheses.

Using a Cournot oligopoly model, *Neumann* shows that increasing monopoly power should yield a higher level of risk, while restricted monopoly power produces a higher share of risk bearing assets in the portfolio. A decline in demand generally elicits increased efforts to reduce risk. A data set of 16 West German industries from 1976 to 1989 shows empirically that leverage was inversely related to concentration. The data also confirm that increased demand in a particular industry actually decreases the ratio of risky assests to net wealth. Thus, Neumann's paper demonstrates that careful portfolio modelling by oligopolistic firms yields testable hypotheses for empirical research and implications relevant to competition policy and macroeconomic stabilization.

Domberger & Hensher's contribution regarding the economics of competitively tendered contracts is innovative in two respects. Initially, they compare different approaches of selecting winners in the public and private sectors. Secondly, they relate the approaches to quality variables.

Their compiled data consists of 46 public and 18 private buyers. A first set of equations (of the binary probit type) shows amongst other noteworthy results, that private firms more often utilize prequalification, the duration of their contracts is shorter, and they obtain fewer bids.

The second set of equations deals with quality or performance aspects. It has often been claimed that the contractor selected as the lowest bidder tends to provide low quality service or may altogether fail to fulfil the contract specification. Domberger and Hensher provide the first empirical evidence that this plausible hypotheses does not hold. In the public sector there is no correlation between contract performance and the contract having been awarded to the lowest bidder. Even more surprisingly, lowest bid contractors selected in the private sector performed better than contractors with higher bids.

For policymakers, several related observations are equally important. Performances can indeed be enhanced by prequalification procedures. They are more effective than such procedures as weighting price and subjective performance projections at the bid selection stage, or contractial attempts to insure performance.

Another avenue leading to problems regarding the multiplicity of game theoretical models is Sutton's approach. Economists should screen models for robust implications, i.e. implications which are produced in different model settings. Such a test is performed by *Dröttboom & Leininger*, who propose a mechanism under which a regulator can force an incumbant monopolist to increase output and reduce price by offering a subsidy to a potential entrant. Setting the subsidy at a level where the monopolist is induced to deter entry, the regulator achieves a zero cost regulation (since the subsidy never has to be paid). Dröttboom and Leininger show that the result depends on the assumption that the monopolist always honers his pre-entry commitment. It turns out that no commitment on behalf of the incumbant can credibly deter entry by choosing an output level in excess of the monopoly output, after successful entry deterrence. Thus the scheme is ingenious but not robust.

Where will Applied Industrial Organization go to?

Industrial Organization is a science which has been and will be applied to an enormous variety of problems. The papers in the current volume address problems of innovation, profitability, productivity, growth, regulation, tendering and portfolio choice. While for some scholars this may encompass too many topics, the issues addressed are only a minor subset within all the topics which can and should be addressed in Industrial Organization.

To date, theoretical developments and particularly the ever more dominant strand of non cooperative game theory, have not greatly influence applied, industrial organization. It appears that two new dimensions have been added to the deplorable multiplicity of empirical adhoc studies along the SCP paradigm, namely the multiplicity of models and the multiplicity of equilibria. This comes inter alia to what Fisher (1989) calls the tendency that game theory has developed as an "exemplifying theory", in which it is shown what could happen (instead of being a generalizing theory proceeding from wide assumptions to inevitable consequences).

But there are some signs that the current division between theory and empirical research will soon be bridged, at least to a certain degree. The first indication is that even papers which do not claim to test game theoretical models are now more eager to provide some theoretical foundations. This holds true for papers modelling conjectural variation, and papers specifying demand equations and supply relations (called NEIO, new empirical industrial organization, in Bresnahan (1989)). Secondly a wealth of empirical papers has appeared, which explicitly claim to derive their hypotheses from game theoretical models (see Shapiro (1989), Schmalbach (1993) or Aiginger (1994) for a review). These papers do not test theory, because the environment and the variables in the models differ from that in the tests and because many of the hypotheses could be derived from alternative – non game theoretical – models, also. But at least there are spillovers from theory to empirical research and maybe some feedback, too. In the third place, the general feeling prevailing within the science is that the production of more models will be of "diminishing returns" (Shapiro (1989), Fisher (1989)). Sutton proclaims this most explicitly by calling for robust predictions of a broad class of theories, and provides nice examples of how empirical work may best be performed, when the predictions tested are to some extent related to game theory. Last but not the least, the next step will be to narrow the gap between game theoretical theory and empirical research, utilizing the richness in the data bases, now available to empirical researchers.

The data will in any case provide sources for an increasing number of empirical research projects; hopefully many applications will be related to theoretical work.

The largest return to researchers in Industrial Organization will probably lie in the derivation of rather robust predictions from theory, in the application of these results to an empirical data set, and in the derivation of either contradictions or stylized facts. Any of these results can be used to remodel theory or to indicate which other subset of available theoretical models should be tested next. The papers in the volume have each performed a small part of this task, hopefully encouraging other researchers to tackle complementary tasks.

References

Aiginger, K. (1987) *Production and decision theory under uncertainty*. Blackwell.

Aiginger, K. (1994) The use of game theoretical models for empirical research – some examples in recent industrial organization literature, Berlin: Humboldt University.

Andrews, P.W.S. (1952) 'Industrial Economics as a specialist subject', *Journal of Industrial Organization*.

Brauike, M. (1993) 'Quo Vadis IO? Stand und Entwicklungsperspektiven der Industrieökonomik'. *IFO Studien*, pp. 255–269.

Bresnahan, T. (1989) in: Schmalensee R. and Willig R.D. (eds.) *Handbook of Industrial Organization*. Elsevier.

Fisher, F.M. (1989) 'Games economists play: a noncooperative view', *Rand Journal of Economics* **20(1)**, Springer, pp. 113–124.

Güth, W. Spieltheorie und Industrieökonomik – Muss Liebe weh tun? Ifo Studien 1993, pp. 271–316.

Neumann, Industrial Organization: Ein Überblick über die quantitative Forschung, *ZFB Enzyklopädie*, ZFB 7/1979, S 654–660.

Nelson, R.R. and S.G. Winter (1992) An evolutionary theory of economic capabilities, Cambridge, M.A.

Peltzman, S. The Handbook of Industrial Organization: A Review Article, Journal of Political Economy, **99**, February 1991, pp. 201–217.

Porter, R.H. A Review Essay on Handbook of Industrial Organization, Journal of Economic Literature, **29**, pp. 553–72.

Salinger, M. The Concentration – Margins Relation Reconsidered, Brookings Papers: Microeconomics, 1990, pp. 287–335.

Schmalensee, R. The New Industrial Organization and the Economic Analysis of Modern Markets, MIT Working Paper 1133–80.

Schmalensee, R. (1982) Antitrust and the New Industrial Economics, AER **72(2)**, pp. 24–28.

Schmalensee, R. (1989) in: Schmalensee, R. and Willig, R.D. (eds.) *Handbook of Industrial Organization*. Elsevier.

Schwalbach (1994) Stand und Entwicklung der Industrieökonomik, Forschungsbericht 94-1. Berlin: Humboldt Universität.

Shapiro, C. (1989) 'The theory of business strategy', *Rand Journal of Economics* **20(1)**, Spring 1989, pp. 125–137.

Sutton, J. (1990) 'Explaining everything, explaining nothing', *European Economic Review* **34**, pp. 505–12.

Sutton, J. (1991) Sunk costs and market structure, MIT Press, Cambridge, Mass.

I. THE ROLE OF INNOVATION

K. Aiginger and J. Finsinger (eds.), Applied Industrial Organization, 15–34.

Lagging Productivity Growth: Measurement, Technology, and Shock Effects

F.M. SCHERER
Kennedy School of Government, Harvard University, Cambridge, U.S.A.

Abstract. One of the most important problems about which economists have professional knowledge is lagging productivity growth. After illustrating some significant developments this paper addresses three questions: (1) To what extent does R&D activity drive productivity growth, (2) how do alternative measures of productivity affect the conclusions and (3) how did the oil price shocks and the increased openness of the U.S. economy affect productivity growth? After removing the influence of the extremely dynamic computer industry, average manufacturing industry productivity in the U.S. throughout the 80s grew at a disappointing pace. And it didn't improve in the most dynamic industries. But there is good news as well. First, part of the 1970s productivity slump is clearly attributable to the 1973–74 oil price shock. Second and more important, technological innovation does not appear to have lost its power in driving productivity growth forward. Indeed there is evidence of stronger and more consistent productivity effects from R&D investment during the 1980s, although the exact channels through which R&D enhances manufacturing sector productivity are left in doubt. Estimates of the role inter-industry technology flows play are sensitive to aggregation and the conventions used to construct the industry price deflators underlying productivity measures.

Key words: Productivity, technology, R&D.

JEL codes: D24, L60, O47.

1. Introduction

Next to containing the proliferation and use of nuclear weapons, the most important problem about which I have professional knowledge is lagging productivity growth. I begin by illustrating the sharp productivity growth declines that have afflicted most of the world's industrialized nations. I then turn to the special case of the United States, for which there have been hopeful signs of a possible recovery. Determining how robust those indications are poses peculiarly difficult measurement problems, especially for a single leading sector, the computer industry. Having raised but not solved those problems, I proceed to three further questions, in each case testing for the sensitivity of my findings to differing methods of handling the computer industry. First, to what extent does formal industrial research and development (R&D) activity continue to drive the growth of productivity in manufacturing? Second, how do alternative measures of productivity growth affect one's conclusion as to where the gains from industrial R&D are captured? And finally, how did the shocks resulting from oil price increases and the U.S. economy's greatly increased openness to international trade affect productivity growth?

2. The Slump

Following World War II, most of what are now the world's leading industrial nations experienced unusually strong productivity growth, carrying the citizens of those nations to unprecedented levels of material well-being. Around 1970, and almost surely before the first OPEC shock in 1973–74 sent much of the world into an economic tailspin (see Scherer, 1986), the growth of productivity began to ebb.

An indication of how serious the slump has been is provided by U.S. data. Between 1950 and 1970, real output per hour of work in the private business sector of the U.S. economy increased at annual average rate of 2.76 percent (U.S. President, 1992, p. 348). During the 1970s and 1980s, the comparable growth rate dropped to 1.16 percent. Had productivity growth continued in the 1970s and 1980s at the rates it achieved during the 1950s and 1960s, real output in the U.S. private sector during 1990 would have been 38 percent greater than it actually was. That huge amount of extra output could have been used to strengthen lagging educational efforts, rebuild deteriorating infrastructure, widen medical insurance coverage, generate additional savings to support industrial investment, and quite generally, to solve many of the problems the United States finds so nettlesome today.

Table I provides roughly comparable productivity growth statistics for a cross section of individual nations and for all European OECD member nations. Two general points stand out. First, for nations other than the United States, productivity growth has been an even more powerful engine of advancement than for the Americans. Average growth rates during the 1960s were such that real GDP per person employed was doubling every 15 years. Second, the 1970s, and especially the years following 1973, saw a productivity growth decline in Europe and Japan at least as severe as that experienced by the United States. Equally importantly, the decline for Europe continued and even intensified during the 1980s.

The manufacturing sectors of industrial economies have had somewhat different productivity growth experiences. Productivity is probably measured with greater precision for manufacturing than for such sectors as services and government, and on average, recorded annual growth rates have been higher. Table II presents data spanning three decades for eleven representative nations. During the 1960s, the eleven-nation average was 5.7 percent. Average growth rates dropped during the 1970s and continued to decline, although less precipitously, during the 1980s. However, within the averages are some more favorable indications. The Anglos – the United Kingdom, the United States, and Canada – experienced substantial manufacturing productivity growth rate gains during the 1980s, kindling hopes that a turnaround might not be far away for other nations too. About the U.S. experience I shall have much more to say subsequently.

Many hypotheses have been advanced to explain the decline in productivity growth rates. Whatever explanation one accepts, it must account for the fact that the slump has been world-wide, and not confined to only a few industrialized

TABLE I. Annual growth in real gross domestic product per person employed

Nation	Time interval			
	1960–68	1968–73	1973–79	1979–89
Austria	4.9%	5.1%	2.5%	1.1%
Belgium	4.0	4.9	2.3	2.0
Germany	4.2	4.1	2.9	1.5
Finland	4.0	5.8	1.6	2.8
France	4.9	4.3	2.4	2.0
Italy	6.3	4.9	2.8	2.1
Sweden	3.9	2.9	0.5	1.4
Switzerland	2.9	3.0	0.6	1.0
United Kingdom	2.7	3.2	1.3	1.7
Total OECD-Europe	*4.5%*	*4.2%*	*2.4%*	*1.6%*
U.S.A.	2.6%	1.0%	0.2%	1.1%
Canada	2.6	2.5	1.3	1.2
Japan	8.5	7.6	2.9	3.0

Source: Organization for Economic Co-operation and Development, *Historical Statistics: 1960–1989* (Paris: 1991), p. 51.

TABLE II. Average annual growth in manufacturing output per labor hour

Nation	Time interval		
	1960–70	1970–80	1980–90
Austria	5.67	3.27	2.10[a]
Belgium	6.05	4.15	4.74
Germany	5.51	3.84	2.49
Finland	5.68	5.38	0.74
France	6.45	4.37	3.43
Italy	6.29	5.59	3.74
Netherlands	6.91	5.74	3.21
Norway	4.44	2.57	2.78
Sweden	6.46	3.33	2.04
United Kingdom	3.60	2.39	4.78
U.S.A.	2.79	2.24	3.46
Canada	3.99	0.83	1.98
Japan	10.28	5.72	4.04
Average of Thirteen	*5.70*	*3.80*	*3.04*

Source: U.S. Bureau of Labor Statistics, *Monthly Labor Review*, March 1992, p. 91, except Austria, which is estimated from incomplete OECD data.

[a] 1979–89.

nations.

For a while, hypotheses linked to sharply rising oil prices received the greatest emphasis, in part because the first OPEC shock coincided so closely in time with the first dramatic evidence of falling growth rates. The oil shock nexus no longer claims much support, mainly because, with only brief exceptions, real oil prices since 1986 have hovered at levels not much higher than they commanded before November 1973.

The most credible remaining contender is the "convergence" theory explored at length by Baumol *et al.* (1989). An elaboration emphasizes three considerations. First, since the recovery from World War II commenced, the United States has experienced much slower productivity growth rates than most other industrialized nations because it is harder to keep moving ahead when one is the leader (with the highest *absolute* productivity levels) than it is to absorb the leader's technology and catch up. Quite generally, among those nations that have not become mired in under-development, the higher starting productivity *levels* were, the slower subsequent productivity growth rates have been. Second, as many nations have moved to the technological frontier and approached the United States in absolute productivity levels, they have had to make the transition from being absorbers to being frontier-extenders. Since being a frontier-extender is more difficult, average growth rates necessarily declined. Third, and least compelling logically, for both the frontier nations and those that were moving rapidly toward the frontier, growth rates during the 1950s and 1960s were extraordinarily rapid by historical standards – too rapid to be sustained. Fatigue, the depletion of opportunities, and retarded growth had to follow. Or in an explanation that places less emphasis on causation, William Nordhaus (1989) argues, the productivity growth rates of the 1950s and 1960s *happened*, perhaps by chance, to be high. Galtonian regression makes it likely that after a run of unusually good fortune, more disappointing results will follow.

The third of these conjectures is not inconsistent with the notion of Schumpeter-Kondratief long swings. I am skeptical whether there is any solid mechanism (other than chance) that ensures *regular* wave-like fluctuations in economic growth and prosperity. But I believe that Schumpeter's insights do provide a plausible framework for explaining the world-wide fluctuations in productivity growth experienced since World War II. During the 1930s much of the world lay deep in the throes of depression. Investment and dramatic technological innovations were held back by unpropitious demand. Private sector consumption and investment were then suppressed owing to war materiel demands. But especially in the United States, the war's end unleashed a vast hoard of purchasing power, driving a consumption and investment boom. At least equally importantly, the spectacularly successful application of science and technology for military purposes during the war set an example that spurred private sector research and development efforts after the war. The result was an outpouring of technological innovations that was, among other things, manifested in unusually high productivity growth rates. This is precisely the sort of pattern Schumpeter visualized for a Kondratief upturn. After two decades of such technology-based growth, however, the supply of unexploited technological possibilities began to dwindle. Company-financed research and development spending, which had been growing in the United States at an average rate (after price deflation) of 6.4 percent per year during the 1950s and 1960s, suddenly stopped growing and for several years remained stagnant (see Scherer, 1986). When brisk growth resumed after 1976, R&D spending stagnation became evident again in the 1986–92 period.

3. Manufacturing Productivity in the 1980s

If there is any regularity to Schumpeter-Kondratief fluctuations, one might expect an upturn to be commencing soon. Or perhaps it has already begun, forshadowed by the increased productivity growth rates reported for U.S. manufacturing during the 1980s – a leading sector in a leading economy. Closer examination of the U.S. experience is therefore warranted. Two main questions must be addressed. First, was the accelerated manufacturing productivity growth of the 1980s real, or was it merely a statistical anomaly? And second, assuming that it was real, what were its principal causes? In particular, was it rooted in technological advances, or was it more closely related to unusual shocks that struck the U.S. economoy during the 1970s and 1980s?

Let us begin with the measurement question. Except in industries with relatively standardized output (such as flour, cotton cloth, heating oil, or steel beams), the "real" output measure comprising the numerator of a productivity index must be calculated by dividing the value of industry output, calibrated in monetary terms, by a price deflator index. Real output measures can be no more meaningful than the price deflators used in their construction.

Problems arise when there are changes over time in product specifications, most commonly, as a result of technological innovations (see Griliches, 1979). The method normally used in the United States, and I assume elsewhere, to adjust price indices for product quality change, is linking in the prices for new products by splicing. Usually after some time has elapsed to ensure that a new product is not just a passing fad, its price is added to the bundle of prices making up an industry's price index. This procedure implicitly assumes that at the year of linking, if the index for previously included product prices is 100, the index for the new product's price is also set at 100. For products whose technology is changing rapidly, this introduces two biases, usually on the side of understating the rate of price decline, or exaggerating the rate of inflation. First, linking in the new product at price index parity with the products it replaces or makes obsolete implicitly assumes that no improvement in product quality, or no increase in the value of the consumer's purchasing power, has occurred with the new product's appearance. Second, by waiting until the new product is well-established in the marketplace, price index compilers exclude that early period during which the product's price may be falling particularly rapidly due to learning-by-doing or the pursuit of a "skimming" pricing policy by the innovator. Only continuing, possibly milder, price reductions that occur once the new product has been linked into the index show up in the form of price index decreases and, monetary sales volume held constant, output increases.

Computer Industry Productivity

These procedures are imperfect, systematically understating the amount of real product value enhancement reflected in price indices, but they may be the best price index compilers can do in an extremely complex and changing environment. However, for the dynamic and increasingly important digital computer industry, it was recognized that the standard procedures were not good enough. While the unit costs of carrying out standardized data processing and storage operations by computer were declining at a fairly consistent average "real" rate of 28 percent per year during the 1960s and 1970s (see Flamm, 1987, pp. 27–28), the official price deflators for computers were declining much more slowly. To correct what appeared to be a serious problem, beginning in 1985, and with retroactive adjustments to 1969, the group compiling official U.S. national income estimates shifted to a "hedonic price index" method of estimating real output in computers (Young, 1989). With the new price deflators exhibiting more rapid price decreases, productivity growth estimates increased correspondingly. Thus, in an earlier study of productivity growth by industry (Scherer, 1982), I worked with data estimating the average growth of real output per work hour in computers and related products between 1973 and 1978 to be 7.3 percent per annum. With the new data used in subsequent portions of this paper, the productivity growth rate for the corresponding period is estimated to be 23.9 percent.[1] For 1978–1988, the new estimates indicate computer industry productivity growth of 26.8 percent per year.

Over any moderately lengthy period of time, such rapid productivity growth can have astounding output effects. To illustrate, suppose one begins, as my new data series does, with the year 1973. Price deflators for that year are implicitly set equal to 1.0. At the time, the computer industry originated 0.85 percent of all U.S. manufacturing industry sales, and with a price deflator of 1.0, the same fraction (ignoring some minor estimation differences) of manufacturing sector real output. Now let real output be estimated by the current dollar value of shipments in a given year divided by that year's price deflator. By 1988, the computer industry's estimated real output has grown so much more rapidly than the other 446 four-digit industries in my data set that it originates 43 percent of total manufacturing sector real output!

This, of course, is impossible. One cannot tour the United States and find nearly half of all manufacturing establishments dedicated to cranking out computers. In fact, by 1988, the computer industry's share of current-dollar manufacturing plant sales had risen to 2.34 percent. Falling prices elicited an expansion of activity relative to to other industries, but not nearly as great an expansion as suggested by the hedonic index-based statistics, which in effect measure the burgeoning supply of raw computing power. Nor does a measure of raw computing power properly capture the computer industry's productivity growth contribution to the aggregate U.S. economy. Upon those businesses and individuals who would have used computers even at the old, much higher, prices, the industry's dramatically falling prices per billion floating point operations conferred large consumer surpluses. But as Austrian economists taught a century ago, the important action is at the margin. As computing power prices fell, the use of computers was extended to activities of descending marginal value – e.g., improving the readability of students' term papers (a high-value activity indeed!), speeding the design of automobile parts, zapping Martian space ships on a computer game screen, and carrying out extensive computations on productivity data sets (an activity whose value the author hesitates to judge). Use expanded to the margin where the value of computation equalled its new and very much lower cost.

Those who estimate real industry output for purposes of national income determination have a simple method of avoiding the absurd 43 percent computer output share result suggested by my previous calculations. Following the logic of marginal productivity theory, they weight the real output estimates (for computers, now very large) by base year price index values (for computers, by 1988, quite small) to arrive at sector aggregate outputs. But given the very large changes that have occurred in computer prices and outputs, this sensible procedure is not without residual difficulties. Until 1992, estimates of real U.S. gross domestic product were published using 1982 fixed price weights. When a routine change was made in the spring of 1992 to 1987 price weights, the rapidly growing real output of the computer industry received much lower weight owing to its diminished prices, and because the computer industry is such a sizable component of all manufacturing, total reported manufacturing output estimates dropped appreciably.[2] Because the manufacturing output aggregates are used to calculate sectoral productivity growth, indicated productivity growth also dropped. Thus, for the period 1979–1990, the average annual growth of manufacturing sector output per labor hour fell from 3.1 percent using 1982 price weights to 2.5 percent using 1987 weights. The 1982-weighted data were the basis inter alia for the productivity growth estimates of Tables I and II. With the new 1987-weighted data, it is less clear that U.S. productivity growth in manufacturing actually did revive briskly, as suggested by Table II. Whether, and how strongly, revival did occur is a question of no small moment.

ALTERNATIVE GROWTH COMPARISONS

To shed further light on the issue, I have analyzed an array of central tendency measures in data on productivity growth for 447 four-digit manufacturing industries over the years 1973 through 1988. The data were prepared at the National Bureau of Economic Research by Wayne Gray (1989); therefore they will be called "the

TABLE III. Average annual productivity growth tendencies, 447 U.S. manufacturing industries, 1973–78 and 1978–88

	Time interval	
	1973–78	1978–88
Weighted average, using 1973 real output weights		
Including computers	2.08%	2.63%
Excluding computers	1.86	2.38
Weighted average, using 1978 real output weights		
Including computers	3.12	3.49
Excluding computers	2.19	2.45
Simple unweighted average		
Including computers	1.64	2.28
Excluding computers	1.59	2.23
Median	1.24	2.00
First quartile	−0.33	0.85
Third quartile	3.54	3.39
Top quartile mean	6.06	5.27

NBER data". Real output and input measures were chosen for three years, all peaks in the business cycle: 1973, 1978, and 1988. Productivity growth is measured as the average annual compounded growth of real output per hour of labor input, with salaried personnel assumed to work 2,000 hours per year. To evaluate the sensitivity of measures to the extreme productivity growth values in computers (23.9 percent for 1973–78, 26.8 percent for 1978–88), mean industry growth rates were calculated with and without computers. The central tendencies are reported in Table III.

By most measures, productivity did increase during the 1980s relative to the 1973–78 period – a period, to be sure, of unusually low growth owing to the first OPEC shock and efforts by the U.S. government to combat the inflation resulting from it and other shocks. Weighted average growth is seen to be more rapid when later year output weights are used, putting more emphasis on the industries whose output has increased inter alia as a result of above-average productivity improvements. By all conventions, the central tendencies, with the computer industry excluded, are well below the 2.5 percent threshold generally considered to represent "strong" manufacturing productivity growth.[3] The median industry's growth rate was only 2.00 percent – an improvement, to be sure, over the median industry during the mid 1970s. The first quartile estimates for 1973–78 suggest that a cluster of industries were unusually hard-hit by the turbulent economic conditions following 1973. The third quartile (75 percent point) estimates reveal a most interesting deviation from the general pattern: for the top 112 industries, the minimum growth rate was actually higher over 1973–78 than in 1978–88. Within those select cohorts, each with its own top industry rankings, the unweighted average of annual productivity growth was 6.06 percent for 1973–78 and 5.27 percent for 1978–88. (The difference between the two averages is statistically significant; $t = 3.04$.) Thus, in the top-performing industries, productivity growth was actually stronger during the mid 1970s than during the 1980s. The slump following 1973 and recovery during the 1980s appears to have been concentrated in industries, often sizable, that for one reason or another were particularly weak performers.[4] In sum, although the data for the 1980s provide some grounds for optimism, unmitigated joy is hardly warranted.

INTER-INDUSTRY TECHNOLOGY FLOWS

Before we pursue these leads farther, an additional complication must be considered. The analysis thus far has proceeded as if each industry were an isolated entity. However, complex interactions among industries and their relationship to the measurement of productivity growth must be taken into account.

Suppose, for example, that changes in the value-creating or hedonic value of computers were underestimated, as they almost surely were before new price deflators were introduced in 1985. As a consequence of rapid technological progress in computers, other industries ranging from automobile manufacturing to banking to airlines have been able to do their own work more economically and/or to improve service to their consumers.[5] Thus, unless further measurement errors intrude, the use of computers leads to enhanced labor productivity growth in "downstream" industries. But suppose we adopt a more expansive total factor productivity approach, measuring productivity not merely as output per unit of labor input, but output per weighted unit of all inputs – labor, capital, and purchased materials. Whether the contribution of computers to productivity growth will be observed at the using industry depends now upon two additional variables – how competition affects prices, and how the productivity of computer (or other upstream product) makers is measured (see Griliches, 1979).

Competition among computer manufacturers has forced incessant price reductions as the technology has advanced, permitting computer users to enjoy most of the benefits from new technology in the form of reduced capital equipment input prices, rather than letting computer makers capture those benefits in the form of increased profits. The degree of benefits appropriability for firms introducing new technology in computers, and in many other high-technology industries, has been relatively low; most of the newly-created benefits flow as externalities or spillovers to downstream using industries.

This is a fact, but it is not necessarily mirrored in the productivity statistics used to characterize reality. As we have seen, price deflators for technologically dynamic industries often underestimate the magnitude by which those industries' customers have benefited from lower prices or, equivalently, from improved product quality at more or less constant prices. To the extent that the price deflators do measure real price decreases accurately, the real (i.e., price-deflated) *inputs* used by downstream industries will have higher measured values than they would have if (as often happens) the deflators underestimate actual price decreases or quality increases. The more technological improvements are translated through the measurement process into price decreases for the products of the originating industries, the higher will be the measured value of capital (in the case of computers) or purchased material inputs at the using industry stage. This in turn reduces measured total factor productivity growth for the using industry, ceteris paribus.

In the specific case of computers, product quality and price improvements that were not captured by the deflators, as in the United States before 1985, were not necessarily lost in the measurement of productivity growth more generally. They should have had a positive impact, to be sure, subtly disguised, in downstream using industries.

The belief that using industries captured a sizable fraction of the measured benefits from upstream technological advances because price deflators were not on average hedonic led me to construct a matrix of inter-industry technology flows for the United States. Technological advances were traced from the industries that originated them to the industries that used them (Scherer, 1984a, Chapters 3 and 15). How the benefits from new technology are actually divided between originating and using industries is an empirical question whose answer will vary as the methods used to construct price deflators change. Thus, one task to be addressed in the final section of this article is to see how well my technology flow variables account for productivity improvements, using the new price deflators and productivity growth measures. To that and related objectives we turn.

4. Explaining Labor Productivity Growth

We attempt now to "explain" inter-industry differences in productivity growth, using the basic Cobb-Douglas production function approach pioneered by Robert Solow (1957). Real output per unit of labor Q/L is assumed to depend upon capital intensity K/L, energy intensity E/L, the intensity of other purchased materials use M/L, and the stock of knowledge T accumulated from research and development investments, as well as upon unmeasured inputs impounded in a residual. Taking logarithms and then differencing with respect to time, we have:

$$\Delta\, Q/L = a + b_1\, \Delta\, K/L + b_2\, \Delta\, E/L + b_3\, \Delta\, M/L + b_4\, \Delta\, T + e_i\ , \tag{1}$$

where all variables are in logarithms, the Δ indicates time differentiation, and i is indexed over the sample of industries. From Terleckyj (1974), we note that $b_4 = (\partial Q/\partial T)\,(T/Q)$, which permits us to rewrite the technology term as $(\partial Q/\partial T)\,[(\mathrm{d}T/\mathrm{d}t)/Q]$. The second (bracketed) term in the latter expression is the *change* in the technology stock per unit of time divided by output, which, to the extent that additions to the technology stock depreciate slowly, is approximated by the *flow* of research and development expenditures as a percentage of industry output in any given year. This flow ratio can be measured using industry R&D expenditure sources. The first term is the marginal productivity of the R&D

(or technology) stock, approximating the real social rate of return on research and development investment (see Scherer, 1982, note 7). It can be estimated as a regression coefficient on an R&D/output flow variable.

Two sets of data will be used. One is the NBER four-digit manufacturing industry productivity data set, augmented by company-financed research and development / sales ratios from Federal Trade Commission Line of Business surveys for 1976 and 1977 and by 1974 technology flows indices whose compilation is explained in Scherer (1984b).[6] The second data set, called the BLSIO series (for Bureau of Labor Statistics input-output data) covers 87 more highly aggregated manufacturing and nonmanufacturing industries for the years 1973–78 only. It is drawn without modification from Scherer (1982).

THE ROLE OF RESEARCH AND DEVELOPMENT

The first question with which we confront the data is, to what extent were changes in labor productivity growth explained by the 1976–77 research and development intensity of the various industries? And assuming (because disaggregated data for a longer span of years are lacking) that R&D/output ratios remain stable over time, is productivity growth in the 1978–88 period driven more or less systematically than growth in the 1973–78 period by inter-industry differences in research and development intensity?

Table IV presents the principal (ordinary least squares) regression results. Regressions (4.1) and (4.2) include all 447 industries with complete data for the years 1978–88 and 1973–78 respectively. Regressions (4.3) and (4.4) are identical except for deletion of the computer industry, which had the highest measured productivity growth rates in both time periods and the second highest R&D/sales ratio (8.7 percent).[7] These deletions test for any "outlier" effect the computer industry might have had.

All regressions have the anticipated positive coefficient signs. For the full sample, the productivity-enhancing effect of R&D inputs is statistically significant in both years. The implied rate of return on R&D investment is 29.3 percent for 1978–88 and 23.3 percent for 1973–78. However, this result is sensitive to inclusion of the computer industry. When that industry's observations are deleted in regressions (4.3) and (4.4), the estimated return on R&D is smaller (18.1 percent) but still statistically significant for 1978–88, but an insignificant 6.5 percent in 1973–78. It seems clear that productivity growth during the 1980s was driven to a considerable degree by changes in technology – more so, apparently, than was productivity growth in the 1973–78 interval. In this sense, the 1980s appear to herald a return to more systematic Schumpeterian "business as usual".

TABLE IV. Regression equations using NBER productivity data[a]

Regression	Dependent variable	N	RD/Q	PRODRD	USED RD	PRODRD	FLOWRD	$\Delta K/L$	$\Delta E/L$	$\Delta M/L$	Constant	R^2
			Explanatory variables									
(4.1)	1978–88 Productivity growth	447	.293 (4.61)					.070 (2.94)	.021 (0.79)	.659 (18.28)	.735 (5.66)	.519
(4.2)	1973–78 Productivity growth	447	.233 (2.27)					.088 (2.61)	.056 (1.80)	.539 (13.01)	.191 (0.83)	.312
(4.3)	1978–88 Productivity growth	446[b]	.181 (3.03)					.066 (3.02)	.018 (0.76)	.601 (17.76)	.935 (7.69)	.479
(4.4)	1973–78 Productivity growth	446[b]	.065 (0.64)					.095 (2.92)	.064 (2.13)	.515 (12.94)	.0002 (0.00)	.310
(4.5)	1978–88 Productivity growth	447		.287 (3.94)	.104 (1.46)			.073 (3.05)	.017 (0.64)	.662 (18.22)	.745 (5.45)	.517
(4.6)	1973–78 Productivity growth	447		.301 (2.62)	.143 (1.21)			.090 (2.66)	.059 (1.89)	.544 (13.17)	.084 (0.36)	.316
(4.7)	1978–88 Productivity growth	447		.260 (3.50)		.450 (2.15)	.046 (0.59)	.072 (3.02)	.023 (0.88)	.663 (18.28)	.675 (4.76)	.520

[a] T-ratios are given in subscripted parentheses.
[b] Computer industry excluded.

TABLE V. Comparison of 1973–78 productivity growth regressions from two data sets

Regression	Data source	N	Explanatory variables				R^2
			PRODRD	USEDRD	$\Delta K/L$	Constant	
(5.1)	BLSIO	87	.288 (2.01)	.742 (1.89)	.347 (3.29)	−.142 (0.25)	.192
(5.2)	BLSIO	81[a]	.330 (2.29)	.511 (1.23)	.294 (2.64)	.096 (0.17)	.167
(5.3)	BLSIO	80[b]	.209 (1.26)	.538 (1.30)	.307 (2.77)	.152 (0.26)	.141
(5.4)	NBER	448	.307 (2.24)	−.104 (0.74)	.141 (3.68)	1.03 (3.94)	.037
(5.5)	NBER	447[b]	.056 (0.41)	−.091 (0.67)	.146 (4.00)	1.17 (4.69)	.029

[a] Manufacturing industries only.
[b] Computer industry excluded.

PRODUCT R&D VS. "USED" R&D

Regressions (4.5) and (4.6) break the research and development variable down into two components – one, PRODRD, reflecting industry spending on new and improved *product* technologies; the other, USEDRD, measuring from a technology flows matrix the R&D *used* within industries, whether that usage came from work on production process improvement by the industry itself, or whether the new technology was embodied in capital goods or materials purchased by an industry from other industries. Both variables are measured as percentages of subject industry sales. The computer industry is included in each regression. For 1978–88, both R&D flow measures have the predicted signs, although PRODRD implies higher returns on investment (28.7 percent) than USEDRD (10.4 percent) and is more robust statistically.[8] For 1973–78, PRODRD is statistically significant, while USEDRD has an implausible negative sign but is insignificant. Regression (4.7) analyzes 1978–88 productivity growth with the research and development data subdivided even more finely into three mutually exclusive ratios: PRODRD, i.e., product R&D as a percentage of sales; PROCRD, i.e., process R&D conducted within the industry as a percentage of sales; and FLOWRD, i.e., R&D flowing from other industries for the benefit of the industry whose productivity is measured. Both PRODRD and PROCRD have statistically significant coefficient estimates, while FLOWRD does not. The implied rate of return on own process investment, which on average comprised one-fourth of all company-financed R&D, is a substantial 45 percent.

To provide further perspective on these results, Table V repeats the 1973–78 analysis with the aggregated BLSIO data employed in Scherer (1982) and then supplements it with the new, more finely disaggregated NBER data. No separate energy and other material inputs variables were available for the earlier analysis, posing a possible omitted variables problem. Regression (5.1) covers 87 industry groups, including six from nonmanufacturing.[9] Both the product and "used" R&D coefficients are statistically significant at the 0.05 level. The returns on product R&D are similar in magnitude to those estimated with more disaggregated NBER data. Returns of 74 percent are implied for investment in "used" R&D (including both internal process work and R&D flowing from other industry sectors). Regression (5.2) deletes the six nonmanufacturing industry sectors, which perform little R&D on their own, but "import" much new technology from manufacturing industries. The estimated returns on "used" R&D fall and are no longer statistically significant.[10] Regression (5.3) deletes the computer industry, occasioning a ten percentage point drop in the estimated return on product R&D. Regressions (5.4) and (5.5) provide an identically specified analysis of the more disaggregated NBER productivity data, with computers included and then excluded. Regression (5.4) is identical to regression (4.6) except for the omission of energy and materials input variables. The coefficient estimates are similar. Exclusion of computers precipitates a sharp drop in the estimated return on product R&D. In both disaggregated regressions, as in regression (4.6), the coefficients on "used" R&D have an implausible negative sign. It is unclear whether this anomaly comes from the differing degree of industry disaggregation or from differences in the deflators used to estimate real output and hence productivity. Earlier productivity – R&D analyses have shown considerable coefficient estimate instability as the level of disaggregation varied (see e.g. Scherer, 1982, pp. 629–632).

ENERGY SHOCK EFFECTS

Although the regression estimates presented thus far control for *changes* in real energy inputs per unit of labor input, the variable $\Delta E/L$ does not necessarily distinguish industries by their *level* of energy input intensity. Yet our earlier discovery that a cluster of industries experienced particularly poor productivity growth in the 1973–78 period compels a finer-grained investigation of the role energy intensity, and perhaps sensitivity to the OPEC shock of 1973–74, played. We therefore introduce into regressions (6.1) and (6.2) a new variable, ENGSHARE, measuring the share of an industry's 1978 purchased energy inputs as a percentage of 1978 output. The average value of ENGSHARE was 1.70 percent, with a standard deviation of 2.50 percent.[11] The six highest 1978 energy shares were for the following industries:

Lime	25.8%
Industrial gases	15.9
Alkalies and chlorine	15.8
Hydraulic cement	15.7
Primary aluminum	13.2
Nitrogenous fertilizers	13.1%

We begin with regression (6.1) for 1973–78, the period in which the OPEC-induced energy shock was initially experienced. The ENGSHARE coefficient is negative and highly significant statistically. Moving from one standard deviation below the mean in terms of energy intensity to one standard deviation above the mean implies a labor productivity growth decrease of 1.73 percentage points – a very large decrease relative to the average annual growth rate of 1.63 percent for all 447 industries. Industries in the top quartile in terms of energy input intensity had average 1973–78 productivity growth rates of 0.98 percent – a bit more than half the average of 1.84 percent for industries in the lowest three quartiles. (The difference is significant at the 0.05 level, with $F(1,445) = 5.11$.) Thus, the peculiarly low productivity of some industries in the 1970s was associated with their vulnerability to energy shocks.

The source of vulnerability does not appear to be the substitution of labor for energy inputs, as suggested by Dale Jorgenson (1984). For industries in the top energy intensity quartile in 1973, average purchased real energy use as a percentage of output changed very little between 1973 and 1978 – from 4.28 percent to 4.36 percent. The annual *percentage change* in real energy use per unit of labor input from 1973 to 1978 for the top quartile of 1973 was 1.21 percent, compared to 0.41 percent for industries in the lowest three quartiles. This runs contrary to the substitution hypothesis, although the difference in means falls short of statistical significance at the 0.10 level ($F(1,446) = 2.69$). The most energy-intensive industries did experience slightly slower average output growth rates between 1973 and 1978 – 1.15 percent per year for the top quartile in 1973, compared to 1.61 percent for the lowest three quartiles. Here too, however, the difference is not statistically significant; $F = 0.69$. Thus, neither substitution away from energy inputs nor slow growth and hence the working of Verdoorn's law (McCombie, 1987) seems a clear explanation for the weak productivity growth of energy-intensive industries. Apparently, less systematic shock effects were at work.

Regression (6.2) repeats the energy intensity analysis for the later 1978–88 period, marked initially by further oil price increases and then (in 1986) sharp decreases. Now the ENGSHARE coefficient reverses sign but remains statistically significant. A two standard deviation increase in energy intensity was accompanied by a 0.19 point increase in annual labor productivity growth. This productivity improvement was achieved despite a continuation of below-average output growth (for the top energy-using quartile in 1978, –0.11 percent, compared to 0.66 percent for the full sample) and milder increases in energy/labor ratios (0.57 percent per annum, compared to 2.39 percent for the full sample).

Although the exact chain of causation remains unclear, the energy shocks of the 1970s and 1980s appear to have had a substantial impact on productivity growth trends. Energy-intensive industries fared badly following the first great OPEC oil price increases but staged at least a partial recovery during the 1980s.

IMPORT SHOCK EFFECTS

We turn now to a quite different shock effect hypothesis. During the 1980s, U.S. manufacturers were subjected to rapidly rising import competition. Manufactured good imports rose from 6.9 percent of domestic manufactured output value in 1975 to 8.7 percent in 1980 and 14.8 percent in 1986. The main reason for this change was a sharp temporary increase in the value of the U.S. dollar during the early 1980s, which in turn was induced by unusually tight monetary policy. In addition, there were more subtle changes in the mix of imports toward relatively high-technology goods – i.e., those sold by industries sustaining above-average ratios of research and development to sales (see Scherer, 1992, pp. 12–13 and 113–116). These import shocks were widely believed to have provided an impetus to the wave of industrial "restructuring" and belt-tightening actions occurring during the 1980s in America. Here we test for the first time the hypothesis: Industries experiencing particularly rapid import increases raised their productivity at above-average rates, all else equal.

Because many multinational corporations simultaneously export certain product variants from the United States and import other models from their offshore plants into the United States, changes in net exports, i.e., exports minus imports, are a better indicator of varying international competition than changes in imports alone. Our measure of the competitive shock effect therefore focuses on net exports as a percentage of domestic manufactured good sales. If industries were shocked, it must have been from *changes* in net exports, and presumably not from the level of net exports per se. We measure this change by regressing net exports as a percentage of domestic manufactured goods value for each of 447 four-digit industries on a linear calendar year variable running from 1978 to 1986 (after which the trend slowed and then reversed). The resulting NXSLOPE coefficients had a mean value of –1.01 (with a standard deviation of 1.88), indicating that in the average industry, net exports were falling by about a percentage point per year.

Regression (6.3) in Table VI adds the NXSLOPE variable to a specification otherwise identical to Table IV's regression (4.1). The negative coefficient sign on NXSLOPE indicates that as imports rose, causing net exports to fall, productivity rose on average, as predicted. However, the estimate falls short of conventional statistical significance thresholds.[12] It implies that a one percentage point decrease in net exports per year was associated with an increase in the productivity growth rate of 0.054 percentage points, or about 2.3 percent of the mean growth rate. Regression (6.4) excludes the computer industry. Although implied returns on R&D investment drop, as before, there is no appreciable change in the NXSLOPE value. Regression (6.5) excludes two additional industries whose NXSLOPE values were extreme outliers – rice milling, with NXSLOPE = –18.98, and oil field machinery, with NXSLOPE = +15.11.[13] With these exclusions, the NXSLOPE coefficient estimate falls very close to zero. Regression (6.6) substitutes for NXSLOPE industries' average net export level values AVENX over the years 1978–86.[14] The estimated

TABLE VI. Tests of shock effects on productivity growth

			Explanatory variables								
Regression	Years	N	RD/Q	$\Delta K/L$	$\Delta E/L$	$\Delta M/L$	ENGSHARE	NXSLOPE	AVENX	Constant	R^2
(6.1)	1973–78	447	.212	.092	.086	.583	−.347			.293	.369
			(2.16)	(2.82)	(2.84)	(14.46)	(6.32)			(1.25)	
(6.2)	1978–88	447	.293	.070	.037	.660	.075			.566	.524
			(4.64)	(2.94)	(1.37)	(18.40)	(2.21)			(3.76)	
(6.3)	1978–88	447	.289	.069	.019	.656		−.054		.696	.521
			(4.54)	(2.91)	(0.73)	(18.16)		(1.22)		(5.21)	
(6.4)	1978–88	446[a]	.176	.066	.017	.597		−.059		.893	.482
			(2.94)	(2.99)	(0.68)	(17.63)		(1.46)		(7.15)	
(6.5)	1978–88	444[b]	.178	.075	.020	.603		.008		.924	.486
			(2.97)	(3.35)	(0.81)	(17.65)		(0.16)		(7.38)	
(6.6)	1978–88	447	2.84	.069	.021	.662			.003	.750	.520
			(4.40)	(2.89)	(0.80)	(18.26)			(0.79)	(5.71)	

[a] Computer industry excluded.

[b] Computer, rice milling, and oil field machinery industries excluded.

coefficient is small and statistically insignificant. Thus, we are led to conclude that even though productivity may have been affected by import shocks in specific cases (as in the steel industry), there is no evidence of systematic shock effects, favorable or unfavorable.[15]

5. Conclusion

The analysis here offers both bad news and good. The bad news is that, after removing the influence of the extremely dynamic computer industry, average manufacturing industry productivity in the United States throughout the 1980s grew at a disappointing pace, not much more rapidly than during the oil crisis-ridden 1973–78 period. And in the most dynamic industries, there was if anything retrogression, not improvement. The good news is twofold. First, part of the 1970s productivity slump is clearly attributable to the 1973–74 oil price shock – an experience, one hopes, that will not be repeated soon. Second and more important, technological innovation does not appear to have lost its power in driving productivity growth forward. Indeed, if anything, there is evidence of stronger and more consistent productivity effects from R&D investment during the 1980s than during the 1970s. The exact channels through which R&D enhances manufacturing sector productivity are left in doubt. Estimates of the role inter-industry technology flows play are sensitive to aggregation and the conventions used to construct the industry price deflators underlying productivity measures. Edward Denison's (1989) caveat concerning the hazards of productivity growth estimation at the industry level is well taken. Despite the difficulties, however, it is important to understand what is happening at the industry level and how it is affected by technological changes, capital accumulation, shock effects, and other influences. The research reported here should be considered a useful first step, not the last word.

Notes

1. The industry productivity estimates were compiled from government data at the National Bureau of Economic Research and supplied by Wayne Gray, to whom the author is grateful. The data base evolved from an earlier joint effort by the University of Pennsylvania, the U.S. Census Bureau, and SRI Inc. On assumptions adopted in calculating the various components, see Gray (1989).
2. See "Manufacturing Revival Undercut by Revisions", *New York Times*, April 24, 1992, p. D1.
3. Over the course of two centuries, English pin factories made famous by Adam Smith appear to have sustained growth of output per person employed averaging 2.6 percent. Computed from the data in Pratten (1980).
4. On this point, the productivity growth rates for a number of very large or otherwise strategic industries are of interest:

	1973–78	1978–88
Paper mills	3.29%	3.20%
Plastic resins	1.30	3.06
Pharmaceuticals	2.54	2.48
Petroleum refining	3.89	2.34
Basic steel mills	–0.88	3.24
Electric motors and generators	0.42	1.54
Semiconductors	11.60	10.06
Automobiles	4.53	4.08

Except in the case of steel, no striking pattern is evident. The productivity estimates for pharmaceuticals are almost surely too low. Those for semiconductors may also be too low.

5. On the impact of computers in such service industries as banking and transportation, see Baily and Gordon (1988), who also analyze measurement issues similar to those considered in this paper.
6. When the Line of Business data or technology flow indices were available only at a higher level of aggregation, ratios for the broader industry definitions were repeated for each four-digit industry. This introduces measurement error on the right-hand-side.
7. Pharmaceuticals was first with 10.1 percent.
8. Deletion of the computer industry reduces the implied return on product R&D to 14.6 percent ($t = 3.94$) for 1978–88. The return on used R&D is estimated at 10.4 percent ($t = 1.46$).
9. The nonmanufacturing sectors were agriculture, crude oil and gas extraction, railroads, air transport, communications, and electric-gas-sanitary utilities.
10. From the analysis of a data set that was the predecessor of the NBER productivity data, an almost identical result was reported by Griliches and Lichtenberg (1984). They failed to recognize that their more disaggregated sample differed from my original sample by excluding nonmanufacturing industries.
11. Values of ENGSHARE for 1978 were highly correlated with the comparable values for 1973 and 1988, with simple correlations of 0.976 and 0.900 respectively.
12. When the E/L and M/L variables are omitted, causing probable misspecification errors, the NXSLOPE coefficient is –0.115, with a t-ratio of 1.98.
13. The next most extreme observations had NXSLOPE values of –9.26 and +6.03.
14. The mean value of this variable across all 447 industries was –2.30.
15. For the period 1973–78, an appropriately redefined NXSLOPE variable had *positive* but statistically insignificant coefficients.

References

Baily, Martin N. and Robert J. Gordon (1988) 'The Productivity Slowdown, Measurement Issues, and the Explosion of Computer Power', *Brookings Papers on Economic Activity*, No. 2, 347–432.

Baumol, William J., Sue Anne Batey Blackman, and Edward N. Wolff (1989) *Productivity and American Leadership: The Long View*, Cambridge: MIT Press.

Denison, Edward F. (1989) *Estimates of Productivity Change by Industry*, Washington: Brookings.

Flamm, Kenneth (1987) *Targeting the Computer*, Washington: Brookings.

Gray, Wayne B. (1989) 'Productivity Database', unpublished paper, National Bureau of Economic Research, June 1989.

Griliches, Zvi (1979) 'Issues in Assessing the Contribution of R&D to Productivity Growth', *Bell Journal of Economics*, 92–116.

Griliches, Zvi and Frank Lichtenberg (1984) 'Interindustry Technology Flows and Productivity Growth: A Reexamination', *Review of Economics and Statistics*, 324–329.

Jorgenson, Dale W. (1984) 'The Role of Energy in Productivity Growth', in John Kendrick (ed.), *International Comparisons of Productivity and Causes of the Slowdown*, Cambridge: Ballinger, pp. 270–323.

McCombie, J.S.L. (1987) 'Verdoorn's Law', in John Eatwell *et al.* (eds.), *The New Palgrave Dictionary of Economics*, London: Macmillan, vol. 4, pp. 804–806.

Nordhaus, William (1989) 'Comment', *Brookings Papers on Economic Activity*, Microeconomics, 320–325.

Pratten, Cliff (1980) 'The Manufacture of Pins', *Journal of Economic Literature*, 93–96.

Scherer, F.M. (1982) 'Inter-Industry Technology Flows and Productivity Growth', *Review of Economics and Statistics*, 627–634.

Scherer, F.M. (1984a) *Innovation and Growth*, Cambridge: MIT Press.

Scherer, F.M. (1984b) 'Using Linked Patent and R&D Data To Measure Inter-Industry Technology Flows', in Zvi Griliches (ed.), *R&D, Patents, and Productivity*, Chicago: University of Chicago Press, pp. 417–461.

Scherer, F.M. (1986) 'The World Productivity Growth Slump', in Rolf Wolff (ed.), *Organizing Industrial Development*, Berlin: de Gruyter, pp. 15–27.

Scherer, F.M. (1992) *International High-Technology Competition*, Cambridge: Harvard University Press.

Solow, Robert A. (1957) 'Technical Change and the Aggregate Production Function', *Review of Economics and Statistics*, 312–320.

Terleckyj, Nestor (1974) *Effects of R&D on the Productivity Growth of Industries: An Explanatory Study*, Washington: National Planning Association.

U.S. President (1992) *Economic Report of the President*, Washington: USGPO, February 1992.

Young, Allan H. (1989) 'BEA's Measurement of Computer Output', *Survey of Current Business*, July 1989, pp. 108–115.

K. Aiginger and J. Finsinger (eds.), Applied Industrial Organization, 35–50.

Innovation, Profitability and Growth Over the Business Cycle*

P.A. GEROSKI
London Business School, London, U.K.

and

S. MACHIN
University College London, London, U.K.

Abstract. Recent debates about Industrial Policy are dominated by a concern to make firms "more innovative". In order to make progress in assessing the magnitude of the effects of innovation on corporate performance, one needs to know how such effects occur. We have contrasted two views of the effect of innovation – "the product view" and "the process view" – and have provided some evidence to suggest that both effects are evident in the data. Although it is clear that individual innovations themselves have a positive effect on profitability and growth, it is equally clear that the process of innovation seems to transform firms in some way that gives rise to what look like generic differences between innovators and non-innovators. As a consequence, the process by which profitability and growth are generated differs noticeably between the two types of firms. Perhaps the clearest of these differences is that innovating firms seem to be much less sensitive to cyclical shocks than non-innovating firms are.

Key words: Innovation, profitability, firm growth.

JEL codes: L10, O31.

1. Introduction

Debates about Industrial Policy in the UK are dominated by a concern to make UK firms "more innovative". Countless measures of research progressiveness seem to tell the sorry story of a once great industrial power slipping down the international innovation league tables, and each dozen economists who address this problem produce several dozen solutions. Although there is much work yet to be done in measuring social rates of return and assessing the relative efficacy of different policies designed to stimulate innovation, it seems clear that a comprehensive examination of these issues requires one to think carefully about how the performance of innovative firms might differ from that of non-innovative ones. In this paper we woul like to focus directly on this question, and ask "what effects would one expect to observe on UK corporate performance if UK firms became more innovative?".

As in many other situations, the answer turns out to be sensitive to the way one poses the question in the first place. There are (at least) two alternative views about how innovation might enhance the performance of a firm. The simplest and most obvious view is that product or process innovations alter an innovating firm's competitive position against rivals, or strengthen its bargaining power vis-a-vis buyers or suppliers. Each innovation is, therefore, likely to have an effect on performance which occurs immediately after its arrival, but this effect is likely to be transitory: profits and growth will be elevated above "normal" levels for only as long as the innovator can defend itself from rivals. A second and much more subtle view argues that the process of innovation transforms the firm itself, building up its internal capabilities in a variety of ways that create generic differences between innovating and non-innovating firms. This view sees innovation as itself being the consequence of some more fundamental change that transforms a firm's profit and growth performance in both the short and the long term. That is, innovation is an observable signal of a more primal event which has permanent effects on the performance of a firm, effects that do not necessarily manifest themselves only after an innovation occurs. In sum, these two views correspond to the notions that innovation affects corporate performance because *the product of* innovative effort can favourably affect a firm's market position, and because *the process of* innovation can transform a firm's internal capabilities.

Applied econometricians will instantly recognize that these two views of the effects of innovation involve quite different structures of measurement and testing. Adopting the first view leads one to construct models of corporate performance that include, inter alia, an innovation variable, and the parameter of interest is the size of the co-efficient on that variable. Adopting the second view, however, requires one to entertain the hypothesis that the effects of all of the determinants of corporate performance differ between innovating and non-innovating firms. This, in turn, means that one needs to estimate separate performance equations for each sub-set of firms, and test whether they differ from each other. In what follows, we shall concentrate on exploring the second view of the effect of innovation on corporate performance (not least because it nests the first), estimating corporate performance equations for innovative and for non-innovative firms. It turns out that there are discernable generic differences between the two types of firms which reveal themselves most clearly during recessions.

The plan of the paper is as follows. In Section 2 below, we shall outline the econometric models of corporate performance that we intend to use, and then develop a number of arguments supporting the view that innovation is an observable index of a more fundamental generic difference between different types of firm. In Section 3, we shall describe the data which we have used, and discuss the results of applying our models of corporate growth and profitability to that data. A brief summary and a few concluding observations are contained in Section 4.

2. Innovation and Corporate Performance

There are numerous ways to assess corporate performance, and most commentators agree that there is no simple, single measure which captures everything of importance. However, assessing performance using multiple indicators is often made difficult by the conflicting rankings each measure gives of the performance of different firms. For those interested in describing the behavior of firms, performance measures are of interest because of the incentives that they create for managers, and many commentators express differences in the managerial objective functions of different firms in terms of relative preferences between growth and profitability.[1] It follows that one might legitimately start by focusing on these two measures, and that is the course that we shall pursue here. There are, of course, countless different ways to measure profitability and growth, but many of these different measures of each have similar properties.[2] In what follows, we shall concentrate on profitability measured as a return on sales, and growth measured as the first difference in the log of sales.

Developing models of the effect of innovation (and other exogenous variables[3]) on corporate performance measured either as profits or as growth requires one to make two different sets of decisions. The first and most important is the decision about how innovation affects performance, and, as we have seen, there are (at least) two views worth considering in this context: that it is *the product of an innovation* which matters, and that it is *the process of innovation* which matters.[4] The second decision relates to the type of "experiment" which one needs to conduct in order to observe the effect that one is looking for. If one believes that it is *the product of innovation* which matters, then an accurate measurement of the effect of innovation on performance requires one to correct for other determinants of performance which might be correlated with innovation, to allow effects to accumulate over time, and so on. If, on the other hand, one believes that it is *the process of innovation* which matters, then one needs to decide how to identify the firms who have been transformed by this process, and distinguish them from firms who have not. Let us consider each type of decision in turn.

The two views of how innovation might affect performance lead to two quite different types of econometric model. Consider some firm i operating at time t. In an environment characterized by a number of exogenous variables x_{it} and z_{it}, it manages to achieve a profit outcome, π_{it}, and a rate of growth g_{it}. In addition, it may or may not innovate, a state of affairs indicated by positive or zero values of I_{it}. The simplest view of the effect of innovation on performance is that it is transitory and timed to occur with the appearance of specific innovations (referred to as "the product view" hereafter). This view is embodied in the models

$$\pi_{it} = \beta_0(L)\, x_{it} + \alpha_0(L)\, I_{it} + \mu_{it} \tag{1}$$

$$g_{it} = \beta_1(L)\, z_{it} + \alpha_1(L)\, I_{it} + \eta_{it} \,, \tag{2}$$

where the sets of exogenous variables x_{it} and z_{it} may overlap, μ_{it} and η_{it} are white noise residuals and the $\beta(L)$'s and $\alpha(L)$'s denote polynomials in the lag operator L. α_0 and α_1 are the effects that one wishes to measure, and are identified whenever the indicator variable I_{it} is positive. Estimates of the co-efficients in α_0 and α_1 indicate how transitory the effects of innovation on corporate performance are.

The second view of innovation is that it reflects a generic transformation in how a firm operates (referred to as "the process view" hereafter). The core notion here is that a firm is best thought of as a bundle of skills and/or distinctive capabilities. Competitive advantage arises whenever a firm accumulates a set of skills which more than match those of its rivals, and competitive strategy describes the choice of both the speed and the direction of this process of accumulation. Since many of the more important skills which give rise to competitive advantages are knowledge based, it follows that implementing competitive strategies may be as much a matter of learning and developing existing skills internal to the firm as it is of purchasing assets in the appropriate factor markets. The process of innovating affects corporate performance, then, because it helps to develop a firm's internal capabilities, enhancing its ability to learn about new technology, to match technological possibilities with the characteristics of demand and, as a consequence, to sustain its market position in the face of changes in supply and/or demand conditions.[5]

If it is the process of innovation that matters, then the models of profits and growth embodied in Equations (1) and (2) have two major deficiencies. First, the causal presumption that the occurrence of an innovation ($I_{it} > 0$) leads to a (transitory) increase in profits and/or growth makes no sense. When it is the process of innovation (rather than the product of the innovative process) that matters, the effects of innovation which one might expect to observe on profits and growth will occur even when $I_{it} = 0$ at some date t. Indeed, since the primal causal forces affecting a firms performance are its internal capabilities, one might think of the event $I_{it} > 0$ as no less a consequence of superior competitive ability as high profits or fast growth are. Second, since the process of innovation describes a process by which a firms capabilities are transformed, it follows that the effects of innovation are as likely to be observed in differences in the β's between innovating and non-innovating firms as they are to be associated with the occurrence of a specific innovation. That is, innovation is likely to transform the whole process by which profits and growth are generated, and this means that the models of profits and growth described in Equations (1) and (2) may differ between innovating and non-innovating firms.

An appropriate way to model the process view of the effect of innovation on corporate performance is as follows. Using the event $I_{it} > 0$ for any t in the sample period to distinguish innovating firms (denoted with a superscript I) from non-innovating firms (denoted with a superscript N) for whom $I_{it} = 0$ throughout the sample period, then

$$\pi_{it}^I = \beta_0^I(L)\, x_{it}^I + \mu_{it}^I \qquad (3)$$

$$\pi_{it}^N = \beta_0^N(L)\, x_{it}^N + \mu_{it}^N \,, \tag{4}$$

and

$$g_{it}^I = \beta_1^I(L)\, z_{it}^I + \eta_{it}^I \tag{5}$$

$$g_{it}^N = \beta_1^N(L)\, z_{it}^N + \eta_{it}^N \,, \tag{6}$$

where the indicator variable I_{it} may also be an element of the sets x_{it} and z_{it}. The difference in the profits and growth performance of innovating and non-innovating firms is then

$$(\pi^I - \pi^N) = \beta_0^I(x^I - x^N) + x^N(\beta_0^I - \beta_0^N) \tag{7}$$

and

$$(g^I - g^N) = \beta_1^I(z^I - z^N) + z^N(\beta_1^I - \beta_1^N) \,, \tag{8}$$

where we have suppressed the subscripts and the distributed lag notation to reduce clutter.

Equations (7) and (8) suggest that differences in the performance of innovating and non-innovating firms may arise from one of two sources. First, the exogenous determinants of profits and growth may differ between the two types of firm (this corresponds to the term in the first set of brackets in (7) and (8)), say because innovating firms have larger market shares or operate in industries where rich technological opportunities affect the ability of firms to make profits and/or grow. Second, innovating firms may perform differently from non-innovating firms because the effects of an given exogenous determinant of profits or growth is different for the two types of firm (this corresponds to the term in the second brackets of (7) and (8)), say because the effects of a given market share or a given technological environment are more readily transformed into a superior profit or growth outcome by innovative firms. Comparing (3)–(6) with (1)–(2), it is clear that the former models generalize the latter by allowing the data to reveal a performance differential in performance which varies across firms and over time. In (1)–(2), innovating firms outperform non-innovating firms simply because $I_{it}^I > 0$ while $I_{it}^N = 0$; (3)–(6) adds to this the possibility of differences in performance associated with a range of further exogenous factors.

The second decision that one must make when modelling the effects of innovation on corporate performance is the nature of the "experiment" needed to measure the effect one is interested in. The principle consideration of importance is to avoid omitting important exogenous determinants of profitability and growth which are correlated with innovation. Similarly, since we are only interested in measuring the effect of innovation on performance, the omission of important exogenous determinants of profitability or growth is not a major concern if they are not correlated with innovative activity. The literature on the determinants of innovation often focuses on the role played by firm size and market structure, and many scholars believe that innovative activity is pro-cyclical. Hence, we include variables reflecting cyclical shifts in economic activity, and variables measuring the salient features of market structure. In addition, innovations produced or used by one firm may have an effect on the performance of other firms through spillovers, and these spillover effects need to be allowed for.[6]

These considerations have led us to specify the vector of variables x_{it} in (1) as: current and lagged values of the number of innovations produced by firm i, INN_{it}, spillover variables measuring the number of innovations used and the number of innovations produced by firm i's rivals (in the same three digit industry), IPI_{it} and IUI_{it}, the degree of concentration, import penetration and unionization in firm i's industry, CON_{it}, IMP_{it} and UN_{it}, firm i's market share, MS_{it}, and interaction variable between market share and concentration, a lagged dependent variable to capture disequilibrium dynamics, and a full set of firm specific and time dummies to control for other omitted factors.[7] The vector of variables z_{it} in (2) includes: current and lagged values of the basic variables of interest, INN_{it}, the two spillover variables, IPI_{it} and IUI_{it}, firm size lagged, $SIZE_{it}$, several lags of the dependent variable, and current and lagged values of industry and aggregate growth rates, Ig_{it} and Ag_{it}.[8] By and large, these specifications encompass most of the work reported in the literature that has worked with equations like (1) and (2).

3. Innovating and Non-Innovating Firms

Most of the basic data that we will be working with is described on Table I, which also provides a brief characterization of innovating and non-innovating firms. The basic variable of interest is the innovativeness of each firm, and the data that we have used is a count of major innovations produced and used in the UK over the period 1945–1983 constructed by the Science Policy Research Unit at the University of Sussex (for further details, see Pavitt *et al.*, 1987). The selection criteria used by SPRU to assemble this database was that the innovation had to be both a technical breakthrough and a commercial success.[9] The data tape records somewhat in excess of 4000 major innovations over the period 1945–1983, but less than 10% of these were produced by our sample of 539 firms over the period 1972–1983. Using this information on innovativeness, we partitioned the data into one subset of 98 firms who produced a major innovation during the period (about 18% of the sample), and a second subset of 441 firms who did not.[10]

The means displayed on Table I suggest that innovating firms operate in more innovative sectors (that is, sectors in which large numbers of innovations were produced and/or used), and may, therefore, be exposed to more spillovers than non-innovative firms. Innovative firms in our sample are slightly more likely to be unionized than non-innovators, at least partly because they operate in slightly more concentrated industries than non-innovators. It is not, however, unambiguously clear that innovative firms operate in less competitive markets than non-innovators, since import penetration is relatively high in the markets which innovators inhabit. All of these differences are fairly small however, and they all pale into relative insignificance when compared to what seems to be the truly substantive difference between innovators and non-innovators in this sample: namely, that the former have market shares which are, on average, just under five times larger than those enjoyed by the latter.[11]

The top two rows of Table I show that there are, on average, modest performance differences between innovative and non-innovative firms. The former enjoy profits about 11.9% larger than the latter, and their rate of growth is about 5.6% higher. One must, however, be slightly careful about interpreting these differences for three reasons. First, there is a considerable variation in growth rates across the sample that should make one rather leery of reading too much into differences in means. The difference in mean profit margins between the two groups is about 18% of the standard deviation across the whole sample, while the mean difference in growth rates is about 3% of the full sample standard deviation in growth rates (both profit and growth rates are approximately normally distributed).[12]

Second, comparing means in this way attributes all of the difference between the two groups to the fact that the one group of firms produced at least one innovation during the sample period, while the other did not. In fact, work on this and similar samples using (1) and (2) applied to a group of innovating and non-innovating firms suggests that the simple comparison shown on Table I understates the effects of innovation on both profits and growth. In particular, Geroski *et al.* (1991) used a slightly larger sample of firms and found that each additional innovation produced raised margins by 1.57 percentage points, some 16.5% relative to the mean. The instantaneous increase in total profits associated with each additional innovation was £500,000, rising to some £2,100,000 in the longer run. Using the current sample of firms, Geroski and Machin, 1992, found that the production of a single innovation raised growth rates by 1.4 percentage points in the long run, an increase of just under 13% relative to the sample mean.

The third reason why the data displayed on Table I must be read with care is that Table I fails to capture what is arguably the most interesting feature of the data. This is displayed on Figures 1–3. Figure 1 shows the total number of innovations produced by firms in the full sample over the period. The important point to note is that the total number of innovations produced by firms in our sample falls off markedly towards the end of the period, dropping from a high of 45 in 1979 to a low of 7 in 1983. Using (1) or (2), one would immediately infer from this that differences in profits and growth between innovating and non-innovating firms are likely to have decreased during the period: one would expect to see much larger differences in profits and growth between the two subsets of firms in the middle 1970's than in the early 1980's. Figures 2 and 3 show that the average profit and growth rates for the two types of firms throughout the period do not conform to this pattern. Profit differences are rather smaller at the beginning of the period (the difference is 0.008 in 1976) than they are at the end (the differences were 0.016,

TABLE I. The characteristics of innovating and non-innovating firms, 1976–83

Variable	Description	The full sample (539 firms)	Innovators (98 firms)	Non-innovators (441 firms)	Source
g	first difference in the log of sales	0.1083	0.1132	0.1072	Datastream, Item 104
ROR	net profits derived from normal trading activities before tax and interest payments divided by ssles	0.0953	0.1043	0.0932	Datastream, Item 26, Item 104
INN	total number of innovations produced in all innovating units owned by the firm	0.0513	0.2819	0	SPRU Innovations tape
IPI	total number of innovations produced by by all members of the two-digit industry	12.580	15.948	11.831	SPRU Innovations tape
IUI	total number of innovations used by all members of the two-digit industry	6.279	7.207	6.073	SPRU Innovations tape
UN	industry union density across 15 two-digit industries	0.6815	0.7084	0.6755	updated from Price and Bain, 1983
MS	total sales divided by industry total sales work done	0.0282	0.0797	0.168	Datastream, Item 104, ACOP, Table P1002a
CON	five firm concentration ratio by sales	0.3952	0.4033	0.3933	ACOP, Table P1002a
IMP	import intensity, defined relative to home demand	0.2548	0.2671	0.2520	Business Monitor, Table MQ12
$SIZE$	defined as the log of firm sales $(t-1)$	3.2644	4.7762	2.9285	Datastream, Item 104
Ig	first difference in the log of industry sales	0.0972	0.0990	0.0970	ACOP, Table P1002a
Ag	aggregate real GDP growth	0.0165	0.0165	0.0165	Economics Trends

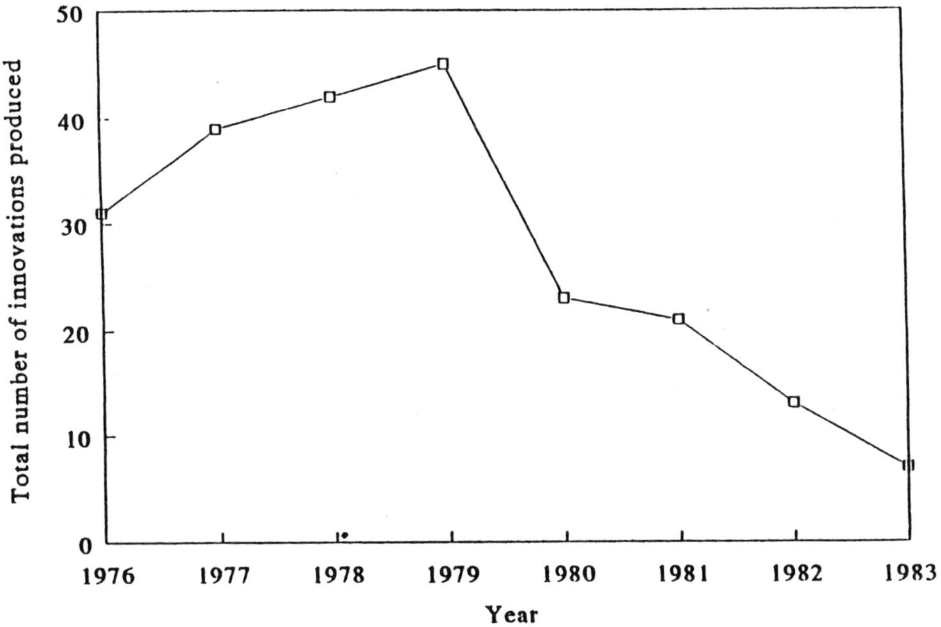

Fig. 1. Total number of innovations produced by firms in the sample.

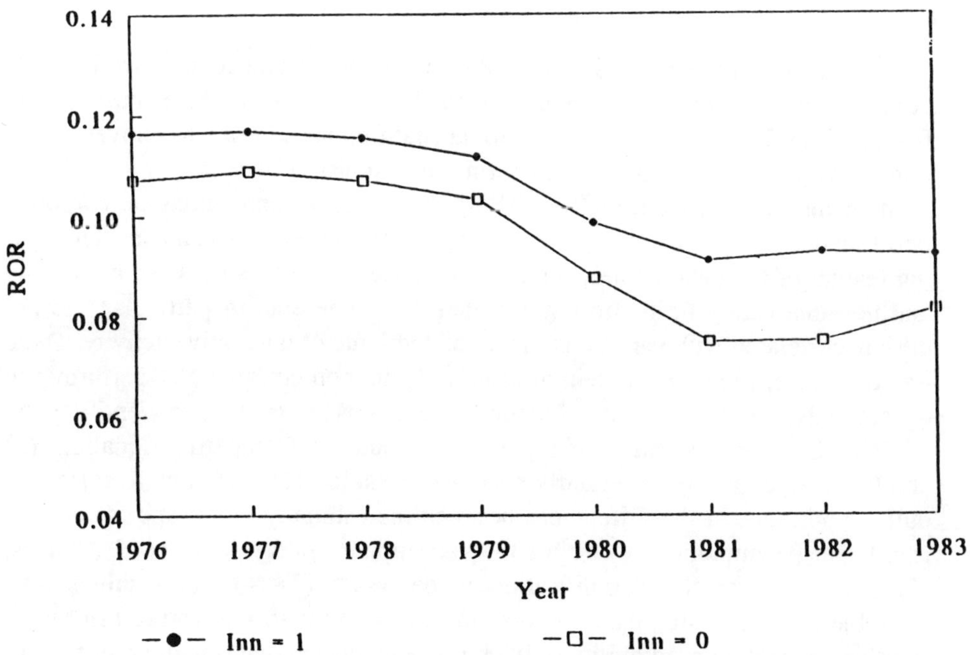

Fig. 2. Average profitability for innovators and non-innovators.

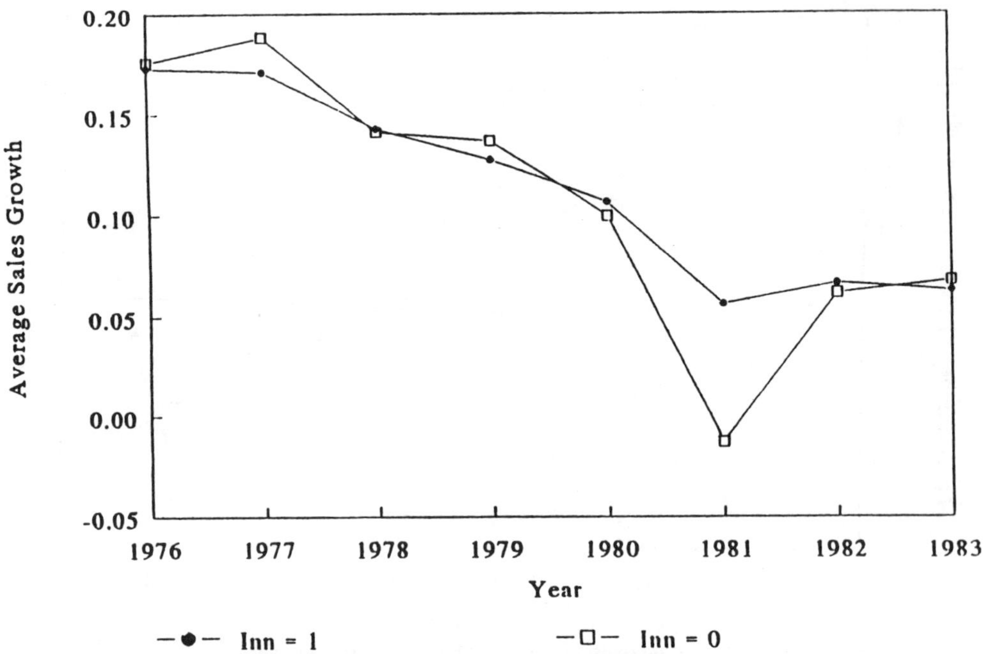

Fig. 3. Average growth rates of innovators and non-innovators.

0.018 and 0.011 in 1981, 1982 and 1983), while the difference in growth rates is negligible in virtually every year except 1981. In fact, what emerges most clearly from Figures 2 and 3 is that the performance differences between innovators and non-innovators are most noticeable during recessions.

It seems evident, then, that modelling the effect of innovations on corporate performance using Equations (1) and (2) misses what seems to be the most intriguing feature of the data: namely, that performance differences between innovating and non-innovating firms are not constant over time and, in particular, are not closely correlated with variations in the total volume of innovative activity. There are, of course, numerous potential causes of this non-constancy in performance differentials, and it seems natural to turn to equations (3)–(6) to help identify them.

Table II reports estimates of Equations (3) and (4). Comparing Equations (3) and (4) to estimates of a similarly specified Equation (1) leads one to reject the null hypothesis that the differences between the estimates of (3) and (4) are not significant (asymptotic p-value for the appropriate Wald test < 0.001); that is, (1) is not an acceptable simplification of the system (3)–(4). The results shown on Table II suggest that each innovation produced by an innovating firm has a short run impact on profitability of 0.23 of a percentage point (raising profitability by just over 2% relative to the mean profitability of innovators), and a long run effect of 0.006 (raising profitability by 5.8% relative to the mean profitability of

TABLE II. Models of profitability estimated using (3) and (4)*

	(i) Innovating firms	(ii) Non-innovating firms
Constant	0.0015 (0.810)	0.0084 (4.764)
INN	0.0023 (3.804)	–
$IPI/100$	0.0078 (0.736)	–0.0047 (0.370)
$IUI/100$	0.0031 (1.812)	0.0061 (0.412)
UN	0.072 (1.853)	–0.0385 (1.741)
MS	0.2205 (2.916)	0.4743 (3.871)
CON	0.009 (0.222	0.1518 (3.735)
$MSxCON$	–0.4822 (4.012)	–0.7781 (3.677)
IMP	–0.0480 (3.686)	–0.0207 (3.677)
$ROR(-1)$	0.1950 (4.710)	0.5601 (15.311)
$INN(-1)$	–0.0008 (1.319)	–
$INN(-2)$	0.0001 (0.121)	–
$INN(-3)$	0.0007 (0.946)	–
$INN(-4)$	–0.0004 (0.507)	–
$INN(-5)$	0.0021 (2.897)	–
$INN(-6)$	0.0009 (1.224)	–
$D1977$	–0.0026 (0.980)	–0.0039 (1.515)
$D1978$	–0.0037 (1.631)	–0.0112 (5.655)
$D1979$	–0.0069 (3.530)	–0.0093 (5.068)
$D1980$	–0.0144 (5.587)	–0.0140 (6.767)
$D1981$	–0.0047 (1.198)	–0.0130 (5.339)
$D1982$	0.0065 (1.584)	–0.0024 (0.832)
$D1983$	0.0021 (0.644)	–0.0045 (1.767)
Average fixed effect	0.037	0.008
Number of firms	98	441
Sample size	784	3528

* The estimation period is 1976–1983; absolute t-statistics in parenthesis; these regressions include firm specific fixed effects, and the variables DN are dummy variables isolating particular years n.

innovators, and 6.4% relative to non-innovators). Innovation spillovers seem to be rather modest in size, and their size is imprecisely determined in both samples. Like many other studies, we find that market share has a positive and significant impact on profitability, as does industrial concentration for non-innovators (it is statistically insignificant in the innovators sub-sample). Industry unionization takes opposite signs but is not very well determined in both cases, whilst import penetration and the market share/concentration interaction exert a negative effect in both samples. Probably the two most important differences between innovators and non-innovators are the coefficients on the lagged dependent variable and on the time dummies. Lagged profitability has a precisely determined effect in both samples, but it is evident that the dynamics of profitability differ significantly between the two types of firm. In particular, the long run impact of any exogenous variables, x_{it}, on the profitability of innovating firms is about 1.25 times larger than its short run effect; for non-innovating firms, long run effects are twice as large as short run effects.[13] The second noticeable difference concerns the common macroeconomic effects captured by the time dummies, especially in the early 1980s. The sum of the time dummy coefficients between 1980 and 1982 is –0.0126 for innovators and –0.0294 for non-innovators; converted to long run analogues these become –0.0156 and –0.0668 respectively. That is, the early 1980's recession saw a more marked fall in the margins of non-innovators (relative to trend profitability) than in the margins of innnovating firms, suggesting that innovators were more able to insulate themselves during this severe downturn than non-innovators were.

Turning to corporate growth, Table III displays estimates of Equations (5) and (6). Comparing (5) and (6) to estimates of a similarly specified Equation (2) once again leads one to reject the null hypothesis that the differences between the two types of firms shown on Table III are not statistically significant (asymptotic p-value for Wald-test < 0.001). Table III shows that each innovation produced by an innovating firm has a short run effect on growth of just under 1 percentage point (raising growth by 8% relative to the mean growth of innovators), and a long run effect of 1.4 percentage points (raising growth by 12.4% relative to the mean growth rate of innovators, and by 13% relative to that of non-innovators). Innovation spillovers are positive, but small and very imprecisely estimated. The lagged sales growth variables have positive and fairly precisely determined effects, and it is evident that the dynamics of growth do not differ too much between innovating and non-innovating firms: the long run effects on growth of a change in any exogenous variable z_{it} is 1.3 times larger for innovating firms but only 1.13 times larger for non-innovating firms. However, the most noticeable difference between the two types of firms is in their sensitivity to macroeconomic shocks. An industry specific shock that increases industry growth rates by 1% raises the growth rate of innovative and non-innovative firms by about 0.5 percentage points. However, a macroeconomic shock which increases aggregate growth raises the growth rate of innovative firms by a mere 0.124 percentage points; the growth of non-innovative firms increases by 1.09 percentage points.

Using (7) and (8) to decompose the differences between innovators and non-innovators shown on Tables II and III adds relatively little to what we have already observed. Most of the profit difference emerges from differences in the fixed effects of the two types of firms (0.037 for innovators and 0.008 for non-innovators), although relatively permanent positive differences are associated with market share and unionization. However, a clearly cyclical component to this difference is evident in the time dummies, and the recession year of 1981 stands out as a year in which profit differences between innovators and non-innovators are relatively large. In fact, the sum of the co-efficients on the 1981, 1982 and 1983 year dummies contributes 0.4 of a percentage point to the mean differential (which is about 1.0

TABLE III. Models of sales growth estimated using (5) and (6)*

	(iii) Innovating firms	(iv) Non-innovating firms
Constant	0.039 (1.364)	0.028 (2.198)
SIZE	–0.002 (0.710)	–0.004 (1.552)
$g(t-1)$	0.097 (2.043)	0.080 (3.229)
$g(t-2)$	0.032 (0.457)	–0.017 (0.800)
$g(t-3)$	0.097 (2.565)	0.054 (1.793)
$INN(t)$	0.009 (1.256)	–
$INN(t-1)$	–0.007 (0.976)	–
$INN(t-2)$	0.001 (0.137)	–
$INN(t-3)$	0.008 (1.077)	–
$Ig(t)$	0.171 (2.190)	0.120 (3.055)
$Ig(t-1)$	0.252 (3.710)	0.187 (5.011)
$Ig(t-2)$	0.070 (1.074)	0.150 (3.521)
$Ig(t-3)$	–0.125 (1.426)	0.013 (0.336)
$IPI/100(t)$	0.061 (0.614)	0.117 (2.085)
$IPI/100(t-1)$	0.039 (0.283)	0.013 (0.191)
$IPI/100(t-2)$	–0.122 (0.682)	–0.079 (0.981)
$IPI/100(t-3)$	0.055 (0.578)	–0.087 (1.326)
$IUI/100(t)$	0.349 (1.949)	0.104 (1.282)
$IUI/100(t-1)$	–0.175 (0.944)	–0.024 (0.324)
$IUI/100(t-2)$	0.220 (1.437)	0.063 (0.903)
$IUI/100(t-3)$	–0.278 (1.863)	0.015 (0.221)
$Ag(t)$	0.177 (0.384)	0.230 (1.183)
$Ag(t-1)$	0.092 (0.180)	1.587 (7.277)
$Ag(t-2)$	–0.204 (0.470)	–1.201 (6.332)
$Ag(t-3)$	0.031 (0.104)	0.352 (2.551)
R^2	0.114	0.128
Number of firms	98	441
Sample size	784	3328

* The estimation period is 1976–1983; absolute t-statistics in parenthesis; these regressions do not include firm fixed effects.

percentage point). Differences in growth performance, by contrast, are more difficult to discern (the mean growth differential is 0.006), and they are not permanent. Most of the difference becomes manifest in 1981, and the most sizeable effect is captured by differences in the co-efficients on the aggregate growth variables. These indicate that a 1% fall in real GDP increases the growth differential by 1.6 percentage points (or 200%).[14]

4. Some Conclusions

In order to make progress in assessing the magnitude of the effects of innovation on corporate performance, one needs to know how such effects occur. We have contrasted two views of the effect of innovation – "*the product view*" and "*the process view*" – and have provided some evidence to suggest that both effects are evident in the data. Although it is clear that individual innovations themselves have a positive (if fairly modest and perhaps rather short lived) effect on profitability and growth, it is equally clear that the process of innovation seems to transform firms in some way that gives rise to what look like generic differences between innovators and non-innovators. As a consequence, the process by which profitability and growth are generated differs noticeably between the two types of firms. Perhaps the clearest of these differences is that innovating firms seem to be much less sensitive to cyclical shocks than non-innovating firms are.

There is something deeply sensible and unsurprising about this result (at least when it is looked at with the benefit of hindsight). Whatever it is that creates a generic difference between innovating and non-innovating firms, the result is likely to be that innovators are more flexible and adaptable. They have the internal capabilities to respond quickly to new technological developments, and to bring technological possibilities into harmony with changing consumer needs. One suspects that in many cases, they have organizational structures designed to cope with the challenge of change. If one thinks of the economic environment as a selection mechanism and asks: "when are these kinds of characteristics are likely to increase a firms survival value?", the answer is: "almost certainly during times of adversity". In particular, recessions are a major exogenous change in a firms market environment, and coping with a recession often requires a fundamental reorientation of a firms activities. If the innovation process really does transform a firm's internal capabilities, then one would only ever expect to see the effects of this transformation during periods of adversity. Most firms, innovative or not, can prosper in a buoyant market, but only a few of the more innovative ones can continue to do so when the going gets tough.

Notes

* We are obliged to the ESRC for support. Some of the work discussed here draws upon joint work with John Van Reenan, and we are obliged to him for his assistance and helpful comments. Jonathan Haskel also provided very helpful comments on an early draft of the paper. We are also obliged to seminar audiences at the University of Ulster, the University of Manchester, the National Institute of Economic and Social Research, NERA, UMIST, University College London, the Centre for Economic Performance at the LSE and the Industrial Organization Conference held at Vienna, June 24–26, 1992, for many stimulating observations. However, the usual disclaimer applies.

1. For example, Odagiri (1992) describes the behavior of Japanese firms in terms of a preference for growth; more generally, see the survey and discussion in Mueller (1987).
2. Measuring profitability has been the source of much recent controversy, the problem being that of insuring that capital inputs are properly valued. This (and other measurement errors) can give rise to large differences between different measures of profitability. However, even when accounting and "economic" profits do diverge, it is nevertheless the case that persistently high

levels of accounting profits imply persistently high levels of economic profits (see Fisher and McGowan, 1983; Fisher, 1987; and Edwards *et al.*, 1987). Measurement problems associated with growth are likely to be no less serious than those associated with profitability, but growth rates are so inherently variable that this additional source of variation is likely to be relatively insignificant (see Hall, 1987).

3. In what follows, we shall presume that innovation is exogenous to current period growth and profitability. While there is no doubt that firms undertake innovative activities to increase their size and improve their profitability and use past profits to finance current R&D efforts, the many lags that occur during the innovation process mean that it is highly unlikely that there exists a strong feedback between current values of profitability and growth on the one hand, and innovation on the other.
4. It is important not to confuse this distinction between "the product of" and "the process of" innovation with the conventional distinction between "product" and "process" innovations. It is conceivable that product and process innovations have different effects on profits and growth, but these effects are transitory and associated with the occurrence of a particular innovation of either type. Effects associated with the process of innovation are generic, and can be observed even when innovations are not produced.
5. For example, Cohen and Levinthal (1989) contrast the view of R&D as a process which produces innovative outputs with the view of R&D as a process which builds up internal capabilities (see also Mowery and Rosenberg, 1989; Pavitt, 1991; Willman, 1991; and others).
6. See Cohen and Levin (1989) for a survey of empirical studies of the determinants of innovation. Much of this work suggests that the role of firm size and market structure in affecting innovation is fairly modest, and is probably dominated by the effects of variations in "technological opportunities". For a survey of work on spillovers, see Geroski (1992).
7. For a justification of the market share/concentration interaction variable, see Kwoka and Ravenscraft (1986), Machin and Van Reenan (1992), and others; Geroski and Jacquemin (1988), and Mueller (1986 and 1990) make the case for allowing for dynamics explicitly in a model like (1). Fixed effects are included to pick up relatively permanent factors which affect the profitability of firms, and might be best interpreted as (indirect) measures of the height of mobility barriers. The time dummies are designed to capture macroeconomic effects which all firms feel. For a fuller discussion, see Geroski *et al.* (1991).
8. The inclusion of a size variable has been standard in growth equations for some time, and reflects an interest in testing the Law of Proportionate Effects. The inclusion of lagged dependent variables, industry growth and aggregate growth rates is designed to capture unobserved firm, industry and macroeconomic shocks, and the persistence of the effects of these shocks on firm growth can be untangled from the estimated co-efficients on these observables. Firm specific effects are not included because there is very little persistence in corporate growth rates over time; see Geroski and Machin (1992), and references cited therein for a fuller discussion.
9. That these innovations are selected into the sample because (*inter alia*) they are commercial successes means that we are unlikely to see negative effects on corporate performance associated with them. If these innovations are set against those that were introduced but failed, then the returns to total innovative activities are likely to be lower than those estimated below.
10. Relatively few of the innovations recorded in this data set were first used by the firm that produced them. That is, the data only identify innovation producing firms, and there are good grounds for thinking that users capture many of the benefits yielded by these innovations (see Geroski, 1991). It follows that however accurately our estimates measure the effects of these innovations on innovation producing firms, they are likely to understate the total effects of these innovations on the profits and growth of all of the firms who are associated with them.
11. The relationship between firm size and innovativeness across all firms and innovations in the SPRU data tape is more complex than this, since very small firms contribute disproportionately to total innovative activity (see Pavitt *et al.*, 1987). What Table I shows is a pro-Schumpeterian positive correlation between size and innovation within the (sub) population of large, quoted firms.
12. Growth rates are far more variable than profits and the range over which they vary is several times larger. What is more – and what is more interesting – most of the variation in growth rates is within firm variation while most of the variation in profitability is between firms (with percentage of variation that is within firm is 86% for growth and 7% for profits). This lack of

persistence in growth over time is particularly evident when one looks at the serial correlation in the data. The correlation between growth rates in 1983 and 1982 is – 0.056, and falls to –0.026 between growth rates in 1983 and 1974; for profitability, the same correlations are 0.914 and 0.459. We have also used robust regression methods to downgrade the importance of outliers in our growth equations, but the resulting estimates were very similar to those reported in the text.

13. That is, thte profitability of innovating firms is less persistent over time (all else constant) than that of non-innovators, although variations in innovators profits are not noticeably less predictable than those of non-innovators.
14. Since most of the innovations in the SPRU data come from engineering or chemicals firms, it is unlikely that the (relative) cyclical insensitivity of innovating firms which we have observed arises because innovators are in cyclically less turbulent markets than non-innovators.

References

Cohen, W. and R. Levin (1989) 'Empirical Studies of Innovation and Market Structure', in Schmalensee, R. and R. Willig (eds.), *Handbook of Industrial Economics*, Amsterdam: North Holland.

Cohen, W. and D. Levinthal (1989) 'Innovation and Learning: The Two Faces of R&D', *Economic Journal* **99**, 569–596.

Edwards, J., J. Kay and C. Mayer (1987) *The Economic Analysis of Accounting Profitability*, Oxford: Oxford University Press.

Fisher, F. and J. McGowan (1983) 'On the Misuse of Accounting Rates of Return to Infer Monopoly Profits', *American Economic Review* **73**, 82–97.

Fisher, F. (1987) 'On the Misuse of the Profits-Sales Ratio to Infer Monopoly Power', *Rand Journal of Economics* **18**, 384–397.

Geroski, P., S. Machin and J. Van Reenan (1991) 'The Profitability of Innovating Firms', mimeo, London Business School.

Geroski, P. and S. Machin (1992) 'The Dynamics of Corporate Growth', Mimeo, London Business School.

Geroski, P. (1991) 'Innovation and the Sectoral Sources of UK Productivity Growth', *Economic Journal* **101**, 1438–1451.

Geroski, P. (1992) 'Technology and Markets', forthcoming in Stoneman, P. (ed.), *Handbook of the Economics of Innovation and Technical Change*, Oxford: Basil Blackwell.

Geroski, P. and A. Jacquemin (1988) 'The Persistence of Profits: An International Comparison', *Economic Journal* **98**, 375–390.

Hall, B. (1987) 'The Relationship between Firm Size and Firm Growth in the US Manufacturing Sector', *Journal of Industrial Economics* **35**, 583–606.

Kwoka, J. and D. Ravenscraft (1986) 'Cooperation vs. Rivalry: Price-cost Margins by Line of Business', *Economica* **53**, 351–63.

Machin, S. and Van Reenan (1992) 'Profit Margins and the Business Cycle: Evidence from UK manufacturing Firms', forthcoming, *Journal of Industrial Economics*.

Mowery, D. and N. Rosenberg (1989) *Technology and the Pursuit of Economic Growth*, Cambridge: Cambridge University Press.

Mueller, D. (ed.) (1990) *The Dynamics of Company Profits*, Cambridge: Cambridge University Press.

Mueller, D. (1986) *Profits in the Long Run*, Cambridge: Cambridge University Press.

Mueller, D. (1987) *The Corporation: Growth, Diversification and Merger*, London: Harwood Academic Publishers.

Odagiri, H. (1992) *Growth Through Competition, Competition Through Growth*, Oxford: Oxford University Press.

Pavitt, K. (1991) 'Key Characteristics of the Large Innovating Firm', *British Journal of Management* **2**, 41–50.

Willman, P. (1991) 'Bureaucracy, Innovation and Appropriability', mimeo, London Business School.

K. Aiginger and J. Finsinger (eds.), Applied Industrial Organization, 51–61.

Empirical Evidence on Schumpeterian Hypotheses in Austria

GERNOT HUTSCHENREITER and HANNES LEO
Austrian Institute of Economic Reserach, Wien, Austria

Abstract. The Schumpterian hypothesis of a more than proportinal increase of innovative activity in relation to firm size is not supported by the empirical results for Austria. The regression of R&D expenditure and innovation expenditure on size variables (employment and sales) produced a proportional relationship. This relationship holds uniformly true if the firms are regrouped around five industrial sectors. If we look at the results from a technology policy perspective we do not find support for a policy which intends to create large business units or something like "national champions".
The regression of R&D employees on the size variables even showed a degressive relationship. On the level of industrial sectors this result was only reproduced for the Construction Materials and Engineering Goods sector. The obvious deviation from the proportional relationship of R&D expenditure and innovation expenditure and size described above is due to size dependent differences in the quality of the R&D labor force or in the factor proportions of R&D.
The regression of the spending for different types of innovation (e.g. product and/or process innovations) on the size variables produced again a proportional relationship. The only exception was the spending for process innovations in office and administration which showed a degressive relationship. Compared to the regression results described above the only remarkable difference was the much lower amount of variance explained by the size variable in this case.

JEL codes: O3, O30, O32.

Key words: Industrial organization, Schumpeterian hypotheses, R&D and innovation, firm size

I. Schumpeterian Hypotheses: Foundations and Empirical Results

Few economists have delivered as many starting points for economic analysis as Joseph A. Schumpeter. His treatment of the role of large firms in his *"Capitalism, Socialism, and Democracy"* (Schumpeter, 1942) inspired what may be the second largest body of empirical literature in industrial organisation.[1] In sharp contrast to standard theory, Schumpeter argued that the model of perfect competition "... has no title to be set up as a model of ideal efficiency" (Schumpeter, 1942, p. 106). The existence of large firms and hence of market power is a precondition to realize "plans of large dimensions". In his view one has to accept that the organization of industry according to the model of perfect competition is less efficient than a system where large firms act as Schumpeterian "engines of progress". Schumpeter did not explicitly explain why large enterprises should perform better as innovators. His successors, however, suggested that large firms had superior access to capital, ability to pool risks, economies of scale in the maintenance of laboratories and advantages regarding the availability and stability of internally generated funds.

Since Schumpeter's conjectures appear rather vague at times, his disciples "... took liberties translating them into testable hypotheses" (Scherer, 1984, p. 169). Although most authors claim that their work belongs legitimately to the "Schumpeterian" tradition, their research efforts in many cases show a substantial distance from the theoretical body laid down by Schumpeter himself.[2] For an overview of empirical results covering the whole range of Schumpeterian hypotheses see, for example, the surveys by Kamien and Schwarz (1982, Chapter 3), Baldwin and Scott (1987, Chapter 3) and Cohen and Levin (1989). Although a considerable amount of resources was devoted to test the size/innovativeness relationship, the results obtained render few "hard facts". As Cohen and Levin (1989) stated, the results are rather inconclusive.

Schumpeter's complex arguments – which are basically dynamic and long-term in character – were translated into two major hypotheses, which were most often formulated in a static context:

(1) Innovation increases more than proportionately with firm size,
(2) Innovation increases with market concentration.

The present paper focuses on the relationship between innovation and *size*. The Schumpeterian hypothesis of a more than proportionate increase of innovative activity in relation to size is not supported by the empirical results presented in this study for Austria. The regression of *R&D expenditure* on size variables (employment and turnover) do not preclude a proportional relationship. This result appears rather robust. It holds uniformly true when production units are regrouped to five industrial sectors and irrespective of the size measure (employment or turnover) chosen. Moreover, the same results hold true for the regression of the more comprehensive variable *innovation expenditure* on size. The regression of *R&D employees* (instead of R&D expenditure) on the size variables even indicated a degressive relationship. The obvious deviation from the proportional relationship between R&D expenditure and innovation expenditure and size described above may be due to size dependent differences in the quality of the R&D labour force or in the factor proportions of R&D.

Up to the early 1970s, the prevalent assumption among researchers was that the empirical relationship between the volume of innovative activities and firm size was an S-shaped one.[3] Recent research casts doubt on the basis for the above mentioned "consensus": In 1984, Scherer reassessed the Schumpeterian hypothesis using 1974 Federal Trade Commission "Lines of Business" data. He finds – in contrast to his 1965 study – that "... in most industries, size appear to be neither stimulating nor retarding" (Scherer, 1984, p. 237). Summarizing the results of recent research, Baldwin and Scott (1987, p. 111) conclude that "... it has been ... well demonstrated that among the larger enterprises in individual industries the causal relationships running from firm size to R&D effort are, if identifiable at all, weak".

Although there is, if any, only limited support for the traditional Schumpeterian hypothesis regarding innovativeness and size, no competing hypothesis seems to have evolved. The reluctance to reject the Schumpeterian hypothesis may be due to the fact that there are still numerous problems associated with the measurement of the variables (so that differences in the results obtained are to a considerable extent due to different measurement procedures and definitions of the data utilized) as well as to the proposition that the relationship may not be invariate of time, industry and country.

II. Method: Specification and Estimation

Up to now, there are no results of formal empirical tests of Schumpeterian hypotheses available for Austria. It was therefore decided to collect empirical evidence regarding the standard Schumpeterian hypothesis that size is conductive to innovative activity. The rich database of the Austrian Technology and Innovation Survey (Leo, Palme and Volk, 1992) of the Austrian Institute of Economic Research (WIFO)[4] enabled us to test not only the well-known Schumpeterian hypothesis that R&D, measured in terms of input variables (R&D expenditure and R&D employment), increases more than proportionately with size but also the relationship between size and innovation expenditure. Furthermore we broke down innovation expenditure into four components (1. product innovations without change in manufacturing technology, 2. product innovations with simultaneous change in manufacturing technology. 3. process innovations in manufacturing technology without product changes, and 4. process innovations in office and administration) and tested the influence of firm size on them.

As compared to R&D expenditure and corresponding employment in R&D, innovation expenditure is a more comprehensive indicator of innovative activity. It comprises spending on R&D, outlays for construction and design, utility patents and licences, expenditure for production and marketing startups as well as for process innovations.[5] It covers not only expenditures which are related to the generation of technological knowledge (R&D spending) but also expenditure related to the adoption of technology (construction and design, utility patents and licenses, expenditure for production and marketing start-ups and process innovation).

On the industry level innovation expenditure therefore reflects to some extent the technological level of a country, i.e. the amount of resources devoted to the creation of new knowledge vs. the adoption of knowledge developed abroad. The history of postwar Austria shows a distinct shift from simple adoption of foreign technology to the development of a – although moderate – capacity to produce technology: during the reconstruction period following the end of World War II, the innovation processes in the Austrian industry were to a considerable extent based on the transfer of technology, mainly embodied in capital goods imported from abroad. Against the background of an industry lagging far behind technological leaders, high growth in productivity was achieved (Steindl, 1977 and 1983). The level of domestic R&D

activities, however, was, and still is, comparatively low. It seems that Austrian industry has not separated itself completely from this pattern of development that emerged in the postwar period.[6] What is more important, even with considerably increased levels of home based R&D activities or generation of technological knowledge in general, technology transfer, embodied or disembodied, remains essential for a small country like Austria and Austrian industry correspondingly devotes more resources to activities which are related to the adoption of technology than that in other countries (see Leo, Palme and Volk, 1992). Innovation expenditure as defined above does include important components of transferred technology in its disembodied (e.g. patents, licences) and embodied (e.g. capital goods for innovative projects) form. It appears, therefore, to be of interest to ask the Schumpeterian question, whether size is conductive to the conduct of innovation in the broader sense explained above.

Like other studies (e.g. Soete, 1979), we chose to specify the equation

$$INNOV = \alpha * SIZE^{\beta} * \varepsilon$$

or, after logarithmical transformation,

$$\log INNOV = \log \alpha + \beta * \log SIZE + \varepsilon,$$

where the dependent variable INNOV represents innovation activity (measured alternately by R&D expenditure, number of R&D employees, innovation expenditure and subsets thereof). The independent variable SIZE (of establishments) is alternately measured by the number of employees and by turnover. The coefficient β may be interpreted as scale coefficient. A value $\beta > 1$ indicates innovative activities increasing more than proportionately with size. $b < 1$ bears a corresponding meaning (less than proportionate increase). A value of $\beta = 1$ indicates that no scale effects are present. Of course, ε represents the error term.

Regarding the choice of the (independent) scale variable Scherer (1965b) argues that variables "neutral in terms of factor proportions" seem to be preferable on theoretical grounds. Sales data, having this property, may serve as a substitute for information on value added which is not obtainable in many cases. Moreover, sales "... appears to be the principal scale variable taken into account by company decision-makers in setting R&D budgets" (Scherer, 1965b, p. 261).

When interpreting the regression results it should be borne in mind that the procedure used may introduce a bias. Specifically, Scherer (1965b, p. 258) pointed out that the deletion of zeros "penalizes the case for bigness". Observations of the innovation variable INNOV with a realization of 0 are deleted, while it is well known that large sized units are more likely to engage in R&D at all than small firms.

For illustrative purposes it may be mentioned that in Austria 4.2% of total industry R&D is performed by firms with less than 100 employees. These firms account for 23.5% of total industry employment. On the other hand, firms with more than 500 employees spend 79.4% of total industry R&D, but employ just

TABLE I. Effects of size on R&D expenditure and R&D employment

	Logarithmic regression results					
	Size measured by number of employees			Size measured by turnover		
	Scale Coef-ficent b	Standard Error	R^2	Scale Coef-ficent b	Standard Error	R^2
R&D expenditure						
All industries	1.079*+	0.063	0.54	0.990*+	0.055	0.56
Basic goods	1.202*+	0.199	0.60	1.002*+	0.170	0.58
Chemicals	1.183*+	0.147	0.61	1.119*+	0.120	0.68
Construction materials	1.032*+	0.129	0.62	0.915*+	0.128	0.56
Traditional consumer goods	0.656*+	0.174	0.24	0.731*+	0.187	0.25
Engineering goods	1.033 *+	0.096	0.53	0.950*+	0.084	0.56
R&D employement						
All industries	0.884*	0.055	0.51	0.796*	0.049	0.51
Basic goods	0.948*+	0.172	0.55	0.740*+	0.158	0.47
Chemical	0.945*+	0.127	0.57	0.913*+	0.100	0.67
Construction materials	0.766*	0.113	0.54	0.662*	0.113	0.46
Traditional consumer goods	0.780*+	0.148	0.38	0.839*+	0.161	0.38
Engineering goods	0.902*+	0.090	0.50	0.816*	0.080	0.51

* H_0: b significantly different from 0, at the 0.05 level
+ H_0: b not significantly different from 1, at the 0.05 level

38.7% of employees in industry. Assuming that the variance in the distributions is only partly explained by varying R&D intensities, it may be inferred that the propensity to perform R&D increases with firm size.

In the following, we first run the standard regressions of R&D indicators (R&D expenditure and R&D employees) on size. This exercise is followed by substituting the broader innovation expenditure variable and a breakdown thereof for the R&D indicators.

III. Results

Regression *R&D expenditure* on size (measured either by number of employees or turnover) gives an estimate scale coefficient b close to unity and R^2 of 0.54 and 0.56, respectively (Table I). The null hypothesis that the scale coefficient b is equal to unity (proportionate increase) cannot be rejected (at the 0.05 significance level). The same holds true for each of the five industrial sectors or, briefly, industries.

The lower scale coefficients for turnover as independent variable (size measure) as compared to that for number of employees may be caused by the fact that the latter "underestimates" the size of large capital intensive production units. For this reason, Jacquemin and De Jong (1977, p. 154), for example, give preference to turnover as measure of size. The differences in the results obtained for different size measures (turnover and employment) thus conform to those of previous studies.

TABLE II. Effects of size on innovation expenditure

	Logarithmic regression results					
	Size measured by number of employees			Size measured by turnover		
	Scale Coefficent b	Standard Error	R^2	Scale Coefficent b	Standard Error	R^2
Innovation expenditure						
All industries	1.067*+	0.055	0.60	0.940*+	0.051	0.57
Basic goods	1.194*+	0.208	0.57	0.972*+	0.183	0.53
Chemicals	1.140*+	0.109	0.72	1.029*+	0.097	0.73
Construction materials	1.098*+	0.127	0.66	0.989*+	0.124	0.62
Traditional consumer goods	1.000*+	0.174	0.43	0.943*+	0.206	0.32
Engineering goods	0.943*+	0.083	0.56	0.858 *+	0.073	0.58

* H_0: b significantly different from 0, at the 0.05 level
\+ H_0: b not significantly different from 1, at the 0.05 level

Already Scherer (1965b, p. 258) had found that the scale coefficient was higher when employment – rather than sales or assets – was used as a size measure.

Contrary to the behaviour of R&D expenditure, *R&D employment* increases, irrespective of the size measure chosen, less than proportionately with size. The scale coefficient b – estimated at 0.88 and 0.80, respectively – is significantly smaller than unity at the 0.05 significance level ($R^2 = 0.51$). On the industry level less than proportionate increases can be identified in the Construction Materials and Engineering Goods industries.

The difference in the results concerning R&D expenditure on the one hand, and R&D employment on the other, may be explained by size dependent differences in the quality of the R&D labour force (leading to higher labour costs of R&D personnel) or in the factor proportions in R&D. It should be borne in mind, that R&D expenditure – as defined in the WIFO survey following OECD (1981) – apart from labour costs of R&D personel also includes other current costs as well as capital expenditures. In both cases, however, the results do not give support to the hypothesis that innovative activity (at least when measured by R&D input indicators) increases more than proportionately with size.

As explained above, in a next step *innovation expenditure* was substituted for R&D indicators as dependent variable and subsequently regressed on size ($R^2 = 0.60$ or 0.57, respectively). The results (see Table II) resemble rather closely those obtained for R&D expenditure. Again, the null hypothesis that innovation expenditure increases proportionately with size cannot be rejected either at the aggregate industry or at the industry level. As may be expected, the scale coefficient b varies less across industries in the equation for innovation expenditure than that in the equation for R&D expenditure.

In the Technology and Innovation Survey, innovation expenditure as defineda bove was broken down into four components (types of innovation), viz., expenditure on:

(1) product innovations without change in manufacturing technology,
(2) product innovations with simultaneous change in manufacturing technology,
(3) process innovations in manufacturing technology without product changes,
(4) process innovations in office and administration.

This decomposition was also used to compute regressions on size. Regression results are presented in Table III. Generally speaking, size explains only a small part of the variation of innovation expenditure in its different uses. Taking the first three types of innovation expenditure, R^2 varies from 0.07 to 0.11.

In cases (1)–(3) – *product innovations without change in manufacturing technology, product innovations with simultaneous change in manufacturing technology, process innovations in manufacturing technology without product changes* – the null hypothesis of proportionate increase of the respective type of innovation expenditure cannot be rejected (at the 0.05 significance level), irrespective of the size measure chosen.

The fourth type of innovation expenditure, viz., that on *process innovations in office and administration*, is set apart as a special case. R^2 is even lower than before (0.03 and 0.04, respectively). The scale coefficient b differs from zero only at the aggregate industry level (with just one exception at the industry level) and is significantly smaller than unity.

IV. Conclusions

The Schumpeterian hypothesis of a more than proportionate increase of innovative activity in relation to size is not supported by the empirical results presented in this study for Austria. The regression of *R&D expenditure* on size variables (employment and turnover) do not preclude a proportionate relationship. This result appears rather robust. It holds uniformly true when production units are regrouped to five industrial sectors and irrespective of the size measure (employment or turnover) chosen. At least as regards the aggregate industry level, this result confirms *a priori* reasoning on structural characteristics of Austrian industry. Moreover, the same results hold true for the regression of the more comprehensive variable *innovation expenditure* on size.

The regression of *R&D employees* (instead of R&D expenditure) on the size variables even indicated a degressive relationship. The obvious deviation from the proportionate relationship between R&D expenditure and innovation expenditure and size described above may be due to size dependent differences in the quality of the R&D labour force or in the factor proportions of R&D.

These results indicate that in the Austrian context no support for the proposition that large firms are powerful Schumpeterian "engines" in the process of generation

TABLE III. Effects of size on innovation expenditure (by type of innovation)

	Logarithmic regression results					
	Size measured by number of employees			Size measured by turnover		
	Scale Coef- ficent *b*	Standard Error	R^2	Scale Coef- ficent *b*	Standard Error	R^2
Product innovations without change in manufacturing						
All industries	0.870*+	0.182	0.08	0.741*+	0.164	0.07
Basic goods	1.714*+	0.748	0.15	1.177	0.653	0.09
Chemicals	0.953*+	0.383	0.11	1.003*+	0.329	0.19
Construction materials	0.665	0.403	0.04	0.545	0.376	0.03
Traditional consumer goods	0.727	0.548	0.02	0.296	0.605	0.02
Engineering goods	0.827*+	0.285	0.07	0.795*+	0.254	0.08
Product innovations with simultaneous change in manufacturing						
All industries	1.131*+	0.196	0.11	0.951*+	0.177	0.09
Basic goods	1.805*+	0.711	0.19	1.108	0.636	0.08
Chemicals	1.482*+	0.424	0.22	1.190*+	0.392	0.17
Construction materials	0.783	0.471	0.04	0.641	0.441	0.03
Traditional consumer goods	1.910*+	0.508	0.23	2.120	0.546	0.25
Engineering goods	0.727*+	0.342	0.03	0.631*+	0.308	0.03
Process innovations in manufacturing technology without product changes						
All industries	1.022*+	0.186	0.10	0.844*+	0.169	0.09
Basic goods	0.755	0.636	0.02	0.548	0.540	0.00
Chemicals	0.921*+	0.419	0.09	0.722	0.382	0.06
Construction materials	0.861	0.460	0.06	0.907*+	0.421	0.09
Traditional consumer goods	1.076*+	0.509	0.07	0.760	0.569	0.02
Engineering goods	0.972*+	0.327	0.07	0.768*+	0.297	0.05
Process innovations in office and administration						
All industries	0.539*	0.175	0.03	0.512*	0.157	0.04
Basic goods	0.599	0.711	0.01	0.590	0.595	0.00
Chemicals	0.196	0.367	0.01	0.326	0.327	0.00
Construction materials	0.556	0.396	0.02	0.615	0.364	0.05
Traditional consumer goods	0.974*+	0.472	0.07	0.602	0.529	0.00
Engineering goods	0.345	0.311	0.00	0.413	0.278	0.01

* H_0: *b* significantly different from 0, at the 0.05 level
\+ H_0: *b* not significantly different from 1, at the 0.05 level

and adaptation of technology could be found. Considering the results from a technology policy perspective, one has to be sceptical towards a simple-minded support for the creation of large business units or "national champions" in order to push innovative activities. On the other hand the structural characteristics of the Austrian economy suggest that it cannot safely be assumed that the relationship between R&D activity and size fully corresponds to the one observed in major industrial economies or even in technologically advanced small economies. It has to be mentioned, that – by Austrian standards – "large" industrial producers fall into three categories:

(1) Austria's nationalized industries – historically strong in basic industries – which, in the recent past, exhibited an R&D intensity below the industry average.
(2) Subsidiaries of multinational enterprises. Despite a tendency towards increasing internationalisation of R&D activities within multinational enterprises, R&D so far remains concentrated at corporate headquarters.[7] On the other hand, there is no Austrian multinational enterprise of European, let alone global standards.
(3) The remaining "large" industrial producers are often to be found in less R&D intensive consumer goods or basic industries (e.g. pulp and paper).

Considering this setting, at least as regards the aggregate industry level, one may *a priori* doubt whether in Austria large firms are "powerful engines" of R&D. Therefore empirical results obtained for countries with research intensive large enterprises may differ from the Austrian estimates.

Regression of the spending for different types of innovation (product and/or process innovations) on the size variables again does not preclude a proportionate increase with size. The only exception was the spending for process innovations in office and administration which indicated a degressive relationship. Compared to the regression results described above, the only remarkable difference was the much lower part of variance explained by the size variable in this case.

The rather low explanatory power of the size variables for the allocation of resources between different types of innovations (in contrast to overall R&D spending or innovation expenditure) indicates that the size of the firm is important for determining the relative amount of money to be spent on innovations. The actual allocation of funds seems to be guided by factors not included in this analysis. In this respect one has to allow for additional degrees of freedom concerning the organisation of markets (concentration, international activities, networks, etc.) and the wider environment of the firm (e.g. scientific advances stemming from universities, the role of national technology policy, etc.).

Appendix: The Data Base

The present study is based on data of the WIFO Technology and Innovation Survey for the year 1990.[8] The industrial establishments responding to the 1990 survey (about 600) represent this approximately 1/3 of industrial sales. This data base has several advantages:

(1) The WIFO Technology and Innovation Study covers a variety of indicators of innovative activities, reflecting both inputs (R&D expenditure, R&D employees, innovation expenditure) as well as outputs (patent applications, number

of innovations) of the innovation process. Contrary to many other studies, the data base allows for differenciation between product and process innovations.

(2) The WIFO Technology and Innovation Survey covers relatively homogeneous reporting units (establishments) as compared to the large conglomerate firms used in other studies. As Cohen and Levin (1989, p. 1070) point out, the choice of statistical units is by no means irrelevant, since the arguments behind the Schumpeterian hypotheses refer to different levels of aggregation (e.g. firms as a whole or "lines of business"). Arguments with regard to financing innovation activities or to risk spreading might refer to the level of the firm as an entity, whereas arguments concerning cost spreading might rather refer to the level of lines of business. Economies of scale in R&D, in turn, may refer to one or the other level. One may even go one step further and argue that – with increasing importance of cooperative relations (strategic alliances etc.) of firms with other actors – the boundaries of the firm are becomming "fuzzy". In suitable cooperative structures or arrangements, small firms might be able to perform functions of larger integrated firms (Teece, 1991, p. 410). If this holds true, however, it would clearly undermine the traditional Schumpeterian exercises.

(3) Integration of innovation related data of the Technology and Innovation Survey with WIFO's industrial enterprise data base (including WIFO's Business Cycle and Investment Surveys) offers a wide range or analytical possibilities for future research.

(4) Contrary to the data base of most empirical studies in the Schumpeterian tradition which build on available data for large firms, the WIFO survey also includes medium and small sized industrial production units.

The sample used in this study includes 252 units of production designed as "innovators", defined as establishments reporting non-zero R&D expenditure, R&D employment and innovation expenditure. With more than 122,000 employees they account for about 23% of total employment in Austrian industry. Almost half of the establishments in the sample have less than 200 employees, just below three quarters less than 500 employees. However, in the sample, about 2/3 (66.3%) of turnover and 3/4 (74.2%) of R&D expenditure is concentrated on units with 1,000 or more employees.

Notes

1. According to Cohen and Levin (1989) it is exceeded in volume only by the literature investigating the relationship between concentration and profitability.
2. See the critical comments in Markham (1965) and Fisher and Temin (1973).
3. See, for example Pavitt, Robson and Townsend (1987). This consensus was strongly influenced by the works of Scherer, e.g. Scherer (1965a).
4. The data set is described in more details in the appendix.
5. The results obtained for Austria indicate that R&D expenditure accounts for roughly 1/3 of total innovation expenditure.
6. For a recent assessment of the role of R&D in Austrian manufacturing see Hutschenreiter (1993).

7. See, for example, Dunning (1990).
8. For details, see Leo, Palme and Volk (1992).

References

Baldwin, W.L. and J.T. Scott (1987) *Market Structure and Technological Change*, Chur: Harwood.

Bound, J., C. Cummins, Z.Griliches, B.H. Hall and A. Jaffe (1984) 'Who does R&D and who Patents', in Z. Griliches, ed, *R&D, Patents, and Productivity, University of Chicago Press for the National Bureau of Economic Research*, Chicago.

Cohen, W.M. and R.C. Levin (1989) 'Empirical Studies of Innovation and Market Structure', in R. Schmalensee and R.D. Willig, eds, *Handbook of Industrial Organization*, Volume II, North Holland, Amsterdam, pp. 1059–1107.

Cohen, W.M., R.C. Levin and D.C. Mowery (1987) 'Firm Size and R&D Intensity: A Re-Examination', *The Journal of Industrial Economics* **35(4)**, pp. 543–565.

Dunning, J.H. (1990) 'Multinational Enterprises and the Globalization of Innovatory Capacity', *Discussion Papers in International Investment and Business Studies*, No. 143, University of Reading, Department of Economics.

Fisher, F.M. and P. Temin (1973) 'Returns to Scale in Research and Development: What does the Schumpeterian Hypothesis Imply', *Journal of Political Economy* **81(1)**, pp. 56–70.

Hutschenreiter, G. (1993) *Innovation and Produktivitätsentwicklung in der österreichischen Industrie*, Paper presented at the Annual Meeting of the Austrian Economic Association, Graz, 14–16th April 1993, Austrian Institute of Economic Research, Vienna.

Jacquemin, A.P. and H.W. De Jong (1977) *European Industrial Organization*, Macmillan, London.

Kamien, M.I. and N.L. Schwartz (1982) *Market Strukture and Innovation.* Cambridge: Cambridge University Press.

Kraft, K. (1989) 'Market Structure, Firm Characteristics and Innovative Activity', *The Journal of Industrial Economics* **37(3)**, pp. 329–36.

Leo, H., Palme, G. and Volk, E. (1992) *Die Innovationstätigkeit der österreichischen Industrie.* Austrian Institute of Economic Research, Vienna

Markham, J.W. (1965) 'Market Structure, Business Conduct, and Innovation', *American Economic Review*, Papers and Proceedings, **55(2)**, pp. 323–332.

OECD (1981) *The Measurement of Scientific and Technical Activities ("Frascati Manual" 1980)*, Paris.

Pavitt, K., M. Robson and J. Townsend (1987) 'The Size Distribution of Innovating Firms in the UK: 1945–1983', *The Journal of Industrial Economics*, **35(4)**, pp. 297–316.

Scherer, F.M. (1965a) 'Firm Size, Market Structure, Opportunity, and the Output of Patented Innovations', *American Economic Review* **55**, pp. 1097–1125.

Scherer, F.M. (1965b) 'Size of Firm, Oligopoly, and Research: A Comment', *Canadian Journal of Economics and Political Science*, **31(2)**, pp. 256–66.

Scherer, F.M. (1984) *Innovation and Growth. Schumpeterian Perspectives*, Cambridge, Mass: MIT Press.

Schumpeter, J.A. (1942) *Capitalism, Socialism, and Democracy*, New York: Harper.

Soete, L.L.G. (1979) 'Firm Size and Inventive Activity', *European Economic Review* **12**, pp. 319–40.

Steindl, J. (1977) 'Import and Production of Know-How in a Small Country: The Case of Austria', in C.T. Saunders ed, *Industrial Policies and Technology Transfer between East and West*, Wien, New York: Springer-Verlag, pp. 211-8.

Steindl, J. (1983) 'Innovation, Forschung und Technologie', in H. Kramer et al., eds, *Perspektiven der österreichischen Industrie*, Wien, pp. 63–74.

Teece, D.J. (1991) 'Technological Development and the Organization of Industry', in OECD, *Technology and Productivity – The Challenge for Economic Policy*, The Technology/Economy Programme, Paris.

K. Aiginger and J. Finsinger (eds.), Applied Industrial Organization, 63–81.

New Experiments in Industrial Organisation

JOHN D. HEY*
Department of Economics, University of York, U.K.

Abstract. Experimental economics has devoted much of its relatively short life to the study of issues of industrial organisation, and has achieved notable successes, of considerable value to the development of both the theoretical and empirical aspects of the subject. The general message emerging from the market-level experiments is that the existence of, and convergence to, the (market) equilibrium of neoclassical theory is, in general, well-supported by the experimental evidence; on the other hand, the general message emerging from the individual level experiments is that the foundations of the neoclassical market theories are seriously flawed. This paper argues for new types of experiments in industrial organisation, ones that are theory-suggesting rather than theory-testing, and ones that are more ill-defined than those carried out to date. There is a need to shed some light on how people tackle extremely complicated ill-defined problems as opposed to experiments confined to testing well-defined theories of simple problems with complicated solutions.

Key words: Experimental economics, industrial organisation, R&D.

JEL codes: B41, C90, L00, O32.

1. Introduction

Experimental economics has devoted much of its relatively short life to the study of issues in industrial organisation, and has achieved notable successes, of considerable value to the development of both the theoretical and empirical aspects of the subject. Indeed, the very earliest developments in experimental economics were specifically directed towards answering key questions of concern to industrial organisation experts. Here one particularly thinks of the early experiments of Chamberlain, of Siegel and of Smith. Their legacy lives on, in a host of market experiments of one form or another.

Such work has often been cited in support of economists' claims that economics is indeed a science: that it, like the "hard" experimental physical sciences (physics, chemistry and biology) can rightly claim that it uses experimental methodology underlying a truly Popperian scientific strategy. Yet, from a methodological perspective, these early experiments are something of an enigma – not really qualifying as genuine "theory-testing experiments", like those carried out in the physical experimental sciences and those required by the Popperian methodology. For they were not testing any well-defined theory; rather they were testing to see whether the equilibrium claimed by the theory would actually be attained in reality.

I will have more to say on such methodological issues later. For the moment, let me pass on to another set of experiments, found more commonly elsewhere in economics (experiments on individual decision taking under risk, for example) but now becoming increasingly common in the field of industrial organisation theory. Most of these are genuine theory-testing experiments, for example like those testing the axioms of Neumann–Morgenstern utility theory, and here, particularly, is the Popperian methodology alive and well and kicking. Indeed, primarily because of experimental work, we now have in economics a very active sub-culture, busily re-building the foundations of individual (and increasingly strategic) behaviour under risk (and uncertainty), with a multitude of new models as extensions to, and generalisations of, Expected Utility (EU) theory, as well as a growing number of "refinements" to solution concepts in Game Theory.

There is, however, a strange dichotomy between these two types of experiments, and a growing divergence between their implications: the general message emerging from the market-level experiments is that the existence of, and convergence to, the (market) equilibrium of neoclassical theory is, in general, (though with some minor qualifications), well-supported by the experimental evidence; on the other hand, the general message emerging from the individual level experiments is that the foundations of the neoclassical market theories are seriously flawed.

One potential explanation of this apparent contradiction is based on the fact that equilibrium in markets is driven, and determined, by the marginal traders, and, as long as these marginal traders are rational agents in the neoclassical sense of the word, then, in equilibrium, the market will behave as if it were *entirely* composed of rational agents: the strange non-EU agents may have some influence on out-of-equilibrium behaviour, but their influence disappears as equilibrium emerges. Moreover, the experimental evidence would suggest that the nature of the equilibrium (though perhaps not the convergence to it) is not affected by the presence of "irrational" agents.

An alternative explanation (of the apparent discrepancy between the findings of market level experiments and individual level experiments), usually proffered by relatively hard-line neoclassical theorists, is that the market mechanism not only punishes non-EU behaviour, but also makes it obvious to the market participants that non-EU behaviour is not very sensible. Proponents of this line of argument would continue by suggesting that the magnitude of the incentives offered to participants in many individual level experiments is insufficient to force the participants to think carefully through the implications of their actions. In other words, the payoff function is relatively flat-topped, with little implied incentive to choose the "optimal" response appropriately.[1] So, non-EU behaviour in such experiments is simply the result of lack of incentive, lack of care and lack of experience. The implication, of course, is that if one makes the rewards large enough, introduces some appropriately large losses, and repeats the experiment often enough with the same subjects, then EU-behaviour would emerge.

Of course, many of the market level experiments do indeed have a large number of repetitions: often it takes several market days for convergence to be reached. There is some experimental interest in the question of *how long* it takes to reach convergence, and whether the length of time is influenced by the particular market structure, but usually the out-of-equilibrium behaviour is not analysed in any further detail.

[A methodological aside might be in order here. This concerns the nature of market level experiments, and, in particular, whether they are theory-testing experiments. Given that there is no, or very little, theory of out-of-equilibrium behaviour in such markets, the experiments cannot be construed as testing any such out-of-equilibrium theory. Nor can they be construed as testing the hypothesis that markets will converge, say, to their competitive equilibrium, for the theory of competitive market equilibrium makes no such claim: it merely states that, under certain conditions, an equilibrium exists in the sense that, if all agents are price-takers, then there exists a price at which aggregate demand equals aggregate supply; it says nothing about convergence to such an equilibrium price. Nor, indeed, can the observation that experimental markets usually converge to this equilibrium price be taken as evidence for the validity of this existence property – for in the experimental markets, agents are price-setters, whereas they are price-takers in the theoretical markets, so, these experiments are not theory-testing, merely descriptive.[2]]

Thus we have descriptive experiments at the market level and theory-testing experiments at the foundation level. In between, there is relatively little experimental work, either of a theory-testing or a theory-suggesting type. But there is enormous scope for such work. More importantly, the way that economics currently operates makes experimental testing the natural way to proceed. Consider the following quote from Judge *et al.* (1980, p. 4):

> "Economic theory, through a formal deductive system, provides the basis for experimental abstraction and the experimental design . . ."[3]

With Industrial Organization theory as currently practised, there is enormous scope for experimental work: as I have remarked elsewhere, the definitive book by Tirole (1989) is like a manual for would-be experimental doctorates – nearly every page contains a nice neat simple model that can be exactly replicated in the laboratory.[4]

I, like others, have followed this route, and I suspect that many others will follow in the years to come. But I am increasingly tempted to the conclusion that this is precisely the wrong route to follow – mainly because I think that theory itself is following the wrong route. Instead of following theory, experimental work should be leading the way. This requires a new type of experiment.

I need to build up my argument carefully. Let me begin on familiar ground and then move on to unfamiliar ground.

2. Familiar Ground

I use as the starting point for my discussion an experiment I have talked about before (in 1990) to the Austrian Economic Association. It is an experimental investigation of Fudenberg *et al.*'s (1983) patent race. The race itself is simple to describe: there are 2 firms, who start at the same point and who are racing to a winning post, a known fixed number of steps away from the starting point. There is a known fixed prize for the first past the winning post, which is shared equally if both pass it at the same time. The race proceeds in a sequence of rounds, in each of which the two firms independently and simultaneously decide whether to go 0, 1 or 2 steps in that round. Going 0 steps costs nothing, going 1 step costs C_1 and going 2 steps costs C_2; C_1 and C_2 are known and fixed and C_2 is more than twice C_1, which makes going 1 step per round more efficient than going 2 steps per round. But there is the problem that the rival might get to the winning post first.

Although the race is simple to describe, and indeed, simple for subjects in an experiment to understand, the solution, as described in Fudenberg *et al.* (1983), and extending over many of the 29 pages of that article, is extremely complex. Indeed, I am repeatedly tempted to the conclusion that the sheer complexity of the solution was the reason for the article's publication in the *European Economic Review*.

The solution (the symmetric Nash equilibrium solution, which exists for certain constellations of parameter values) can be described as follows, where $S_i(k_1, k_2)$ denotes the optimal response of firm i when firm 1 has k_1 steps left to the winning post and firm 2 has k_2 steps left, where $[x_1, \ldots, x_n;\ p_1, \ldots, p_n]$ denotes a mixed strategy involving playing x_i with probability p_i $(i = 1, \ldots, n)$, where $[x_i]$ denotes the pure strategy of playing x_i, and where k^* is $\min\{k;\ \frac{V}{2} \geq \frac{k}{2} C_2\}$ where V is the prize.

If k_1, k_2 *both* $> k^*$

$$S_1(k_1, k_2) = \begin{cases} [0, 1, 2;\ r_0^k, r_1^k, r_2^k] & \text{if } k_1 = k_2 \\ [0] & \text{if } k_1 > k_2 \\ [1] & \text{if } k_1 < k_2 \end{cases}$$

If $k_1 = k^*$ *and* $k_2 > k^*$

$$S_1(k_1, k_2) = [1]$$

If $k_1 > k^*$ *and* $k_2 = k^*$

$$S_1(k_1, k_2) = [0]$$

If k_1, k_2 *both* $\leq k^*$

$$S_1(k_1, k_2) = \begin{cases} [2] & \text{if } k_1 = k_2 \\ [0, 2;\ p_0^k, p_2^k] & \text{if } k_1 = k_2 + 1 \\ [1, 2;\ q_1^k, q_2^k] & \text{if } k_1 = k_2 - 1 \\ [0] & \text{if } k_1 > k_2 + 1 \\ [1] & \text{if } k_1 < k_2 - 1 \end{cases}$$

(The expressions for $S_2(k_1, k_2)$ are found using symmetry.) The probabilities r_i^k $(i = 0, 1, 2)$, p_i^k $(i = 0, 2)$ and q_i^k $(i = 1, 2)$ are functions of V, k, C_1 and C_2. They can be derived recursively.

This patent race model I have replicated in the laboratory; the results are described in detail elsewhere (Hey and Reynolds, 1992). In summary they are as follows: almost 84% of all decisions taken by the experimental subject were *not inconsistent* with the Nash Equilibrium strategy as defined above; but a test of the hypothesis that subjects were using the relevant probability distributions (for the mixed strategies) is rejected at virtually any significant level one cares to specify. What does one make of this? An 84% "not-inconsistency rate" seems, at first glance, remarkably high (and, indeed, almost contradictory to the second finding) but on closer inspection it is not so remarkable: for example, subjects soon realised that when they got 2 steps behind they should give up, and that when they got 2 steps ahead they should play 1. Sophisticated reasoning, like that underlying the Nash Equilibrium solution, was not needed to get this result. The inconsistency between the theoretical probability distributions and the observed relative frequency distributions does not surprise me: I can see no way that the subjects could have calculated the correct probabilities.[5]

I am tempted to the conclusion that the subjects, faced with a very simple task with an extremely complicated "solution", reacted in a relatively simplistic fashion – moreover, in a manner which resembled in certain respects the structure of the optimal solution. This could be taken as vindication of the theory (but note I say resembled the "structure" – not the detail of the theory), but I would prefer to conclude that it is an indication of the triumph of common sense. Subjects were responding in a reasonable manner: tending to try things out ("adopt a mixed strategy") when things looked unclear, and becoming more positive when things became clearer. In summary: we have a very simple problem, with a very complicated "optimal solution", but one which is tackled in a relatively simplistic fashion by the subjects.

Let us now stand back, and ask ourselves about the theory which I have been testing experimentally. The theory was designed as a description of R&D behaviour, of Patent Race behaviour, and is very typical of the *genre*. The authors are very explicit about their motivation for constructing the model presented in the paper: they wanted a story in which a firm which falls behind in a patent race *might* catch up and then overtake its rival; the authors call this leapfrogging. Most early papers on R&D races could not explain such leapfrogging behaviour, and Fudenberg *et al.*'s main motivation was to construct a simple story in which such leapfrogging was possible. (So the theory was empirically motivated.) And the basic structure of the story is indeed simple: no exogenous uncertainty of any type – only the endogenous uncertainty generated by strategic considerations: the probabilistic behaviour of the mixed strategy being the appropriate optimising response.

I say that the "theory was empirically motivated" but only in the sense that the authors wanted a model in which a stylised fact (leapfrogging) could emerge as an implication of the optimising behaviour of the participants. The actual "rules of the game" themselves were *not* empirically motivated: not even the authors, I presume, would pretend that the model mimics the behaviour of rival R&D departments. So what does one make of the theory: a theory which is constructed in order to illustrate leapfrogging and which actually does exhibit leapfrogging?

Does one conclude that the model mimics reality; or does one simply conclude by admiring the model-building skills of the authors?

I am not decrying the simplicity *per se* of the model, nor the fact that it is an abstraction of reality (which all useful models must necessarily be). Rather, I am trying to emphasise that here we have an extremely simple (or simply-stated) problem with an extremely complex solution. I ask again: why was the paper accepted for publication in the *European Economic Review*? Or to put it another way: would it have been published if the solution had taken up just 1 page and been extremely simple? And if the sheer complexity of the solution is the reason for its publication – that four high priests of the profession had spent many hours working out the optimal solution – what credence can we give for the solution as a description of actual behaviour?

Let me now state my opinion: the Industrial Organisation theory literature (and trailing after it the Experimental IO literature) is heading off in the wrong direction, particularly in the crucial area of Research and Development. The Fudenberg *et al.* model is an extremely simple problem with an extremely complicated solution. Real life R&D behaviour is not like this; on the contrary it is almost exactly the opposite: an *extremely complex problem tackled* (usually and almost necessarily) *in an extremely simplistic manner*. The problem, of course, is that modern (neoclassical) theoretical methodology does not have a way of tackling the latter problem: locked in its optimising mode, and obliged to solve optimally any problem it sets itself, it almost inevitably leads to increasingly complex solutions to apparently trivial problems, particularly strategic ones. Consider the development of the literature, and, for example, imagine the response of (constructive) neoclassicists to my criticism of the "reality" of the "rules of the game" of the Fudenberg *et al.* model; they would increase the number of firms; they would make the prize a random variable; they would make the costs random variables; they would make the number of steps to the winning post a random variable; they would allow more than 0, 1 or 2 steps in each round; etc., etc. True one would be moving closer to reality, but all the time the optimal strategy would be becoming ever more complex, not just taking four high priests of the profession many hours to work out, but rather dozens of high priests many weeks to work out. Relevant to this final observation is the answer to the question: why did Fudenberg *et al.* stick with such a simple model? Because even then its solution was extremely complex?

3. Unfamiliar Ground

I would now argue that Experimental Economics should, at least in part, abandon its almost total concern with theory-testing experiments and return to one of its original motivations: theory-suggesting experiments. Concomitant with such a shift of emphasis would be a move towards *ill-defined* experiments. This is a much more difficult move, and takes experimental economics into relatively untrodden territory.

It is safe to say that virtually all experiments conducted so far have been well-defined experiments, whether they have been theory-testing or theory-suggesting/descriptive. Such a statement is almost tautological when one is discussing neo-classical theory-testing experiments since the theory that is being tested is itself well-defined (being neoclassical) and since the experiment, of necessity, must replicate the theory. The market level experiments I discussed earlier were also well-defined in the sense that all participants were completely informed about the "rules of the game", even if they were not informed about all the numerical parameters of the experiment.

It is extremely difficult to set up and run ill-defined experiments. Of necessity (otherwise the experimenter loses control) they must be well-controlled, but the subjects must not be fully informed about all aspects of the experiment. Ill-defined experiments appear ideally-suited for R&D problems, since R&D, possibly of all areas of economics, is an area in which economic agents face ill-defined problems: they do not know the "rules of the game", they do not know the objective distribution of time to the discovery of the patent (as a function of the expenditure on R&D) and even if they have some subjective probability distribution for this time, I suspect that Expected Utility theory cannot be mechanically applied, because of the nature of the uncertainties associated with that distribution.[6]

There are, inevitably, enormous practical difficulties involved in setting up and running genuinely ill-defined R&D experiments. Consider, to illustrate this point, the difficulty of setting up some kind of experiment in which subjects undertake genuinely innovative research activity of some kind – crucially of a kind that none of them have had any prior experience of. Almost tautologically this is impossible, for if the research is not genuinely innovative, then some of the subjects may have had experience of it, whereas if it *is* genuinely innovative, then one is not only carrying out experimental economics work, but also genuine research activity. And what is the guarantee that any of the subjects will actually discover whatever it is (inevitably undefined?) that they are meant to be discovering? How then can one motivate them?

Given such difficulties, it is natural to try to think up some kind of stylised model of R&D behaviour (just like the neo-classical theory of course!) that attempts to mimic the real world, but which is equally familiar (or unfamiliar) to all subjects. This is what I and some of my collaborators, particularly Patrizia Sbriglia of the University of Naples, have been trying to do. "Unfortunately", we have ended up, at least for the time being, with a rather well-defined experimental situation. But at least it is not simplistic.

The motivation for these experiments is the vision I have of research biochemists trying to discover a new cure for some old or new illness. I picture the biochemist in his or her laboratory surrounded by masses of bottles and jars full of ingredients and chemicals, busily mixing together various combinations of these ingredients and trying them out to see if they work. Some combinations will work better than others, and one hopes to find the Perfect Combination that miraculously cures the illness. Bingo!

In actuality the situation is rather complicated: the Perfect Combination, if it exists, consists of an unknown number of ingredients, mixed in different proportions (and there may well be complications concerning the mixing process). Moreover, the biochemist is never completely certain whether he or she is getting closer to the Perfect Combination, because of noise, false alarms and general confusion. The crucial difficulty here is the modelling of the connection between the information obtained from incorrect combinations and the Perfect Combination itself.

An analogy which some might find fruitful is that of an explorer who is trying to locate some destination, and who has a map of the surrounding terrain. To begin with, the explorer does not know where he or she is, other than somewhere in the terrain covered by the map. Now the way that the explorer tries to locate the destination depends crucially on the information that he or she gets from the present location. Suppose, for example, that the only information conveyed by the map is that of *height* (it is simply a contour map), and that the only information that the explorer has about the present location is its *height*. Then the explorer has quite a difficult problem to solve, involving building up a picture of the neighbourhood of the initial location, and locating that on the map. I suppose that some clever theorist will tell me that there is a well-defined "optimal" solution to this problem, but I would find it more constructive (at least initially) to observe what the explorer did. I suppose if the explorer was given lots of such problems to tackle, then his or her expertise would probably improve – though the resemblance of the problem to an R&D problem would recede.

This is one of various scenarios that I have considered; in due course we hope to implement it experimentally. In the meantime, one we have particularly concentrated on is that with Patrizia Sbriglia which we call The Combination Race.[7] This takes us back to the vision of the research biochemist surrounded by millions of jars. Naturally, it is a simplification of that vision, but not, we hope, a simplistic one.

There are N subjects/participants/firms in the experiment. We have a set of m letters of the alphabet from which n are selected at random without replacement. These n letters (nor the residual $m - n$) are not told to the subjects; they form the Winning Combination. The purpose of the Combination Race is to discover the Winning Combination: the first subject so to do earns a rather serious prize of V (shared equally if two or more subjects discover the Winning Combination at the same time); the rest earn nothing, except any residual from an initial participation fee. The Race proceeds in a sequence of rounds, the precise way depending upon the information given to the subjects. There are 2 basic versions: deterministic information and noisy information.

In the deterministic information version, the Race proceeds in a sequence of rounds, in each of which each of the N subjects buys as many or as few Trial Combinations as he or she wishes, at a constant and known cost per combination

C_1. (Initially these costs are subtracted from the participation fee, but after this is exhausted, subjects must actually pay their own money if they want to continue in the Race.) At the end of each round, each subject is told, for each of their Trial Combinations, how many letters in that Trial Combination appear in the Winning Combination. This information is given accurately, without noise. In the noisy information version, however, this information is given with noise, the precise implementation being as follows: if the correct number of letters in a Trial Combination appearing in the Winning Combination is j then the subject will be told that i of them are correct, where the relationship between i and j is as follows:

$$\text{if } 0 < j < n \qquad i = \begin{cases} j-1 & \text{with probability '1/4} \\ j & \text{with probability 1/2} \\ j+1 & \text{with probability 1/2} \end{cases}$$

$$\text{if } j = 0 \qquad i = \begin{cases} 0 & \text{with probability 3/4} \\ 1 & \text{with probability 1/4} \end{cases}$$

$$\text{if } j = n \qquad i = \begin{cases} n-1 & \text{with probability 1/4} \\ n & \text{with probability 3/4.} \end{cases}$$

Subjects are told these relationships.

In the noisy information version, a distinction needs to be made between Trial Combinations and Declarations. Because subjects may not know whether a Trial Combination actually is the Winning Combination, they need to Declare it as such. Only if a correct Declaration is made is the subject deemed to be the winner. (Obviously such a distinction is not necessary in the deterministic information version, for once the Winning Combination is tried, it is immediately discovered.) For obvious reasons, Declarations cost more than Trial Combinations: a constant and known cost per declaration of C_2. $(C_2 > C_1)$.

As with any experiment, considerable thought needs to be given to the appropriate choice of parameters, in this case N, n, m, V, C_1 and C_2. When we initially conceived this experiment, we had no idea of any "optimal" strategy (we remain somewhat hazy about this, though we do have rather more ideas than originally), nor did we have any notion of how people might actually tackle this in practice. So we naively constructed a "random choice" model, simulated the implications of this on a computer, and decided in a monstrously *ad hoc* fashion, to assume that subjects would take only one-half of the time implied by this "random choice" model. We then chose the parameters so that the experiment would last a reasonable number of rounds (obviously this is a stochastic variable in the "random choice" model) so that we would get a reasonable number of observations, and so that (average) payment per subject would provide a sensible incentive (somewhat above the marginal wage rate of the subjects) while providing a serious-enough amount of money as a prize. I seem to recall (though I must admit that I prefer not to remember too well) that the initial pilot experiment (involving 2 identical sessions) had $N = 8$, $m = 26$, $n = 3$ $V = 50$, $C_1 = 10$p (and C_2 irrelevant as it was a deterministic information version). We thought this would last about 6 rounds.

In practice the first session lasted just 2 rounds: all 8 subjects correctly identifying the Winning Combinations in the 2nd round. What most had done was to specify 18 Trial Combinations in the first round, along the following lines:

ABC	DEF	GHI	JKL	MNO	PQR	STU	VWX	YZA
ADG	BEH	CFI	JMP	KNQ	LOR	SVY	TWZ	UXA.

Whatever the Winning Combination, these 18 Trial Combinations were sufficient to identify it.[8] We had to cancel the second session of the Pilot.

Naturally we were rather chastened by this – yet at the same time heartened: subjects were actually using intelligence (logical reasoning) to tackle the problem, rather than some form of mathematical technique. I appreciate that the distinction between these two is not clear-cut in general, but this Pilot did bring home to us clearly the fact that many, though not all, economic theories involved the use of some kind of mathematical apparatus. In contrast, this experiment involved the use of logic.

[An aside: in other, unconnected experiments, I have found that the match between theory and behaviour is often much closer when the theoretical result being tested has some intuition lying behind the mathematics of the result; for example, subjects are better at understanding reservation price rules rather than marginality conditions.]

The Pilot took us back to the drawing board. We again tried to determine the appropriate experimental parameters, but now armed with some notion of the strategies that subjects might be using. Further explorations showed us that, in addition to the "matrix rule" described above, a popular strategy was one where $(n - 1)$ of the letters in the Trial Combination were kept fixed while the n'th was varied across the remaining letters of the m in the set. Whether this was more efficient than the matrix rule depended partly on n, and, depending upon its precise implementation, partly on luck.

We have now converged on $N = 5$, $m = 26$ and $n = 7$ as "reasonable" parameters. We have now run 7 deterministic information versions, all with $V = 30$, and 4 with $C_1 = 10$p and 3 with $C_1 = 30$p, and 5 noisy information versions, all with $V = 35$, $C_1 = 10$p and $C_2 = 20$p. All except one of these experiments were run on an individual basis; in the final one we tried, but without success, to induce "Joint Venture" behaviour; the participants who were ahead did not want to join forces with those who were behind, whilst those who were behind did not want to join forces with others who were also behind.[9]

The results of these experiments are reported in detail elsewhere (Sbriglia and Hey, 1992), but I can give a little flavour here. Consider Table I in which the results of one of the deterministic information experiments is reported. A variety

TABLE I. An example of the output from the Combination Race. Race Number 2: Prize $25, cost 10p, no noise. Winning Combination: BFMKPRY

Subject 1	Subject 2	Subject 3	Subject 4	Subject 5
ABCDEFG	ABCDEFG	ABCDEFG	ABCDEFG	ABCDEFG
ABCDEFH	DEFGHIJ	HIJKLMN	ACDEFGH	HIJKLMN
ABCDEFI	BCDEFGH	OPQRSTU	ACDEFJK	OPQRSTU
ABCDEFJ	CDEFGHI	VWXYZAD	AHIJKLM	VWXYZAB
ABCDEFK		GJMPSVY		CDEFHIJ
ABCDEFL		BEHKNQT		HNOLPQR
ABCDEFM		WZCFILO		STUVWXY
ABCDEFN		RUXAEIM		ZABCDEH
ABCDEFO		QUYCGKO		
ABCDEFP				
ABCDEFQ				
ABCDEFR				
ABCDEFS				
ABCDEFT				
ABCDEFU				
ABCDEFV				
ABCDEFX				
ABCDEFY				
HIJKLMA				
HIJKLMB				
HIJKLMC				
HIJKLMD				
HIJKLME				
HIJKLMF				
FKMPRYB	NOPQRST	GJMPSVY	BAJPQRS	GBADFEI
	CDEFGKL	BCDEFGK	BKANORS	SHGABMN
	DEFGKLM	AHILNOQ	BWXYZTU	
	EFGKLMN	TUWXZPD	BLVYZSR	
	FGKLMNO	KMCGYJV	BANPTOW	
	GKLMNOP			
	KLMNOPQ			
	LMNOPQR			
	MNOPQRS			

Winner was Subject Number 1.

of strategies is illustrated here: the eventual winner (subject 1) employs the strategy of keeping $(n-1)$ letters fixed and varying the n'th, finally varying the $(n-1)$ fixed letters in combination with another fixed set of $(n-1)$ letters. This yields the Winning Combination directly. Subject 2 started out doing this, but rather half-heartedly. Subject 3 has a variant on the matrix strategy discussed above, though does not get too far with it. Subject 4 is similar to subject 2. Finally, subject 5 goes through the alphabet twice, producing overlapping combinations. Elsewhere other subjects tried variations on this latter theme, and there were other variations too – like going round the keyboard rather than through the alphabet.

This research is still ongoing, but I can describe the thrust of our current work. We are identifying the various strategies used, and their dependence on the subject's relative position in the Race. Sometimes there are no clear strategies: subjects seem to be trying randomly in the hope of getting lucky. What we plan to do then is to simulate the effects of different strategies meeting each other. This will take some time, as there is much richness in the results.

The final set of experiments I would like to describe are some we are just piloting. They differ in certain respects from The Combination Race, but they share the feature of trying to get a rich environment in which the "optimal strategy" is not immediately apparent, and is certainly rather complicated – because of the complicated nature of the environment itself. An Industrial Organisation theorist would describe these as repeated two-stage oligopoly problems: the first stage involving the choice of capacity (and implicitly the decision as to whether to enter the market or not) and the second stage involving the price or the output decision, depending on whether one is in a price- or a quantity-setting market. Where our experiment differs from any that may have gone before (though we are not aware of any with the same structure as ours) is that we specifically want more participants in the experiments than the market can optimally sustain. Unfortunately, the pilot experiment on which we report here did not achieve this latter objective – there was a problem with the design which we did not realize until after the pilots were completed; this perhaps emphasises further that setting up these new types of experiments is considerably more difficult than would initially appear. However, we now think that we have a viable design that achieves our objective; I will describe this briefly later.

Let me be more specific about the basic structure of the experiment. Consider first a quantity-setting market in which aggregate demand is given by

$$Q = a - bP$$

and in which each of the N firms in the market have identical marginal and average production costs of c per unit. The rules of the game specify that each firm i $(i = 1, \ldots, n)$ chooses output q_i independently and simultaneously, and the market price is determined from

$$\sum_{i=1}^{n} q_i = a - bP.$$

Simple algebra shows that the Nash Equilibrium when there are N firms in the market is for each firm to put

$$q_i = \frac{(a - c)}{(N + 1)b}$$

from which it can be shown that Nash Equilibrium profits are

$$\frac{(a-c)^2}{(N+1)^2 b} \text{ per firm.}$$

Now what we wanted was to set up an experiment in which the actual/optimal number of firms in the market was less than the number of participants in the experiment. So we required an earlier stage – in which firms decided whether to entry the market or not. For reasons which are no longer clear to us, we decided that firms should also decide their *capacity* and that there should be a (constant) capacity cost (per unit). Output could not exceed this capacity. We then argued that firms (if they could coordinate entry) would enter until the capacity cost equalled the profits per firm, that is:

$$\frac{(a-c)\,d}{(N+1)b} = \frac{(a-c)^2}{(N+1)^2 b}$$

from which it follows that the number of firms in the market should "optimally" be N^* given by

$$N^* = \frac{a-c}{d} - 1$$

and overall profits per firm entering the market are zero. We then thought that if firms could not coordinate entry, the problem would become horrendously difficult. Unfortunately, as we discovered rather too late, the participants adopted a much simpler strategy: after a brief initial period of uncertainty, they all ended up with output effectively equal to capacity.[10] This effectively reduced the problem to a one-stage quantity-selecting model with total marginal cost equal to the production cost plus the capacity cost. In our next set of experiments we will replace the constant capacity cost per unit with a fixed entry cost (in the quantity-setting experiments) and with a fixed entry cost *plus* a constant capacity cost per unit (in the price-setting experiments).

We have piloted the experiment in both a price-setting and a quantity-setting environment. The quantity-setting version is as described above. The price-setting version requires firms choosing capacity first, and then, when all the capacity decisions have been announced, choosing a price. The capacity decisions are taken, independently and simultaneously, in the morning of each day; the price (or output) decisions are taken, independently and simultaneously, in the afternoon of each day. In the pilots we ran the experiment for 20 days, the first 4 of which were for practice. Subjects were paid a participation fee of £5 plus their cumulative profits over the final 16 days of the experiment. The following four sessions have been run:

Q-setting 1: $a = 100, b = 1, c = 10, d = 15, N = 8$

P-setting 1: $a = 100, b = 1, c = 10, d = 15, N = 8$

TABLE II. Quantity-setting experiment 1

Capacity/output decisions									
Subject	1	2	3	4	5	6	7	8	Price
Day									
1	1/1	10/10	30/30	5/5	3/3	5/5	50/50	10/7	0
2	1/1	8/8	15/15	5/5	10/10	5/5	10/10	9/9	37
3	2/1	10/10	20/20	6/6	11/11	5/5	14/14	12/11	22
4	2/2	15/13	10/10	6/6	10/10	5/5	10/10	9/9	35
5	1/1	15/13	12/12	6/6	10/10	8/8	10/10	9/9	31
6	2/2	10/9	10/10	6/6	10/10	9/9	12/12	10/10	32
7	3/3	15/14	10/10	7/7	11/9	10/9	10/10	11/10	28
8	5/5	8/8	11/11	7/7	15/15	12/10	13/11	11/11	22
9	2/2	15/13	10/10	7/7	15/15	8/8	10/10	10/10	25
10	5/5	10/10	10/10	7/7	15/15	6/6	8/8	10/10	29
11	5/5	10/10	13/13	8/8	16/16	6/6	10/10	11/11	21
12	2/2	10/10	10/10	8/8	16/16	6/6	12/12	11/11	25
13	2/2	8/7	10/10	7/7	16/16	6/6	9/9	11/11	32
14	2/2	8/7	10/10	7/7	17/17	7/7	11/11	10/10	29
15	5/5	8/8	10/10	10/10	17/17	8/8	9/9	11/11	22
16	4/4	9/8	10/10	10/10	17/17	8/8	10/10	11/11	22
17	2/2	7/6	8/8	9/9	16/16	8/8	12/12	11/11	28
18	3/3	10/9	9/9	9/9	16/16	8/8	12/12	10/10	24
19	2/2	8/7	9/9	7/7	16/16	8/8	12/12	10/10	29
20	2/2	8/7	9/9	6/6	16/16	8/8	12/12	10/10	30

Q-setting 2: $a = 100, b = 1, c = 20, d = 10, N = 8$

P-setting 2: $a = 100, b = 1, c = 20, d = 10, N = 8$.

Note, in the first 2, N^* is 5; in the last 2, N^* is 7. Participants were not allowed to talk to each other. Each session lasted some $2\frac{1}{2}$ hours. A brief summary of the results follows.

Q-setting 1: (For details see Table II.) After initial variation, the capacity and output decisions tended to yield a market price which fluctuated around the total marginal cost of 25 ($= c + d$); when it was above 25 all subjects made positive profits, when it was below 25 all subjects made losses. Output tended to equal capacity when aggregate capacity was less than 75, and was generally below otherwise. Most interestingly, capacity and output varied not only for each subject through time but also varied, and to a much greater extent, *across subjects*. This did not appear to concern subjects. Finally, no participant "dropped out" – that is, chose zero capacity – despite the obvious attractions of such a strategy. (We should note that the £5 participation fee required *attendance* until the end of the experiment, but not *active* participation in the market.)

P-setting 1: (For details see Table III.) The first four days of the experiment (the

TABLE III. Price-setting experiment 1

Capacity/price decisions (Blanks indicate infinitely high price)

Subject	1	2	3	4	5	6	7	8	Total capacity
Day									
1	25/35	50/20	15/60	20/26	60/29	10/30	40/27	20/40	240
2	30/26	50/25	25/26	35/26	20/26	20/27	20/17	20/26	220
3	10/25	10/26	60/20	25/26	10/26	25/27	30/21	15/26	185
4	10/26	10/26	20/50	40/26	10/26	20/30	80/20	5/30	195
5	0/	0/	10/50	0/	2/40	5/70	10/20	3/70	30
6	6/34	10/30	10/45	0/	5/45	6/40	15/49	5/43	57
7	10/35	5/30	10/35	8/29	5/32	10/45	14/44	6/32	68
8	20/29	10/29	8/28	10/28	10/26	5/35	12/38	7/20	82
9	0/	15/26	10/26	20/26	10/27	10/28	8/6	8/24	81
10	5/25	10/26	5/26	22/26	10/25	15/25	15/25	8/25	90
11	5/48	0/	6/59	8/26	5/59	5/45	5/26	7/59	41
12	7/45	6/30	5/49	8/26	10/49	5/49	5/42	5/49	51
13	6/54	5/45	7/55	2/40	8/55	5/55	5/48	7/55	45
14	6/53	7/55	5/53	3/49	8/53	6/53	5/55	7/53	47
15	6/49	5/45	8/49	4/49	8/49	6/49	7/50	7/49	51
16	6/50	8/49	5/50	3/51	8/50	6/50	7/48	7/50	50
17	6/44	8/44	8/44	5/44	8/44	6/44	7/49	8/44	56
18	7/48	5/48	5/48	6/48	10/48	6/48	6/48	7/48	52
19	7/41	6/41	6/41	8/41	10/41	6/41	8/41	8/41	59
20	7/33	5/33	10/33	10/33	10/33	6/33	10/33	9/33	67

practice days) showed considerable uncertainty on the part of the participants and rather an erratic set of decisions. If these had been "for real" the subjects would have lost rather a lot of money! In days 5 and 6 (the first two days for which profits counted towards actual payment) several participants stayed out of the market, and this happened occasionally thereafter. But usually all subjects participated in virtually all market days after day 7. There was a general tendency for subjects to reduce their capacity level through time. Prices in days 5 through 10 tended to be only slightly above total cost per unit (production cost per unit plus capacity cost per unit), but as capacity drifted down there was a general tendency for prices to drift upwards. Around day 14 a curious phenomenon emerged – at first with just a few subjects, but then with growing numbers, the prices charged came to equal 100 *minus* the total capacity: subjects came to realise that if they charged this price, they would be guaranteed to sell all their capacity, irrespective of what the other subjects were charging. By day 17, 7 of the 8 subjects were charging this price, and by day 18 all 8 subjects. In the final 2 days all subjects charged this price. However, the price was steadily drifting down (48 in day 18, 41 in day 19 and 33 in day 20) as subjects realised that if all subjects were using this pricing

TABLE IV. Quantity-setting experiment 2

Capacity/output decisions Subject	1	2	3	4	5	6	7	8	Price
Day									
1	10/10	20/10	6/0	7/7	50/25	10/10	5/4	44/44	0
2	10/10	16/16	6/6	2/2	12/8	5/5	5/5	15/15	33
3	8/8	17/17	6/2	15/12	12/12	12/12	8/8	20/20	9
4	8/8	5/5	6/6	5/4	9/9	20/20	7/7	12/10	31
5	6/6	10/9	5/5	7/5	11/11	12/12	7/7	10/10	35
6	6/6	8/5	6/6	10/10	9/9	10/10	7/7	10/10	37
7	6/6	14/10	7/7	10/9	11/11	12/12	7/4	10/9	32
8	6/6	10/9	7/7	9/9	10/10	14/14	7/6	10/9	30
9	6/6	9/9	7/7	11/11	10/10	10/10	6/6	9/9	32
10	6/6	12/12	7/7	10/10	10/10	12/12	6/6	10/10	27
11	6/6	10/10	7/7	11/11	8/8	12/12	6/6	9/9	31
12	6/6	10/10	6/6	7/7	11/11	11/11	6/6	8/8	35
13	6/6	10/10	7/7	8/8	11/11	12/12	6/6	8/8	32
14	6/6	10/10	10/10	9/8	11/11	13/13	6/6	8/8	28
15	6/6	10/8	10/10	10/9	10/10	13/13	6/6	9/9	29
16	6/6	10/10	10/10	10/10	11/11	12/12	6/6	8/8	27
17	6/6	5/5	8/8	7/7	9/9	10/10	6/6	8/8	41
18	6/6	8/8	8/8	7/7	9/9	11/11	6/6	8/8	37
19	6/6	8/8	7/7	8/8	9/9	11/11	7/7	8/8	36
20	6/6	9/9	7/7	7/7	9/9	10/10	7/7	8/8	37

strategy, then they personally would benefit if they increased their own capacity somewhat. Of course, there is a limit to this process – when the total capacity has been increased to 100 *minus* the total cost per unit (production cost plus capacity cost). The pricing rule discussed above would imply profits of zero for all subjects at this limit. This limit was not, however, reached and one can only speculate as to whether it would have been if the experiment had continued for more days. I suspect that further fluctuations would have been observed.

Q-setting 2: (For details see Table IV.) Here prices fluctuated:

Day:	5	6	7	8	9	10	11	12	13	14	15	16	17	18	19	20
Price:	35	37	32	30	32	27	31	35	32	28	29	27	41	37	36	37

Since total (marginal) costs per unit were 30 (production cost = 20 and capacity cost = 10) subjects made losses (unless their capacity was zero) whenever the price was less than 30 (in days 10, 14, 15 and 16) and positive profits (unless their capacity was zero) whenever price was greater than 30. In the practice days capacity tended to be higher than the market could sustain with the result that large (notional) losses were made in those days. After day 4 capacity was generally in the range 5 to 12, though typically there were larger variations across subjects each day than across days for each subjects. Some subjects always had relatively low

TABLE V. Price-setting experiment 2

Capacity/price decisions (Blanks indicate infinitely high price)									
Subject	1	2	3	4	5	6	7	8	Total capacity
Day									
1	10/60	10/50	5/50	16/31	68/32	10/40	4/25	10/45	133
2	10/25	5/35	10/33	30/31	40/28	6/33	10/30	25/40	136
3	50/25	6/32	7/31	10/32	50/31	20/20	6/33	15/20	164
4	5/29	6/35	5/32	5/50	15/31	4/30	10/36	12/25	62
5	10/29	6/37	7/38	5/31	15/31	4/31	7/38	5/30	59
6	15/30	5/42	8/40	5/44	8/32	4/33	5/41	6/35	56
7	6/39	5/42	10/40	5/42	15/33	4/34	6/40	7/38	58
8	10/38	5/33	15/33	1/99	15/38	4/35	9/33	8/40	67
9	15/37	5/23	15/40	5/31	15/35	4/35	11/31	7/35	77
10	17/36	5/32	15/32	5/33	15/36	4/35	8/32	7/37	76
11	16/34	5/31	7/33	5/34	20/33	4/35	10/32	7/32	74
12	23/30	5/30	50/31	10/29	25/31	10/31	8/31	7/31	138
13	20/32	5/30	10/32	5/31	15/31	8/31	5/31	7/32	75
14	40/29	5/30	15/31	5/30	15/31	4/31	6/31	6/31	96
15	35/30	5/30	5/30	5/30	8/36	5/31	6/31	5/31	74
16	15/36	5/44	6/38	5/46	8/33	5/31	6/44	6/42	56
17	15/36	5/30	7/30	5/32	16/36	10/31	7/32	6/32	71
18	20/34	5/30	7/30	5/30	20/33	10/31	7/31	6/30	80
19	15/40	10/30	7/31	5/31	15/30	6/31	7/32	7/31	72
20	15/34	5/49	7/48	5/40	3/50	1/30	8/49	7/49	51

capacities (and outputs) while other had relatively high capacities (and outputs). The former made smaller profits and smaller losses than the latter; possibly this reflects risk aversion?

P-setting 2: (For details see Table V.) The pricing rule observed in the closing stages of *P-setting 1* showed itself briefly for some of the subjects around day 8, but it disappeared again. Thereafter prices generally sunk to around or a little above total cost per unit (30 = unit capacity cost *plus* unit production cost), recovering later in the experiment as total capacities were reduced. By day 20 there was a partial re-emergence (among some of the subjects) of the pricing rule observed earlier.

This rule is an interesting one: given the capacities chosen, it is very much a safe rule rather than an optimising one. I have yet to explore its implications, but it would appear to be very much a satisficing rule rather than an optimising rule.

A fuller description of the results of these pilot experiments, and further experiments on the same basic theme, will appear elsewhere.

4. Conclusions

I have been arguing in this paper for new types of experiments in Industrial Organisation, one that are theory-suggesting rather than theory-testing, and ones that are more ill-defined than those carried out to date. In a sense, it is a plea to return to earlier concerns. These types of experiments are frustrating to carry out and to analyse, and difficult to sell to one's neo-classical colleagues. Yet we need to shed some light, particularly in the field of IO in general and R&D in particular, on how people tackle extremely complicated ill-defined problems. If all experiments are confined to testing well-defined theories of simple problems with complicated solutions, we are little better than the drunk who was asked if he had dropped his keys near the lamp-post and replied: "No – but I can see better here".

Notes

* I am particularly grateful to the ESRC, the Leverhulme Trust and the Fondazione Ivo Vanzi for financing the experiments discussed in this paper. I would also like to pay tribute to Patrizia Sbriglia, who has carried out much of the work on The Combination Race, and to Cristina Pitassi, who has worked with me on the Oligopoly Experiment discussed at the end of the paper. Finally, my especial thanks to Norman Spivey, for writing the software for two of the three experiments discussed here, and to Jo Hall for typing this paper faster than I could write it.

1. Recent experiments (Hey, 1992) which attempt to *estimate* EU and non-EU preference functionals suggest that there is, indeed, a considerable amount of noise in subjects' responses.
2. At one stage, they were considered theory-suggesting (suggesting theories of out-of-equilibrium behaviour) but this now seems not to be of particular interest to the experimentalists carrying out such experiments.
3. They also go on to say "... but society in most cases carries out the experiment, possibly using its own design".
4. On page 4 of Tirole (1989), there is a splendid remark on which all economists should dwell: "Still another method of collecting evidence that can benefit from the theoretical developments is the running of controlled experiments in laboratories".
5. It presumably took Fudenberg *et al.* some time to work out the solution; and it took me about 3 months to write a computer program specifying the Nash Equilibrium strategy.
6. Here it is instructive to note the significance of the Ellsberg Paradox for the problem of R&D, and to recognise the bulk of evidence which clearly seems to support the notion that subjects, when tackling Ellsberg Paradox type problems, do not have well-defined subjective probabilities which are manipulated according to the Subjective Expected Utility rules.
7. The experiments conducted on The Combination Race have been financed by a generous grant from the Fondazione Ivo Vanzi, to whom we are extremely grateful.
8. This is not necessarily the most efficient way to identify the Winning Combination, but it *guarantees* finding it.
9. At the end of every round, we gave a table of information to all subjects showing how many trial combinations everyone had bought, and how many of them had 0, 1, 2 ..., n reported letters correct. From this table, subjects could get some idea of how well they were doing relative to others.
10. This was when total capacity was less than a minus the total marginal cost, in which case the price would necessarily exceed total marginal cost so that all participants would make positive profits; when total capacity exceed a minus the total marginal cost – in the early stages of the experiment – the output of some participants was less than their capacity.

References

Fudenberg, D., Gilbert, R., Stiglitz, J., and Tirole, J. (1983) 'Preemption, Leapfrogging and Competition in Patent Races', *European Economic Review* **22**, 3–31.

Hey, J.D. (1992) 'Circles, Triangles and Straight Lines: Estimation of Betweenness-Satisfying Non-EU Preference Functionals Using Experimental Data', EXEC Discussion Paper, University of York.

Hey, J.D. and Reynolds, M.R. (1992) 'Experiments, Games and Economics', Chapter 6 of Moss, S. and Rae, J., *Artificial Intelligence and Economic Analysis*, Edward Elgar.

Judge, G.G., Griffiths, W.E., Hill, R.C., and Lee, T.-C. (1980) *The Theory and Practice of Econometrics*, Wiley.

Sbriglia, P. and Hey, J.D., 'The Combination Race', EXEC Discussion Paper, University of York.

Tirole, J. (1989) *The Theory of Industrial Organization*, MIT Press.

II. THE EVOLUTION OF MARKETS AND FIRMS

K. Aiginger and J. Finsinger (eds.), Applied Industrial Organization, 85–93.

Entry, Growth, and Survival: The New Learning on Firm Selection and Industry Evolution

DAVID B. AUDRETSCH and TALAT MAHMOOD
Wissenschaftszentrum Berlin für Sozialforschung, Berlin, Germany

Abstract. This paper tries to shed some light on the seeming paradox posed by the findings in the industrial organization literature that (1) the bulk of firms in an industry are not only very small, but also sufficiently small so that they are operating at a sub-optimal scale of output, and (2) entrepreneurs are apparently not deterred from starting new firms even in industries where scale economies play an important role. A dynamic view of the process of firm selection and industry evolution is that new firms typically start at a very smal scale of output. Because this level of output may be sub-optimal, the firm must grow in order to survive. The empirical evidence supports such a dynamic view of the evolutionary nature of industries. Viewed through a dynamic lens, the often-observed asymmetric size distribution of firms becomes more understandable. The persistence of an asymmetric firm-size distribution skewed towards small enterprises presumably reflects a continuing process of entry into industries and not necessarily the survival of such small and suboptimal enterprises over a long period of time.

Key words: Firm size, entry, firm selection.

JEL codes: L11.

1. Introduction

One of the more striking stylized facts to emerge in the industrial organization literature has been the pervasiveness and persistence of an asymmetric firm-size distribution predominated by small enterprises. Empirical studies, dating back at least to the seminal study by Simon and Bonini (1958) have identified such a skewed firm-size distribution to exist across a wide range of industries, nations, and time periods.[1] The pervasiveness of an asymmetric firm-size distribution is consistent with the observation by Weiss (1964 and 1976), Scherer (1973), and Pratten (1971) that most firms in virtually every industry are operating at a suboptimal level of output.[2]

A second finding which has emerged only in recent studies is that the entry of new firms into an industry is apparently not substantially deterred in industries where capital intensity and scale economies play an important role. For example, Acs and Audretsch (1989 and 1990, Chapter 5), Evans and Siegfried (1992), Austin and Rosenblaum (1991), and two of the five country studies summarized in Cable and Schwalbach (1992) found evidence that entrepreneurs are not noticeably deterred from entering industries characterized by substantial scale economies.

Why are most firms small and why is their entry not deterred in the presence of scale economies? The purpose of this paper is to resolve these seeming paradoxes. By combining the recent evidence regarding the pattern of entry into industries with the post-entry performance of new firms, it is possible to shed light on the overall process of firm selection and industry evolution. In the second section of this paper, a theory of firm selection and industry evolution is presented. This theory purports to explain the actual observed behavior of entrepreneurs starting firms and to predict their post-entry experience. In the third section, issues related to measuring the post-entry performance of firms are explored. Based on a large longitudinal data base tracking more than 11,000 new manufacturing start-ups in the United States, the hazard duration model is used in the fourth section to identify the ability of firms to survive subsequent to start-up.

Finally, in the fifth section a summary and conclusion are provided. In particular, we find considerable evidence supporting the dynamic view of the selection process of new firms which is at the heart of industry evolution. The persistence of an asymmetric firm-size distribution skewed towards small enterprises presumably reflects a continuing process of entry into industries. However, this does not at all imply that such new firms survive over a long period of time. Rather, new firms are typically engaged in the selection process, whereby the successful enterprises grow and ultimately approach or attain the optimal size, while the remainder stagnate and may ultimately be forced to cease operations. Thus, although the skewed size distribution of firms persists with remarkable stability over time, it does not appear to be a constant set of small and sub-optimal scale firms responsible for this skewness.

2. Firm Selection and Industry Evolution

Why should entrepreneurs start a new firm? The traditional model in industrial organization offers one answer: Entry occurs because profits in excess of the long-run equilibrium profit rate prevail in the industry. That is, as Geroski (1989) characterizes the underlying motivation for entry,

$$E = \lambda[\pi - \pi^*(BE)] \tag{1}$$

where E represents entry, π represents the actual profit rate realized by firms in the industry, and π^* represents the long-run equilibrium rate of profit, after controlling for the extent of barriers, to entry, BE. According to this model, the product, production technology, inputs, and input prices all remain constant. Entry is about business as usual – it is just that the entrants provide more of it. Thus, entry serves an equilibrating function in the market, in that the additional output offered by the new firms restores the levels of price and profitability back to their equilibrium levels.

A different answer was provided by Schumpeter (1950), who argued that new firms may be the result of an inherent "subjectivity of knowledge". Schumpeter

(1950, p. 132) observed that, "... the function of entrepreneurs is to reform or revolutionize the pattern of production by exploiting an invention or, more generally, an untried technological possibility for producing a new commodity or producing an old one in a new way ... To undertake such new things is difficult and constitutes a distinct economic function, first, because they lie outside of the routine tasks which everybody understands, and secondly, because the environment resists in many ways."

That is, entrepreneurs may start new firms not merely to replicate the incumbent firm, but rather to do something different. In this sense, new firms can be viewed as "agents of change". If there were not subjectivity of economic knowledge, there would be no need for new firms, because both managers of the incumbent firms and the inventor of an idea would reach the same valuation of the economic value of that idea. The inventor would merely transfer the idea to the incumbent firm for roughly the value of that idea. However, the greater the subjectivity of information, the greater the gap is likely to be between the evaluation of a potential innovation by the incumbent firm and by the inventor. Acs and Audretsch (1989 and 1990, Chapter 5) argue that if this gap becomes large enough, entrepreneurs will tend to start a new firm rather than transfer their ideas to the incumbent enterprises. The empirical evidence clearly shows that start-up activity tends to be greater in those industries characterized by the entrepreneurial regime, or where the conditions of technological knowledge are the most subjective.

Entrepreneurs will start new firms when the gap between the expected value of their potential innovations by themselves and the incumbent firms tends to be the greatest.[3] However, because knowledge is subjective, not all inventions, or potential innovations, actually become successful innovations. What happens to those new firms whose potential innovations do not materialize? The answer is: "It depends". Subsequent to entering an industry, a firm must decide whether to maintain its output (Q_{it}), expand, contract, or exit. The probability of a firm remaining in business in period t, or $P(Q_{it} > 0)$, is essentially determined by the extent to which a firm is burdened with an inherent size disadvantage, and the probability of actually innovating, i

$$P(Q_{it} > 0) = f[i_{it}, c(Q_{it}) - c(Q_i^*)] \tag{2}$$

where $c(Q_{it})$ is the average cost of producing at a scale of output Q_i, $c(Q_i^*)$ is the average cost of producing the MES level of output, or the minimum level of production required to attain the minimum average cost, Q_i^*. Thus, in deciding whether to remain or exit from the industry, a firm will weigh the extent to which it is confronted by a scale disadvantage against the likelihood of innovating or otherwise growing to attain scale economies. As the firm size grows relative to the MES level of output, the more likely the firm is to decide to remain in the industry. This suggests that either an increase in the start-up size of the firm or a decrease in the MES level of output should increase the likelihood of survival.

The firm's actual level of output in period t is determined by its innovative activity, I_{it}, plus some factor of its output in the previous period, $\bar{Q}_{it}$,

$$Q_{it} = \bar{Q}_{it} + Q(I_{it}) \tag{3}$$

where

$$\bar{Q}_{it} = \lambda(Q_{io} + Q_{it-1}) \tag{4}$$

and Q_o is an autonomous level of output and λ is a factor representing the portion of the previous period's output that can be maintained in the market. Factors such as market growth presumably influence the value of λ. That is, if market growth is sufficiently high, a new firm may be able to grow enough so that $Q_{it} = Q_i^*$, even in the absence of innovative activity.

An important implication of the above process is that firms are more likely to be operating at a sub-optimal scale of output if the underlying technological conditions dictate a higher subjectivity of knowledge. If firms successfully innovate, they grow into viably-sized enterprises. If not, they will be doomed to stagnate and ultimately to exit from the industry. This suggests, just as some empirical studies have recently found, entry and the start-up of new firms is not greatly deterred in the presence of scale economies. As long as entrepreneurs perceive that there is some prospect for growth and ultimately survival, such entry will occur. Thus, in industries where the MES is high, firms not able to grow and attain the MES level of output would presumably be forced to exit from the industry, resulting in a relatively low likelihood of survival. In industries characterized by a low MES, neither the need for growth, nor the consequences of its absence are as severe, so higher survival rates would be expected. In industries where the subjectivity of knowledge is particularly high, that is in highly innovative industries, more entrepreneurs may be motivated to start a new firm. In such industries the likelihood of the firm surviving would presumably be lower.

We analyse the post-entry performance of new firms through the lens of the hazard duration model, which was first proposed by Cox (1972 and 1975) and later by Kiefer (1988). The partial likelihood model has the advantage of compensating for censored observations in the estimation procedure and of not imposing any parametric form on the precise time to failure.

3. Measurement Issues

The greatest constraint in analysing the post-entry performance of firms has been the lack of longitudinal data sets consisting of individual plants and firms that identify the actual start-up and closure dates. While Dunne, Roberts, and Samuelson (1988 and 1989), Audretsch (1991), Evans (1987), Hall (1987), Phillips and Kirchhoff (1989) all had access to such a longitudinal data set, none of these studies explicitly estimated the hazard rate model. One reason why the U.S. Bureau of Census data employed by Dunne, Roberts, and Samuelson do not lend themselves to estimation of the hazard model, is that while observations over time are available, they are identified only at five-year intervals.

Thus, we employ a data set which provides bi-annual observations on firms and plants – the U.S. Small Business Administration's Small Business Data Base (SBDB). The data base is derived from the Dun and Bradstreet (DUNS) market identifier file (DMI), which provides a virtual census on about 4.5 million U.S. business establishments every other year between 1976 and 1986.

While the raw Dun and Bradstreet data have been subject to considerable criticism (FitzRoy, 1989), the SBDB data have been adjusted by the U.S. Small Business Administration to clean up the raw data in the original DMI files. Several important studies have compared the SBDB data with analogous measures from the establishment data of the U.S. Census of Manufactures (Acs and Audretsch, 1990, Chapter 2), and from the establishment and employment records of the Bureau of Labor Statistics (Brown and Phillips, 1989) and have concluded that the SBDB data are generally consistent with these other major data bases providing observations on firms and plants.

The essential building block of the SBDB is the establishment, which is defined as a particular economic entity operating at a specific and single geographic location. While some establishments are legally tied to parent firms through either a branch or subsidiary relationship, other establishments are independent and therefore are firms (enterprises) in their own right. The data base links the ownership of all establishments to any parent firms, thereby enabling the performance of establishments which are independent firms to be distinguished from those which are branches and subsidiaries of parent firms.

Besides a detailed identification of the ownership structure of each establishment, the USELM file of the SBDB links the performance of each establishment within two-year intervals beginning in 1976 and ending in 1986, thereby tracking each establishment over what constitutes a ten-year longitudinal data base.

4. Empirical Results

The semi-parametric hazard duration model is used to test the hypothesis that the exposure to risk of new establishments is shaped by the extent to which scale economies play a role in the relevant industry, the initial start-up size of the establishment market growth, and the technological environment. Measurement of the MES has proved to be challenging at best. Here we adapt the standard Comanor-Wilson (1967) proxy for measuring MES, which is defined as the mean size of the largest plants in each industry accounting for one-half of the industry value-of-shipments, 1977. This measure is derived from the Census of Manufactures of the U.S. Bureau of the Census. While the Comanor-Wilson measure is crude, it has prove in numerous studies to at least reflect the extent to which scale economies play an important role in an industry (Scherer and Ross, 1990). This MES measure is expected to exert a positive influence on the rate of hazard confronting new

TABLE I. Regression results for hazard duration model, 1976–1986[a]

Independent variables	All plants (1)	New firms (2)	Branches & subsidiaries (3)	All plants High-tech (4)	All plants Low-tech (5)
Minimum efficient scale	0.0051	0.0053	–0.0002	–0.0017	0.0158
	(3.480)	(3.500)	(–0.028)	(–0.674)	(4.390)
Start-up size	–0.0014	–0.0027	–0.0007	–0.0006	–0.0016
	(–3.780)	(–3.753)	(–1.617)	(–0.685)	(–2.910)
Growth	0.1273	0.1727	–0.9561	–1.2840	–1.0900
	(0.622)	(0.828)	(–0.890)	(–1.270)	(–1.600)
Total innovation rate	0.0325	0.0401	–0.0343	–	–
	(1.125)	(1.338)	(–0.302)		
No. of objects	8109	7717	392	881	3474
Chi. square	32.5	35.6	3.89	2.6	30.3
Log of likelihood	–46783.	–44364.	–1417.	–3945.	–18428.

[a] T-statistics in parenthesis.

establishments.

The most reliable and consistent measure of the size of the establishment when it was founded is the number of employees. As already explained, a larger start-up size is expected to reduce the hazard rate. Market growth is measured as the percentage change in the total scales of the four-digit standard industrial classification (SIC) industry within which the establishment operated between 1976, the year that all of the establishments were founded, and 1986, which is the final year of analysis. This measure is derived from the annual Survey of Manufactures of the U.S. Bureau of the Census. Market growth is expected to increase the growth potential of new establishments, and therefore should increase their ability to survive. That is, all boats should be lifted by a rising tide.

The measure the degree to which new technological knowledge in an industry is subjective, the innovation rate, defined as the number of innovations in 1982 divided by industry employment, is used.[4] The innovate rate is employed rather than the absolute number of innovations in order to standardize the amount of innovative activity by the size of the industry. Presumably an industry with more innovative activity can be characterized by higher technological uncertainty and therefore greater subjectivity.

Using the 7070 manufacturing establishments founded in 1976 for which compatible industry characteristics could be matched, the hazard duration rate was estimated using the semi-parametric model described previously. Equation 1 in Table I shows the regression rates for the estimated hazard function based on all new plants established in 1976. The hazard rate is estimated only for new firms in the second equation. In the third equation the hazard function for new branches and subsidiaries opened by existing enterprises is estimated.

The empirical results indicate that, as expected, the likelihood of survival tends to be reduced in industries where economies of scale play an important role. By contrast, a larger start-up size serves to elevate the likelihood of survival. New plants and firms in highly innovative industries tend to be confronted with a lower likelihood of survival, although the t-ratio is not high enough to be considered statistically significant.

The results also indicate that, just as the likelihood of survival confronting new branches and subsidiaries opened by existing firms is not influenced by the extent of scale economies in the industry, there is little evidence suggesting that an increase in their start-up facilitates the ability to survive.

The hazard rate confronting new establishments in high-technology industries is estimated in Equation 4 and that for low-technology industries is estimated in Equation 5 in Table I. High-technology industries are defined as those four-digit standard industrial classification (SIC) industries where the R&D/sales ratio exceeds five percent. By contrast, low-technology industries are defined as those four-digit SIC industries where the R&D/sales ratio is less than one percent.[5] The likelihood of survival confronting new establishments in low-technology industries is apparently lower in the presence of substantial scale economies. Similarly, a higher start-up size tends to reduce the hazard rate. However, in high-technology industries, neither the minimum efficient scale measure nor the initial start-up size significantly influences the likelihood of survival for new establishments. These results suggest that the greater subjectivity of knowledge found in high technology tends to spur the start-up of new firms, even in the presence of high scale economies.

5. Conclusion

The results of this paper shed at least some light on the seeming paradox posed by the findings in the industrial organization literature that (1) the bulk of firms in an industry are not only very small, but also sufficiently small so that they are operating at a sub-optimal scale of output in most industries, and (2) entrepreneurs are apparently not deterred from starting new firms even in industries where scale economies play an important role. A dynamic view of the process of firm selection and industry evolution is that new firms typically start at a very small scale of output. Because this level of output may be sub-optimal, the firm must grow in order to survive.

The empirical evidence presented in this paper supports such a dynamic view of the evolutionary nature of industries, because the propensity for new firms to survive tends to be shaped by the extent to which there is a gap between the MES level of output and the size of the firm. As this gap increases, the likelihood of any new firm surviving tends to decrease.

Lucas (1978) and Jovanovic (1993) attempt to explain the pervasiveness of small enterprises in the firm-size distribution with a static theory. But viewed through a dynamic lens, the often-observed asymmetric size distribution of firms becomes more understandable. According to this view, the frequent observation of industries dominanted by small firms does not mean that it is the same set of small firms being observed over time. Rather, new firms are engaged in the process of selection, whereby only the successful enterprises are able to grow and ultimately survive. That is, the persistence of an asymmetric firm-size distribution skewed towards small enterprises presumably reflects a continuing process of entry into industries and not necessarily the survival of such small and sub-optimal enterprises over a long period of time.

Notes

1. See for examples the country studies included in Acs and Audretsch (1993).
2. For example, Weiss (1991, p. xiv) observed that, "In most industries the great majority of firms is suboptimal. In a typical industry there are, let's say, one hundred firms. Typically only about five to ten of them will be operating at the MES (minimum efficient scale) level of output, or anything like it."
3. A slightly different approach is undertaken by Jovanovic (1982), who proposes that new entrants face random costs which differ across firms. A central feature of his model is the assumption that a new firm does not know what its costs, that is its relative efficiency, will be, but rather discovers this through the process of learning from its actual post-entry performance. In particular, Jovanovic (1982) assumes that entrepreneurs are unsure about their ability to manage a new start-up and therefore their prospects for success. For further extensions, see Pakes and Erikson (1987), who argue that firms can actively accelerate the learning process by investing in knowledge-generating activities, such as R&D.
4. The total innovation rate was introduced by Acs and Audretsch (1987, 1988, and 1990). It is based on a direct measure of innovative output.
5. The classification of industries by R&D/sales is from the National Science Foundation (1987) for the year 1980.

References

Acs, Z.J. and D.B. Audretsch (1993) *Small Firms and Entrepreneurship: An East-West Perspective*, Cambridge, England: Cambridge University Press.

Acs, Z.J. and D.B. Audretsch (1990) *Innovation and Small Firms*, Cambridge, MA: MIT Press.

Acs, Z.J. and D.B. Audretsch (1989) 'Small-Firm Entry in U.S. Manufacturing', *Economica* **56** (2), 255–265.

Acs, Z.J. and D.B. Audretsch (1988) 'Innovation in Large and Small Firms: An Empirical Analysis', *American Economic Review* **78** (4), 678–690.

Acs, Z.J. and D.B. Audretsch (1987) 'Innovation, Market Structure and Firm Size', *Review of Economics and Statistics* **69** (4), 567–575.

Audretsch, D.B. (1991) 'New-Firm Survival and the Technological Regime', *Review of Economics and Statistics* **60** (3), 441–450.

Austin, J.S. and D.I. Rosenbaum (1990) 'The Determinants of Entry and Exit Rates into U.S. Manufacturing Industries', *Review of Industrial Organization* **5** (2), 211–223.

Brown, H. and D. Phillips (1989) 'Comparison Between Small Business Data Base (USEEM) and Bureau of Labor Statistics (BLS) Employment Data: 1978–1986', *Small Business Economics* **1** (4), 273–284.

Cable, J. and J. Schwalbach (1991) 'International Comparisons of Entry and Exit', P. Geroski and J. Schwalbach (Eds.), *Entry and Market Contestability: An International Comparison*, Oxford: Basil Blackwell, pp. 257–281.

Comanor, W.S. and T.A. Wilson (1967) 'Advertising, Market Structure, and Performance', *Review of Economics and Statistics* **49** (4), 423–440.

Cox, D.R. (1975) 'Partial Likelihood', *Biometrics* **62**, 269–275.

Cox, D.R. (1972) 'Regression Models and Life Tables', *Journal of the Royal Statistical Society* **34**, 187–220.

Dunne, T., M.J. Roberts, and L. Samuelson (1989) 'The Growth and Failure of U.S. Manufacturing Plants', *Quarterly Journal of Economics* **104** (4), 671–698.

Dunne, T., M.J. Roberts, and L. Samuelson (1988) 'Patterns of Firm Entry and Exit in U.S. Manufacturing Industries', *Rand Journal of Economics* **19** (4), 495–515.

Evans, D.S. (1987) 'The Relationship Between Firm Growth, Size and Age: Estimates for 100 Manufacturing Industries', *Journal of Industrial Economics* **35** (2), 567–581.

Evans, L.B. and J.J. Siegfried (1992) 'Entry and Exit in United States Manufacturing Industries from 1977 to 1982', in D.B. Audretsch and J.J. Siegfried (Eds.), *Empirical Studies in Industrial Organization: Essays in Honor of Leonard W. Weiss*, Boston: Kluwer Academic Publishers.

Fitzroy, F.R. (1989) 'Firm Size, Efficiency and Employment: A Review Article', *Small Business Economics* **1** (1), 75–80.

Geroski, P.A. (1989) 'The Interaction Between Domestic and Foreign Based Entrants', D.B. Audretsch, L. Sleuwaegen, and H. Yamawaki (Eds.), *The Convergence of International and Domestic Markets*, Amsterdam: North-Holland, pp. 59–83.

Hall, B.H. (1987) 'The Relationship Between Firm Size and Firm Growth in the U.S. Manufacturing Sector', *Journal of Industrial Economics* **35**, 583–605.

Jovanovic, B. (1993) 'Entrepreneurial Choice When People Differ in Their Management and Labor Skills', *Small Business Economics* **5** (4).

Jovanovic, B. (1982) 'Selection and Evolution of Industry', *Econometrica* **50** (2), 649–670.

Kiefer, N.M. (1988) 'Economic Duration Data and Hazard Functions', *Journal of Economic Literature* **26** (2), 646–679.

Lucas, R.E., Jr. (1978) 'On the Size Distribution of Business Firms', *Bell Journal of Economics* **9**, 508–523.

National Science Foundation (1987) *Science & Engineering Indicators – 1987*, Washington, D.C.: U.S. Government Printing Office.

Pakes, A. and R. Ericson (1987) 'Empirical Implications of Alternative Models of Firm Dynamics', manuscript, Department of Economics, University of Wisconsin-Madison.

Phillips, B.D. and B.A. Kirchhoff (1989) 'Formation, Growth and Survival: Small Firm Dynamics in the U.S. Economy', *Small Business Economics* **1** (1), 65–74.

Pratten, C.F. (1971) *Economies of Scale in Manufacturing Industry*, Cambridge, England: Cambridge University Press.

Scherer, F.M. (1973) 'The Determinants of Industry Plant Sizes in Six Nations', *Review of Economics and Statistics* **55** (2), 135–145.

Scherer, F.M. and D. Ross (1990) *Industrial Market Structure and Economic Performance*, 3rd ed., Boston: Houghton Mifflin.

Schumpeter, J.A. (1950) *Capitalism, Socialism and Democracy*, 3rd ed., New York, NY: Harper and Row.

Simon, H.A. and C.P. Bonini (1958) 'The Size Distribution of Business Firms', *American Economic Review* **48** (4), 607–617.

Weiss, L.W. (1991) (D.B. Audretsch and H. Yamawaki, Eds.), *Structure, Conduct, and Performance*, New York: New York University Press.

Weiss, L.W. (1976) 'Optimal Plant Scale and the Extent of Suboptimal Capacity', R.T. Masson and P.D. Qualls (Eds.), *Essays on Industrial Organization in Honor of Joe S. Bain*, Cambridge, MA: Ballinger, 126–134.

Weiss, L.W. (1964) 'The Survival Technique and the Extent of Suboptimal Capacity', *Journal of Political Economy* **72** (3), 246–261.

K. Aiginger and J. Finsinger (eds.), Applied Industrial Organization, 95–106.

Innovation and Evolution as a Dynamic Game with Rational Behaviour

MATTHIAS BLONSKI
Department of Economics, University of Mannheim, Germany

Abstract. In the recent literature about the explanation of the behaviour of innovating firms there coexist two basically different approaches. To so called *neoclassical* approach assumes maximising behaviour relating to an exogenously given innovation technology and the *evolutionary* approach postulates time constant routine decisions. Both explanations are supported by well known arguments. Nevertheless they seem to be completely separated in the literature. The evolutionary approach even defines itself by the separation of the neo-classical approach. In this paper the two methods or philosophies are linked in a simple duopolistic model. It will be shown, that the strategic maximising behaviour of innovating firms leads in a dynamic model to routine decisions as equilibrium strategies.

JEL codes: L20, O31.

Key words: Economic theory, dynamic game, innovations, R&D investment, evolution.

1. Introduction

Innovation as the result of progress of ideas, invention, exploration and development often requires investment by the entrepreneur who ex ante does not know the true value of this project. That decision thus cannot be modelled as a deterministic maximising problem. In their famous evolutionary approach. Nelson and Winter (1982) even doubt the maximising behaviour of innovating firms. In their model they reject to presume any choice sets or any maximising behaviour of the firms. Instead, they differentiate between 'firms that choose well' and 'firms that consistently make mistakes'. *Evolutionary* in this context means, that the differentiation is ex post. However, Nelson and Winter's explanation for the individual decisions is what they call 'routines' and 'skills', which we imagine to be some kind of bounded rationality.

Unfortunately, economists have not found a theoretical concept for bounded rationality at all, hence the power of explanation on the micro level in the evolutionary approach of Nelson and Winter ends with some distributional assumptions about the heterogeneity of the firms that indeed must be ad hoc.

In the present model, the author tries to link advances of *orthodox* and *evolutionary* models and stresses new aspects of the very complex connection between innovation and market structure. A basic motivation for this model is the problem of connecting rationality of investment decisions with the observable random character of the evolutionary success of innovations. With rationality we identify the payoff maximising assumption. The agents know the model but they do not observe everything in the model, for example their competitor's strategies. This lack of knowledge is replaced by beliefs being consistent with the assumptions of the model.

An important source of inspiration has been the model of Ericson and Pakes (1989). In the general part of their paper (Chapter II), they set up the entrepreneur's decision problem as a Marcovian programming problem over a general discrete state space, that is identified with the success of the entrepreneur's research and development activities, and that is provided with a complete preorder induced by a value function, which itself is derived by expectation values of the discounted payoffs. The existence of a solution for such a discounted dynamic programming problem is well known (see for example Bertsekas (1976)). In order to get more detailed results, Ericson and Pakes are using a much more specific model leading to a life-cycle characterisation and to aggregation results.

The present model is a Marcov game, that explicitly allows for dynamic strategic interaction. Each firm realises the state of the whole system being composed by the state of each participant. But it does not observe the strategies of the competing firms. Thus the change of the state in the system is driven by two elements: (i) maximising behaviour of economic agents; and (ii) stochastic transition between the states. Notice, that the firms are cumulating information over time by realising the state history of each participant. One could imagine, that the resulting strategies are reaction patterns, which possibly are very complicated.

However, in the present model, they are not. Indeed the assumptions about the firm's benefit and the stochastic transition function lead to the simplest imaginable strategies. The behaviour is absolutely constant. There is no reaction on the competitor or state ore time. This leads to a random process on the state space, which we imagine to be *evolution* since optimal behaviour may lead one firm into a better position than others, even if the initial conditions have been opposite. Actually, this is a completely different result than that of Ericson and Pakes, who predict in their competitive context a state dependent investment decision. The reason for this lies in the different specification of the Marcov structure.

The basic hypothesis derived from the present model is the following: As long as the strategic constellation of an interactive system of innovating firms and their beliefs in the expected benefit remain constant, there is a dynamic subgame-perfect equilibrium with constant optimal investment strategies, where the equilibrium path in the periodical innovation benefit of each firm is random. The time pattern of successful innovations may be heterogenous. The most successful firm is not necessarily that one running the biggest reserach program. The present model illuminates the idea of evolving industrial structure where the evolutionary growth is driven by the innovating entrepreneur who behaves rational and may be identified with a *routine*, since the behaviour pattern is endogeneously constant over time.

2. The Model

We consider a duopolistic industry extending over an indefinite number of periods. The strategies of the firms, called *paths of actions*, are investment decisions in research and development (R&D) in each period. R&D-efforts lead in a stochastic way to the discovery of new processes and products. In order to simplify the analysis the current performance of a firm will be described by a one dimensional integer variable, called *the state of the firm*. As a first approach we assume, that this one dimensional variable embraces all relevant information essential to the decision-maker of the firm to assess the success of the R&D-activities. It's possible to generalise the model to a higher dimension and to continuous spaces. However, in the present model we want to focus on the strategic investment decisions. The successful innovation plays just the role of randomly arising profits.

Let the state space S of the game be $\mathbf{Z} \times \mathbf{Z} = \mathbf{Z}^2$. A typical element $s = (s_1, s_2) \in \mathbf{Z}^2$ is called the state of the system, where s_1 is the state of firm 1 and s_2 that of firm 2. The interaction of the two firms will be introduced by the firm's influence on the own state and therefore on the state of the system by the periodical R&D-investment decision, which we shortly call action.

It is convenient to define the action space A_i of each firm $i = 1, 2$ as $I\!R_+$, such that an element $c = (c_1, c_2) \in A := A_1 \times A_2 = I\!R_+^2$ is a pair of R&D-investment in one period. A is obviously convex.

The stochastic q on $\mathbf{Z}^2$ will be described as a cross-product of two for each firm $i = 1, 2$ independently defined stochastics on the own state space. This reflects the fact, that in the present model the motion on the state space is only driven by individual actions, not by any interaction. The interaction will be modelled by period profits, which depend on the state of the system. We describe the stochastic $q_i(s_i|s_i', c_i)$ of firm i, where $q_i(s_i|s_i', c_i)$ is the probability, that firm i changes the state from s_i' to s_i, if it chooses the action c_i, where $i \in \{1, 2\}$ and $q_i(s_i|s_i', c_i) \in [0, 1]$ and $s_i, s_i' \in \mathbf{Z}$ and $c_i \in I\!R_+$.

Assumption 1:

$q_i(s_i|s_i', c_i) = q_i(s_i - s_i'|0, c_i)\ \forall s_i, s_i' \in \mathbf{Z},\ \forall c_i \in I\!R_+$,
here $s_i - s_i'$ is the *standard addition* on $\mathbf{Z}$. By this assumption we shortly write $q_i(s_i, c_i) := q_i(s_i|0, c_i)\ \forall s_i \in \mathbf{Z}$.

Assumption 2:

$$q_i(0, c_i) = 1 - \lambda\ \forall c_i \in I\!R_+ \tag{i}$$

$$q_i(\xi, c_i) = 0\ \forall \xi \in \mathbf{Z} \text{ with } |\xi| > 1,\ \forall c_i \in I\!R_+ \tag{ii}$$

$$q_i(1, c_i) = \lambda f_i(c_i)\ \forall c_i \in I\!R_+ \tag{iii}$$

$$q_i(-1, c_i) = \lambda(1 - f_i(c_i))\ \forall c_i \in I\!R_+, \tag{iv}$$

where $\lambda \in (0,1]$ is an *exogenous parameter*, which reflects the typical velocity of change in the industry driven by the invention of innovative products and processes given by nature. The function $f : I\!R_+ \to [0,1]$ is assumed to have the properties:

$$f_i' > 0, f_i'' < 0 \text{ and boundary conditions } f_i(0) = 0, \lim_{c\to\infty} f_i(c) = 1. \quad \text{(v)}$$

Assumption 1 means, that the probability of the change of state is independent of the state. Actually it depends only on the difference to the new state. This assumption reflects the interpretation of innovation as a sequence of independent inventions. The realisation and the quality of new ideas do not depend on traditional and obsolete ideas.

Assumption 2 is a specification of the stochastics[1]: (i) λ is the exogenous probability of zero-change. Later we use the parameter λ to characterise industry; (ii) The state of a firm changes only to neighbour states. We take this assumption as the simplest case of this model containing all qualitative effects. The function $f_i : I\!R_+ \to [0,1)$ in (iii) and (iv) represents the influence of the R&D-expenditure on the firms own transition probability. Possible specifications for f_i are $f_i(c_i) = 1 - e^{-c_i}$ or $f_i(c_i) = \frac{c_i}{c_i+1}$.

The construction of the transition function $q(\cdot|s,c)$ on the state space of the game S is the following: let $s = (s_1, s_2) \in S = \mathbf{Z}^2$ and $s' = (s_i', s_2') \in S$ and $c = (c_1, c_2) \in A$, then define

$$q(s'|s,c) = q_1(s_1' - s_1, c_1) \cdot q_2(s_2' - s_2, c_2).$$

The interaction of the two firms will be introduced by the current payoff profit mapping $r : S \times A \to I\!R^2$ with $r(s,c) = (r_1(s,c_1), r_2(s,c_2))$, where $r_i(s,c_i)$ is the current payoff profit of firm i, if the state of the system is s and firm i plays action c_i.

Assumption 3:

r is *linear*. We write for $i,j = 1,2$ and $i \neq j$

$$r_i(s_i, s_j, c_i) = r_{ii}s_i - r_{ij}s_j - c_i\,, \quad (1)$$

where $r_{ij} \in I\!R_+$, for $i,j = 1,2$.

Assumption 3 specifies the type of interaction. Firm 1 cannot influence the probability distribution of the state of firm 2, but improving its own state by research investment deteriorates the current payoff profit of firm 2, and vice versa. We may interpret r_{ij} for $i \neq j$ as a measure of interaction between the two firms and r_{ii} as the value of the own state change.

Assumption 4:

$$f_i'(0) > \frac{1}{2\lambda r_{ii}} \quad \text{for } i = 1,2.$$

This is a technical assumption, that guarantees the existence of non-zero equilibrium strategies. The intuition for this assumption is the following: there is a lowest barrier for the slope of the f_i-function at zero. It is consistent to interpret

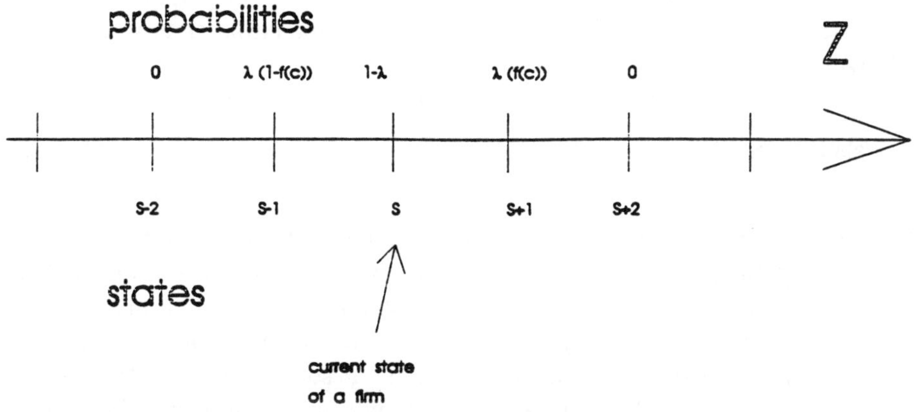

Fig. 1. The picture shows the state space of a firm being in state $s \in \mathbf{Z}$. The transition probability of the firm to be in state $s+1$ is for example $\lambda(f(c))$.

this condition as entry-condition in an extended model, because equality reflects a zero-profit-condition, the equilibrium strategy of zero investment will be called *exit*.

Let time t be indexed by $t = 0, 1, 2 \ldots$. We denote the initial state of the system by $s^0 = (s_1^0, s_2^0) \in \mathbf{Z}^2$. Each of the two firms chooses its R&D-investment decision $c^0 = (c_1^0, c_2^0) \in A$. The state of the system changes from s_0 to s_1 by the transition function q with probability $q(s^1|s^0, c^0)$. Each firm receives its payoff $r_i(s^1, c^0)$. In the next period this procedure repeats with the new initial state s^1 and so on.

Let $\mathbf{c} := (c^0, c^1, c^2, \ldots) = ((c_1^0, c_2^0), (c_1^1, c_2^1), (c_1^2, c_2^2), \ldots)$ be a time path of pairs of actions. It defines a Markov-process on S. Let $q^t(s|s^0, \mathbf{c})$ be the probability, that the system after t periods is in the state s, if s^0 is the initial state and $\mathbf{c}$ is the time path of actions. The expected payoff of firm i in period t conditioned on s^0 is given by

$$E_i^t(s^0, \mathbf{c}) = \sum_{s' \in S} q^t(s'|s^0, \mathbf{c}) \cdot r_i(s', c_i^{t-1}), \tag{2}$$

if actions $\mathbf{c}$ are played. The discounted objective function of firm i will be defined as

$$\Pi_i(s^0, \mathbf{c}) = \sum_{t=0}^{\infty} \delta^t [E_i^t(s^0, \mathbf{c})] \tag{3}$$

with $\delta \in (0, 1)$ as discount factor. We are now ready to define the equilibrium for the dynamic game.

Definition: *'Dynamic Stochastic Nash Equilibrium (DSNE)'*
The time-path $\mathbf{c}^* = ((c_1^{0*}, c_2^{0*}), (c_1^{1*}, c_2^{1*}), (c_1^{2*}, c_2^{2*}), \ldots)$ of pairs of actions is a *Dynamic Stochastic Nash Equilibrium* (DSNE) for the initial state $s^0 \in S$, if the following condition is satisfied:
$\mathbf{c}_i^* = (c_i^{0*}, c_i^{1*}, c_i^{2*}, \ldots)$ for $i = 1, 2$ is solution of the stochastic control problem

$$\underset{\mathbf{c}_i}{\text{Max}} \ \Pi_i(s^0, \check{\mathbf{c}}^*) , \qquad (SMAX)$$

where $\check{\mathbf{c}}^* := ((c_i^0, c_j^{0*}), (c_i^1, c_j^{1*}), \ldots)$ is the path of actions of firm i, given firm j plays the equilibrium path $\mathbf{c}^*$ and firm i maximises over all possible own paths.

Since the action in each period is a function on the space of all histories up to the current period, the strategy spaced of each firm is huge. However, it is well known from the theory of dynamic games, that it suffices to consider stationary strategies, depending only on the actual state. Indeed, an equilibrium in stationary strategies is in particular subgame perfect [see Parthasarathy (1972) or Federgruen (1978)].

Definition: *'Stationary DSNE, Constant SDNE'*
A dynamic stochastic Nash equilibrium $\mathbf{c}^*$ will be called *stationary*, if there exists a map $\tilde{c}_i : S \to A_i$ for $i = 1, 2$, such that $c^{t*} = (\tilde{c}_1(s_t, \tilde{c}_2(s_t)) \ \forall t = 0, 1, 2, \ldots$, where $s_t \in S$ is the realised state in period t. A DSNE is called *constant*, if there is a constant state-independent strategy c_i^* with $c_i^* = c_i^{0*} = c_i^{1*} = c_i^{2*} = \ldots$ for each firm $i = 1, 2$.

Proposition 1:
Given assumptions 1, 2 and 3, there exists a constant DSNE $c^* = (c_1^*, c_2^*)$ for the stochastic innovation duopoly game.

Proposition 2:
If assumptions 1, 2 and 3 hold, the equilibrium path in the state space corresponding to c^* from proposition 1 is given by the composition of a random walk of each firm in its own state space.

Proposition 3:
Under assumptions 1 to 4 the constant DSNE exists, is unique, and is given by

$$c_i^* = (f_i')^{-1}\left(\frac{1}{2\lambda r_{ii}}\right) .$$

Proposition 4:
The comparative statics is given by

$$\frac{\partial c_i^*}{\partial \lambda} < 0 \ \text{ and } \ \frac{\partial c_i^*}{\partial r_{ii}} < 0 .$$

(proofs will be found in the appendix).

3. Interpretation and Conclusion

The main parameters of the model are (i) R&D-expenditure of each firm; (ii) the state of each firm; (iii) the exogenous parameter δ, the discount rate; and (iv) the industry characterising parameter λ indicating the velocity of invention.

R&D-expenditure and discount rate are often used variables in the empirical investigations, so there is no need of further explanation. The state of a firm is in this model identified with revenues of invention by the linearity assumption of the payoff function r_i. Notice, that this is not the current payoff itself. The current payoff is depending on the state of both firms. Hence a good empirical measure for the firm's state should be the number and magnitude of realised inventions. The kind of identification with integers should depend on the data source.

The parameter $\lambda \in (0, 1]$ is the probability of change in the state space of one firm. $\lambda = 1$ means no firm remains more than one period in the same state, $\lambda \to 0$ means state nearly changes never. In this model λ is an exogenous parameter, hence it is intuitive to take λ as an industry characterising measure. Again the adequate empirical measure depends on the data source.

We write down our empirically testable hypotheses derived from the propositions as verbal statements.

Hypothesis 1: Consider an oligopolistic industry being characterised by a typical rate of innovation. Then the firm's optimal dynamic strategy is a long term constantly R&D-investment. This is independent on the short term realisation of innovations and on the behaviour of the opponent. In the spirit of evolutionary terminology we call this constant investment strategy *routine.*

Hypothesis 2: The random character of invention leads to different performance of identical firms. Thus the stochastic nature of industry evolution is not reflected in the firms actions but in the firms fate expressed as *random state* and *random profits*.

Hypothesis 3: The choice of the routine strategy depends only on the industry parameter λ and the value of the own state change. It depends not on the degree of interaction.

Hypothesis 4: Optimal routine R&D-investment increases with the typical velocity of change in an industry and increases for a firm with an increasing value of the own state change.

Hypothesis 4 is quite intuitive, hypothesis 1 to 3 are in contrast to many other innovation papers predicting much more sophisticated strategies in an interactive context. However, the result of *routine decisions* is very close to the Nelson & Winter evolutionary approach. The difference of the present model to Nelson and Winter lies in the bigger power of explanation for the firm's behaviour as endogeneously derived *routine decisions*. Thus, the present paper should as well be taken as a methodological connection between the *orthodox approach* and the *evolutionary approach* to the modelling of innovation.

Appendix

The proof of propositions 1 to 4 will be subdivided into five lemmas.

Lemma 1: Assumption 1 implies $q^t(\tilde{s}|s,\mathbf{c}) = q^t(\tilde{s}-s|0,\mathbf{c})\ \forall \tilde{s}, s \in \mathbf{Z}^2,\ \forall \mathbf{c} \in A^t$.

Proof: By induction over t assume, that for $t-1$ holds:

$$q_1^{t-1}(s_1'|s_1,\mathbf{c}_1) = q_1^{t-1}(s_1'-s_1|0,\mathbf{c}_1)\ \forall s_1', s_1 \in \mathbf{Z},\ \forall \mathbf{c}_1 \in A_1^{t-1}\,.$$

Define $\check{\mathbf{c}}_1 = (c_1^0, c_1^1, \ldots, c_1^{t-2})$, then we write

$$q_1^t(\tilde{s}_1|s_1,\mathbf{c}_1) = \sum_{s_1'\in\mathbf{Z}} q_1^{t-1}(s_1'|s_1,\check{\mathbf{c}}_1)\, q_1(\tilde{s}_1|s_1', c_1^{t-1}) =$$

$$= \sum_{s_1'\in\mathbf{Z}} q_1^{t-1}(s_1'-s_1|0,\check{\mathbf{c}}_1)\, q_1(\tilde{s}_1-s_1'|0, c_1^{t-1}) =$$

$$= q_1^t(\tilde{s}-s|0,\mathbf{c}_1)\,.$$

Obviously the same holds for firm 2. Composition of the two equalities yields the assertion of the lemma.

Lemma 2: From assumptions 1 and 2 follows for $i = 1,2 : \forall s, s' \in \mathbf{Z}^2,\ \forall \mathbf{c} \in A^\infty$:

$$\Pi_i(s,\mathbf{c}) - \Pi_i(s',\mathbf{c}) = \frac{1}{1-\delta}\,[r_i(s,c_i) - r_i(s',c_i)] =$$

$$= \frac{1}{1-\delta}\,[r_{ii}\cdot(s_i - s_i') - r_{ij}(s_j - s_j')]\,.$$

Notice, that the RHS of the equation does not depend on c_i, thus it holds for any c_i.

Proof: We calculate by using Lemma 1:

$$\Pi_i(s,\mathbf{c}) - \Pi_i(s',\mathbf{c}) = \sum_{t=0}^{\infty} \delta^t[E_i^t(s,\mathbf{c})] - \sum_{t=0}^{\infty} \delta^t[E_i^t(s',\mathbf{c})] =$$

$$= \sum_{t=0}^{\infty} \delta^t[E_i^t(s,\mathbf{c}) - E_i^t(s',\mathbf{c})] =$$

$$= \sum_{t=0}^{\infty} \delta^t \Big[\sum_{\tilde{s} \in S} q^t(\tilde{s}|s, \mathbf{c}) \cdot r_i(\tilde{s}, c_i^{t-1}) - \sum_{\tilde{s} \in S} q^t(\tilde{s}|s', \mathbf{c}) \cdot r_i(\tilde{s}, c_i^{t-1}) \Big] =$$

(equals by lemma 1)

$$= \sum_{t=0}^{\infty} \delta^t \Big[\sum_{\tilde{s} \in S} q^t(\tilde{s} - s, \mathbf{c}) \cdot r_i(\tilde{s}, c_i^{t-1}) - \sum_{\tilde{s} \in S} q^t(\tilde{s} - s', \mathbf{c}) \cdot r_i(\tilde{s}, c_i^{t-1}) \Big] =$$

(equals by linearity of r_i and permutation of the summation)

$$= \sum_{t=0}^{\infty} \delta^t \Big[\sum_{\tilde{s} \in S} q^t(\tilde{s} - s, \mathbf{c}) \cdot [r_i(s, c_i^{t-1})) - r_i(s', c_i^{t-1})] \Big] =$$

$$= \sum_{t=0}^{\infty} \delta^t [r_i(s, c_i^{t-1}) - r_i(s', c_i^{t-1})] =$$

$$= \frac{1}{1-\delta} [r_{ii} \cdot (s_i - s_i') - r_{ij} \cdot (s_j - s_j')] \text{ q.e.d.}$$

Lemma 3: Given assumptions 1, 2 and 3 let $\mathbf{c}_i^*$ be a solution of $(SMAX)$:

$$\underset{\mathbf{c}_i \in A_i^\infty}{\text{Max}} \quad \Pi_i(s^0, \check{\mathbf{c}}^*)$$

then $\mathbf{c}_i^*$ is a solution for any initial state $s \in S$:

$$\underset{\mathbf{c}_i \in A_i^\infty}{\text{Max}} \quad \Pi_i(s, \check{\mathbf{c}}^*) \,.$$

Proof: Let $s = (s_1, s_2)$ and $s^0 = (s_1^0, s_2^0)$. We compute for firm 1 by using lemma 2:

$$\Pi_1(s, \mathbf{c}) = \Pi_1(s^0, \mathbf{c}) + \frac{1}{1-\delta} [r_{11} \cdot (s_1 - s_1^0) - r_{12} \cdot (s_2 - s_2^0)] \,.$$

Maximisation over $\mathbf{c}_1$ leads to the same solution for s^0 and each $s \in S$, since the difference does not depend on $\mathbf{c}$ by lemma 2, q.e.d.

Lemma 4: (Solution of the one shot game) Under assumptions 1, 2, 3, 4 the solution of the maximisation

$$\underset{c_i \in A_i}{\text{Max}} \quad E_i^1(0, c) = \underset{c_i \in A_i}{\text{Max}} \sum_{s' \in S} q(s', c)\, r_i(s', c_i)$$

is given by:

$$c_i^* = (f_i')^{-1}\left(\frac{1}{2\lambda r_{ii}}\right) .$$

Remark: Remember, that $q(s', c)$ is the probability, that the state of the system changes from 0 to s', if firm 1 plays c_1 and firm 2 plays c_2. Notice, that the solution $c_1^*(c_2)$ does not depend on c_2, which means, that the reaction function is constant (look at the proof). Of course by symmetry the same holds for firm 2.

Proof: There are 3 states for each firm with probability $\neq 0$, hence we have to evaluate 9 cases. Let $c = (c_1, c_2)$ and $0 = (0, 0)$. We calculate using (2):

$$E_1^1(0, c) = \sum_{s' \in S} q(s', c)\, r_1(s', c_1) =$$

$$\begin{aligned}
&= \lambda^2 f_1(c_1)\, f_2(c_2)(r_{11} - r_{12}) + \\
&\quad \lambda(1-\lambda)\, f_1(c_1)\, r_{11} + \\
&\quad \lambda^2 f_1(c_1)(1 - f_2(c_2))(r_{11} + r_{12}) - \\
&\quad \lambda(1-\lambda)\, f_2(c_2)\, r_{12} + \\
&\quad (1-\lambda)^2 \cdot 0 + \qquad (5)\\
&\quad \lambda(1-\lambda)(1 - f_2(c_2))\, r_{12} - \\
&\quad \lambda^2(1 - f_1(c_1))\, f_2(c_2)(r_{11} + r_{12}) - \\
&\quad \lambda(1-\lambda)(1 - f_1(c_1))\, r_{11} + \\
&\quad \lambda^2(1 - f_1(c_1))(1 - f_2(c_2))(r_{12} - r_{11}) - c_1 =
\end{aligned}$$

$$= \lambda[2 f_1(c_1)\, r_{11} - 2 f_2(c_2)\, r_{12} + r_{12} - r_{11}] - c_1 = \qquad (6)$$

$$= 2\lambda f_1(c_1)\, r_{11} - c_1 + k, \qquad (7)$$

where k is a term, that does not depend on c_1. The first order condition is

$$f_1'(c_1) = \frac{1}{2\lambda r_{11}}\,, \qquad (8)$$

which proves together with assumption 3 the lemma. Notice, that the second order condition is fulfilled, since $f_1'' < 0$. The proof for firm 2 is the same, q.e.d.

Lemma 5: Let $\mathbf{c} = (c^0, c^1, c^2, \ldots) = ((c_1^0, c_2^0), (c_1^1, c_2^1), \ldots)$, then

$$\Pi_i(s^0, \mathbf{c}) = \frac{r_{ii}s_i - r_{ij}s_j}{(1-\delta)^2} + \sum_{t=0}^{\infty} \delta^t \, \frac{E_i^1(0, c^t)}{1-\delta} \,. \tag{9}$$

Proof: We compute $\Pi_1(s^0, \mathbf{c})$, the proof for firm 2 is equivalent. Similar as in equation (5) define the vector $\mathbf{q}^t$ as

$$\mathbf{q}^t = \begin{pmatrix} \lambda^2 f_1(c_1^t)\, f_2(c_2^t) \\ \lambda(1-\lambda)\, f_1(c_1^t) \\ \lambda^2 f_1(c_1^t)(1 - f_2(c_2^t)) \\ \lambda(1-\lambda)\, f_2(c_2^t) \\ (1-\lambda)^2 \\ \lambda(1-\lambda)(1 - f_2(c_2^t)) \\ \lambda^2(1 - f_1(c_1^t))\, f_2(c_2^t) \\ \lambda(1-\lambda)(1 - f_1(c_1^t)) \\ \lambda^2(1 - f_1(c_1^t))(1 - f_2(c_2^t)) \end{pmatrix} \quad \text{'probability distribution on the 9 possible states'}$$

and vector $\mathbf{r}$ as

$$\mathbf{r} = \begin{pmatrix} r_{11} - r_{12} \\ r_{11} \\ r_{11} + r_{12} \\ -r_{12} \\ 0 \\ r_{12} \\ -r_{11} - r_{12} \\ -r_{11} \\ -r_{11} + r_{12} \end{pmatrix} .$$

Equation (5) then reduces to:

$$E_1^1(0, c^0) = \mathbf{q}^0 \cdot \mathbf{r},$$

where $\mathbf{q}^0 \cdot \mathbf{r}$ is the scalar product of $I\!R^9$. Define $rs := r_{11}s_1 - r_{12}s_2$, then a simple calculation shows:

$$E_1^1(s, c^0) = \mathbf{q}^0 \cdot \mathbf{r} + rs = E_1^1(0, c^0) + rs \,.$$

Now we are able to calculate the expectation value of the second period using equation (2):

$$E_1^2(s, c^0) = E_1^1(0, c^0) + E_1^1(0, c^1) + 2rs$$

and for period t:

$$E_1^t(s, c^{t-1}) = t \cdot rs + \sum_{\tau=0}^{t-1} E_1^1(0, c^\tau) \tag{10}$$

thus using (3) the objective function $\Pi_1(s^0, \mathbf{c})$ writes as:

$$\Pi_1(s^0, \mathbf{c}) = \sum_{t=0}^{\infty} \delta^t \Big[t \cdot rs^0 + \sum_{\tau=0}^{t-1} E_1^1(0, c^\tau)\Big] =$$

$$= \frac{rs^0}{(1-\delta)^2} + \frac{1}{1-\delta} \sum_{t=0}^{\infty} \delta^t E_1^1(0, c^t) \text{ q.e.d.}$$

Corollary: The solution of $(SMAX)$ exists and is unique and is given as $\mathbf{c}^* = (c^*, c^*, c^*, \ldots)$, where $c^* = (c_1^*, c_2^*)$ is the constant strategy given by (4).

Proof of the corollary and the propositions: Using equation (9) the $(SMAX)$ delivers for every period $t = 0, 1, 2, \ldots$ one first order condition similar to (8):

$$f_i'(c_i^t) = \frac{1}{2\lambda r_{ii}} .$$

Together with assumption 3 this completes the proof and involves the assertions of proposition 1 and 3. The equilibrium profits using (6) in equation (9) are

$$\Pi_1(s^0, \mathbf{c}) = \frac{1}{(1-\delta)^2} \left[rs^0 + \lambda[2f_1(c_1^*)\, r_{11} - 2f_2(c_2^*)\, r_{12} + r_{12} - r_{11}] - c_1^*\right]$$

and similar for firm 2. Proposition 2 is now obvious and proposition 4 then follows from assumption 2,(v): $f_i'' < 0$.

Notes

1. A generalisation of assumption 2 is an interesting question. If we allow for big and small transitions, we may diversify between 'drastic' innovation and 'normal' technical progress [for this and many other generalisations see Blonski (1993)].

References

Bertsekas, D.P. (1976), *Dynamic Programming and Stochastic Control*, New York: Ac Press.

Blonski, M. (1993), Die Theorie der Industriestrukturen und deren Veränderungen durch technischen Fortschritt und neue Produkte, Universität Mannheim, Dissertation, unpublished.

Ericson, R. and A. Pakes (1989), *An Alternative Theory of Firm and Industry Dynamics*, Columbia University Discussion Paper.

Federgruen, A. (1978), 'On N-Person Stochastic Games with Denumerable State Space', *Advances in Applied Probability* **10**, 452–471.

Nelson, R. and S. Winter (1982), *An Evolutionary Theory of Economic Change*, Cambridge, Ma: Harvard University Press.

Parthasarathy, T. (1973), 'Discounted, Positive and Noncooperative Stochastic Games', *International Journal of Game Theory* **2**, 25–37.

K. Aiginger and J. Finsinger (eds.), Applied Industrial Organization, 107–110.

The Division of Labour and Market Structure

CHRISTIAN VON WEIZSÄCKER
University of Köln, Germany

Abstract. Most firms produce most of the time under conditions of substantial economies of scale. The division of labour, according to Adam Smith the mainspring of wealth, is intrinsically an economies of scale phenomenon. Market structure in most industries in characterized by a small number of suppliers and a larger number of customers. I explain this law of small numbers as the equilibrium of two forces: the deconcentration effect of imitation and the market splitting effect of further refinements in the division of labour by innovation. A deconcentrated market creates larger incentives for market splitting (product differentiation) by innovation than a concentrated market. But market splitting raises concentration in the market and it raises the number of different markets in the economy. Before the economies of scale of old products are fully exploited, new products are being offered which again are produced under conditions of economies of scale.

Key words: division of labour, economies of scale, market structure, innovation.

JEL-Code: L 11

The representative businessman tells you that he would like to sell more than he can at the going price. A substantial margin between price and marginal cost is typical for most businesses. Empirical evidence indicates that a price-marginalcost-margin of 30% to 40% is quite typical for manufacturing. Casual observation leads to similar results for the service sector.

Note that this is long run marginal cost.

The profitability of the representative firm is substantially smaller in terms of percentage of sales. Thus we have a substantial difference between average and marginal cost. Substantial economies of scale prevail in our economies. Average cost may exceed marginal cost by 30% of average cost. Doubling of output will then typically lower average cost by 15%.

This empirical evidence contradicts the traditional market structure model of the industrial organisation tradition. It was for decades that economists looked for minimum optimal scale of plants or firms, thereby implying that the equilibrium minimum scale of plants or firms was determined by this minimum optimum scale. By definition the economies of scale cease to exist at the minimum optimum scale.

It appears that the equilibrium size of firms is characterized by substantial economies of scale. Let us try to understand what that means. Let me try to change our economic thinking habits so as to adapt them to this fact.

Everything began of course with Adam Smith. But there are two Adam Smiths. There is the static and there is the evolutionary Adam Smith. Let me call them

Adam S. Smith and Adam E. Smith. Adam S. Smith is the Adam Smith who developed for us the theory of the natural price, the theory of the equalization of profit rates across industries etc. His image was the theory of equilibrium of forces in physics. He became the father of classical and the neoclassical theory of the textbook of Economics as it is taught today – obviously much improved over Adam S. Smith. Adam E. Smith is the man who opened the Wealth of Nations with the sentence: "The greatest improvement in the productive powers of labour, and the greater part of the skill, dexterity, and judgement with which it is anywhere directed, or applied, seem to have been the effects of the division of labour." He is the theorist of the division of labour. He understood that by markets the division of labour could evolve much faster and that therefore it is the market system which provides superior wealth through superior division of labour.

The sons and the grandsons of Adam S. Smith have shown the static efficiency, the Pareto optimality of a system of competitive markets. They have dwelled on the efficiency losses of monopoly by calculating Harberger tringles ("Monopoly creates an efficiency loss of 1 per thousand of GNP")(Harberger, 1954). But Adam E. Smith opened the book by explaining wealth through the division of labour. This explanation cannot be formalized in terms of the first welfare theorem in an Arrow-Debrue world. Your economic policy creates wealth, real big wealth if it allows the division of labour to evolve. This is the message of Adam E. Smith.

Adam S. Smith and his followers have difficulty with the economies of scale. Perfect competition, the market model from Adam S. Smith down to Chicago, exhibits no economies of scale in equilibrium. The complete formalization of the Walras model used convexity of production sets as a model assumption, i.e. it assumed economies of scale away. The economics profession for a long time tended to minimize the importance of the economies of scale. The phenomenon was inconvenient for a static equilibrium theory.

A theory of the division of labour is besides the point without an explicit acknowledgement of economies of scale. "That the division of labour is limited by the extent of the market" allowed Adam E. Smith to explain the superior wealth of maritime civilisations. This is intrinsically an economies of scale argument.

One of Adam E. Smith's heirs is Karl Marx. He emphasized the economies of scale. He understood that the market system, capitalism, created superior wealth by promoting the division of labour. This historical process he called die Vergesellschaftung der Arbeit. Marx believed on the other hand that competition was not possible in the long run due to the economies of scale. He forecasted the transition of competitive capitalism into monopoly capitalism. And he forecasted the downfall of capitalism to be replaced by the planned economy which could rationally cope with the opportunities provided by the economies of scale and the division of labour. Concerning the planned economy it turned out that he was mistaken. He also was mistaken, I believe, in his opinion that competition could not work.

Adam Smith also invented or at least used a distinction which disappeared later in orthodox economics. It is the distinction between productive and unproductive labour. Marx continued to use it, even though he changed its meaning. For Marx unproductive labour in capitalism was labour spent to run, to control, to monitor the system rather than to actually manufacture commodities. Unproductive labour in the sense of Marx largely corresponds to our modern transaction cost, the category of cost which came to the center stage after the Coase Theorem.

But transaction costs are incurred under conditions of incomplete information and change. In a completely tranquil and repetitive situation transaction costs would disappear. They rise with the amount of change in the economy. Change creates situations of incomplete information, the major cause of transaction costs. The Marxist distinction between productive and unproductive labour thus is the distinction between those cost components which occur under static conditions and those cost components which are due to change and evolution.

Market structure as it prevails in most markets must be understood as an evolutionary equilibrium. It is not an equilibrium in any given market. It will change fairly rapidly. But the general structure of most markets will remain the same: a not very large number of suppliers and a much larger number of customers. Each supplier operates with substantial economies of scale at the margin. Each supplier tries to raise his market share, sometimes by lowering price but always by trying to improve and to differentiate his product.

It is unrealistic to think that customers normally select their supplier out of hundreds of competitors. Transaction costs would be much too high in an environment of competition between heterogeneous products under conditions of change.

But is it not possible to have a large number of suppliers, if an intermediary specializes in choosing among a large number of alternatives? He could drastically reduce transaction costs due to specialisation. Traders are of course specialists in choice between product alternatives. But we observe that such professionalism in choosing drastically reduces the product differentiation advantages of suppliers. The suppliers exhibit economies of scale. It their product differentiation potential is low, we observe a shake-out of suppliers with the outcome of an oligopolostic structure.

In many markets, continuous new product differentiation activities occur. New potential for specialization advantages is discovered. Customers are offered new products which compete with old products already in the market. It is technical progress and further refinement of the division of labour which again reduces the number of competitors. Given the size of a firm and hence its potential to devote resources to innovation and further refinement of the division of labour, the incentive to innovate rises with the size of the market. A new product which has the potential to compete successfully with existing products with sales of 10 million dollars is less attractive than a new product able to compete with existing products with sales of 100 million dollars. The drive to differentiate by innovation and thereby reduce the degree of price competition thus rises with the number of competitors with whom you are in price competition. Out of this consideration comes an equilibrium theory of innovation, i.e. an equilibrium theory of the speed with which the division of labour is refined. The incentive to innovate falls as the index of concentration in the market rises. But innovations and new forms of division of labour tend to split markets into a larger number of smaller markets. Hence they lead to a rise in the number of markets but to higher concentration on each of these new markets. On the other hand imitative entry tends to reduce concentration. Out of these processes we obtain a kind of equilibrium level of market concentration. In industrial markets these are oligopolistic levels of concentration. This I call the law of small numbers.

Reference

A.C. Harberger (1954) 'Monopoly and Research Allocation', *American Economic Review* **44**, 77–87.

K. Aiginger and J. Finsinger (eds.), Applied Industrial Organization, 111–130.

The Evolution of the Vertically Integrated Firm: A Transaction Cost Analysis

JOSEF WINDSPERGER
Institute of Business Economics, University of Vienna, Vienna, Austria

Abstract. This paper examines the evolution of the vertically integrated firm in terms of coordination economies. First, we develop the concept of coordination efficiency, which is defined by the sum of transaction, risk and set-up costs of the coordination design. The transaction and risk costs are positively related to uncertainty, transaction specificity, transaction frequency, and the potential volume of transactions. The set-up costs of the coordination design are determined by the complexity, as well as incentive and cognitive compatibility of the coordination design. Second, this concept is applied to the question of the evolution of the vertically integrated firm. We show that the vertically integrated firm evolves the more (less) likely, the more asymmetric (symmetric) the interfirm transactions are. Finally, this result was compared with the Williamsonian governance structure approach which overestimates the likelihood of the evolution of the vertically integrated firm, because Williamson does not differentiate between symmetric and asymmetric specific transactions.

JEL codes: L22, M20

Key words: Vertical integration, theory of the firm.

I. Problem

There are three broad determinants of vertical integration: noncompetitive market structure, production economies and coordination economies. The first are extensively analyzed in the neoclassical theory of vertical integration (Tirole 1988; Perry, 1989); the second are only in combination with the third a determinant of vertical integration because transactional uncertainty and hence transaction costs prevent the firm from designing complete contracts (Williamson 1975, 1985). Consequently, given a competitive situation, if the firm cannot set up complete contracts, vertical integration results primarily from coordination economies. The purpose of this article is to explain the evolution of the vertically integrated firm in terms of coordination economies.

The paper is arranged as follows: the second section develops the concept of coordination efficiency as evaluation criterion of the inter- and intrafirm coordination design. The third section applies this coordination efficiency concept to the question why a vertically integrated firm emerges as coordination mechanism. Finally, based on the results in the third section, we re-analyze the Williamsonian governance structure approach (Williamson, 1986, 1989).

II. The Concept of Coordination Efficiency

Generally, the economic efficiency of the firm refers to the production and coordination efficiency. Production efficiency is defined by the minimum of production costs (including transport costs) and coordination efficiency by the minimum of coordination and risk costs. Coordination costs include transaction costs and set-up costs of the coordination mechanism. Transaction costs result from transactional uncertainty (Buttler and Carney 1983, p. 218) and refer both to direct and opportunity costs of the information flow due to limited cognitive capacities and motivation (Windsperger 1991a). Therefore, transaction costs are metacosts as direct and opportunity costs of the information flow, given a certain coordination design. The set-up costs of the coordination mechanism include the costs of information structure (information technology, communication technology, human capital costs (Radner 1991, p. 2)) and the motivation structure (reward systems, seniority rules (Lawler, 1982)). Since transactional uncertainty cannot be completely eliminated by coordination design, risk costs have to be included in the efficiency evaluation (Lavington 1925). Risk costs represent the degree of uncertainty in the cost and revenue expectations (as risk premium). They increase the cost and decrease the revenue expectations (Windsperger 1991a).

II.1. DETERMINANTS OF COORDINATION EFFICIENCY

In the following, we examine the determinants of coordination efficiency, that is to say, the determinants of transaction, risk and set-up costs of the coordination design.

II.1.1. Determinants of transaction and risk costs

Transaction and risk costs depend on the environmental, transactional, and behavioral uncertainty, transaction specificity, transaction frequency, and the potential volume of transactions.

(I) Environmental uncertainty (including transactional uncertainty): The higher the complexity and change of transactional environment as well as the complexity of transactional object (Masten *et al.*, 1991; Malone *et al.*, 1987), the more information have to be searched, processed and communicated in the pre- and postplanning period, and the higher are the transaction and risk costs due to limited cognitive capabilities (see [A] in Figure 1).

(II) Behavioral uncertainty: The higher the transactors' motivation to behave opportunistically, the higher is the behavioral or strategic uncertainty, and the higher are the transaction costs as opportunity (disincentive) costs and expenses

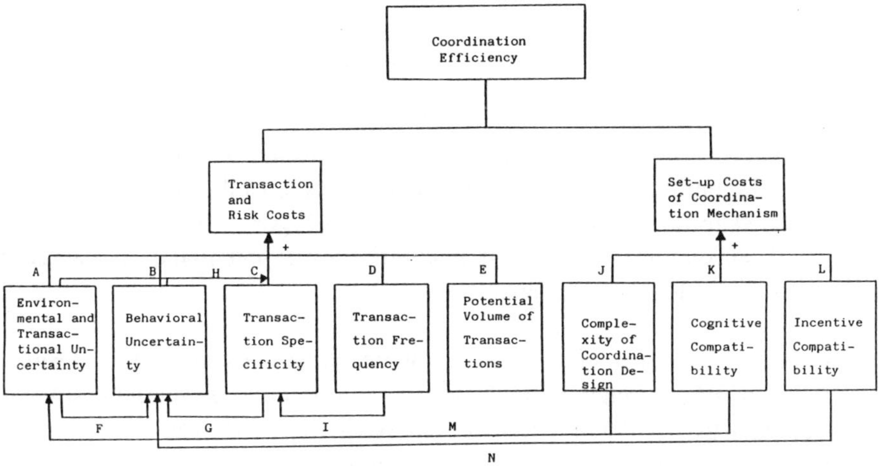

Fig. 1. Determinants of coordination efficiency.

as well as risk costs due to information selection and manipulation in the pre- and postplanning period (see [B] in Figure 1).

(III) Transaction specificity: The higher the transaction specific investments in the pre- and postplanning period, the lower is the degree of transaction substitutability (Stuckey 1983, p. 52), the higher are the quasi-rents of the highest valued transaction, and hence the higher are the adjustment costs (lost quasi-rents and additional transaction costs as expenses) (Windsperger 1991b), if *ex post* adaptability problems arise (see [C] in Figure 1).

Illustrate this point, assume that company A sells product x to company B at a transaction price of P^{AB}. To carry out this transaction, company A has to undertake transaction specific investments. A's supply costs to complete the transaction are c. Hence A's net value of the transaction with B is $g^{AB} = P^{AB} - c$. If, in addition to B, a second company C offered at most $P^{AC} < P^{AB}$, A's net value of this transaction would be $P^{AC} - c = g^{AC}$, which is lower than g^{AB}. Consequently, A's quasi-rent of the transaction with B (as "relationship-specific advantage", Charny 1990, p. 392) is $q^{AB} = g^{AB} - g^{AC}$, which is lost if the contract with B is terminated. On the other hand, if company A does not expect quasi-rents from the transaction with B, no transaction specific investments will be undertaken. This is the case, if the transaction price between A and B is equal to the external market price ($P^{AB} = P^{AC}$). Thus A's lost quasi-rent is zero, if the contract is terminated, i.e. $g^{AB} - g^{AC} = q^{AB} = 0$.

As a result, if the degree of transaction specificity is low (high), the adjustment costs as lost quasi-rents and adjustment expenses are low (high).

(IV) Transaction frequency: The higher the frequency of transactions, the more new information must be processed and transmitted in the postplanning period, and the higher are the transaction and risk costs (see [D] in Figure 1).

(V) Potential volume of transactions: Transaction and risk costs are furthermore higher, the higher the potential volume of transactions or the "potential market" is, respectively (Young 1929, p. 536; Shove 1930) (see [E] in Figure 1). The potential volume of transactions is measured by the number of potential transactors and the volume of individual transactions.

In addition to these direct effects of coordination efficiency determinants, four indirect effects must be included in the efficiency evaluation: (a) interaction between transaction specificity and behavioral uncertainty, (b) interactive between environmental and behavioral uncertainty, (c) interaction between uncertainty (environmental and behavioral) and *ex post* adaptability problem and (d) interaction between transaction frequency and transaction specificity. The first two interaction effects depend on the transactional dependency that varies with the characteristics of transactions. As examined in the Appendix, the transactional dependence (d) between two parties (A, B) can be defined by the ratio of transaction specificities, i.e. $d = k^A/k^B$. Idiosyncratic (symmetric specific) transactions show a high degree of bilateral dependence (k^A and k^B are high, d = 1), symmetric non-specific transactions are characterized by bilateral independence ($k^A = k^B = 0$; $d = 0$), and asymmetric specific transactions by unilateral dependence ($k^A > k^B, d > 1$; or $k^B > k^A, d < 1$).

(VIa) Interaction between transaction specificity and behavioral uncertainty (motivation effect of transaction specificity) (see [G] in Figure 1):

(1) Asymmetric transactions: If asymmetric transaction specific investments are made, an appropriable quasi-rent is created (Barney and Ouchi 1986, pp. 22–23). The higher and more asymmetric the transaction specific investments, the higher are the differences of transactors' appropriable quasi-rents, the lower is the dependence of the transactor with lower transaction specific investments, and the higher is his motivation to behave opportunistically by appropriating the quasi-rent difference. This is the 'hold-up' problem (Rubin 1990, p. 9).

(2) Symmetric non-specific transactions: If neither party undertakes transaction specific investments, no appropriable quasi-rents arise. In this case the motivation to behave opportunistically is high, because the switching costs of both transactors (lost quasi-rents and adjustment expenses) at the external market are low.

(3) Symmetric specific transactions (idiosyncratic transactions): If both transactors undertake transaction specific investments, both transactors' quasi-rents are high. The higher the transaction specific investements, the higher are the lost quasi-rents (sunk costs) in case of contract termination, and the higher is the trans-

actors' motivation to behave cooperatively to appropriate the relationship-specific quasi-rents (Jarillo and Ricard 1987, p. 85; Macneil 1986).

(VIb) Interaction between environmental and behavioral uncertainty (motivation effect of environmental uncertainty) (see [F] in Figure 1):

(1) Asymmetric specific and symmetric non-specific transactions: The disincentive effect due to symmetric nonspecific and asymmetric specific transactions is enhanced by environmental uncertainty. The higher the degree of environmental uncertainty, the higher is the degree of information asymmetry between the transactors in the pre- and postplanning period, the less likely opportunistic behavior can be detected (Mann and Wissink 1984, p. 9), and consequently, the higher is the motivation to behave opportunistically in the pre- and postplanning period, which results in high transaction costs as expenses and disincentive costs as well as high risk costs.

(2) Symmetric specific transactions: The incentive effects due to idiosyncratic transactions varies directly with the environmental uncertainty. The higher the environmental uncertainty, the higher the information asymmetry between the transactors in the pre- and postplanning period, and the more likely relevant information arises which requires mutual plan adjustments, and hence the higher is the transactors' motivation to behave cooperatively.

As a result, the interaction effect between transaction specificity and behavioral uncertainty as well as between environmental and behavioral uncertainty are positive (disincentive effect), if an asymmetric or symmetric non-specific transactional relation exist, and negative (incentive effect), if a symmetric specific transactional relation exist.

(VIc) Interaction between environmental and behavioral uncertainty and ex post adaptability problem (see [H] in Figure 1):

Given transaction specific investments, the higher the environmental and behavioral uncertainty, the larger is the *ex post* adaptability problem (Williamson 1986, pp. 117–118). The higher the environmental uncertainty, the more new information emerge in the postplanning period, and the more frequently adjustment problems arise, if mutual adjustment measures are required. Additionally, the higher the behavioral uncertainty, the more frequently information selection and manipulation occurs in the postplanning period enhancing the *ex post* adaptability problem.

(VId) Interaction between transaction frequency and transaction specificity (see [I] in Figure 1):

In the case of recurrent transactions the interfirm transaction process generates informational economies of scale due to set up costs of information acquisition (Radner 1970) and economies of "cognitive" learning (Windsperger 1992) regarding technical matters, contracting rules, strategies, needs, and capabilities of the parties (Johanson and Mattsson 1987, p. 39). These informational investments as organization capital (Prescott and Visscher 1980) are transaction specific and are positively related to the frequency of transactions.

II.1.2. Determinants of the set-up costs of the coordination design

The creation of a coordination mechanism requires economic resources. The set-up costs of the coordination design are determined by the degree of complexity (Baligh and Burton 1982, p. 441), incentive compatibility and cognitive compatibility of the coordination design. Complexity refers to the degree of decomposition of the coordination task into subtasks by designing a coordination structure, incentive compatibility refers to the "fit" (Van de Ven and Drazin 1985) between the incentive characteristics of the coordination design and the motivation structure of individuals, and cognitive compatibility refers to the fit between the cognitive characteristics of the coordination design and the cognitive capabilities of individuals. The more complex the coordination structure and the higher the degree of incentive and cognitive compatibility, the higher are the set-up costs (see [J], [K], [L] in Figure 1).

II.2. OPTIMAL DESIGN OF COORDINATION MECHANISM

After having analyzed the determinants of coordination efficiency, the question arises how the optimal design of coordination mechanism is determined.

Given output planning (by explicit contracts), the transaction and risk costs are higher, the higher the uncertainty (environmental, transactional, behavioral), the transaction specificity, the transaction frequency and the potential volume of transactions are. On the other hand, setting up structural planning (by designing a coordination mechanism) improves the information acquisition, communication and processing capacity and reduces the environmental, transactional and behavioral uncertainty and hence the transaction and risk costs. The more complex and cognitive compatible the coordination design, the higher the environmental and transactional uncertainty reducing effect (see [M] in Figure 1), and the more incentive compatible the coordination design, the higher the behavioral uncertainty reducing effect (see [N] in Figure 1). Consequently, the degree of complexity, cognitive and incentive compatibility of the coordination mechanism is limited by its uncertainty and hence its transaction and risk cost reducing effect (Leblebici 1985, p. 108). The higher the degree of uncertainty and hence the risk and transactions costs under output planning, the higher the transaction and risk cost savings of a more complex, cognitive and/or incentive compatible coordination design (Geanakoplos and Milgrom 1991, p. 224), and hence the higher is the optimal degree of complexity, cognitive, and/or incentive compatibility of the coordination design. As a result, the optimum design of coordination mechanism is determined by the minimum of transaction, risk and set-up costs of the coordination design. This is graphically

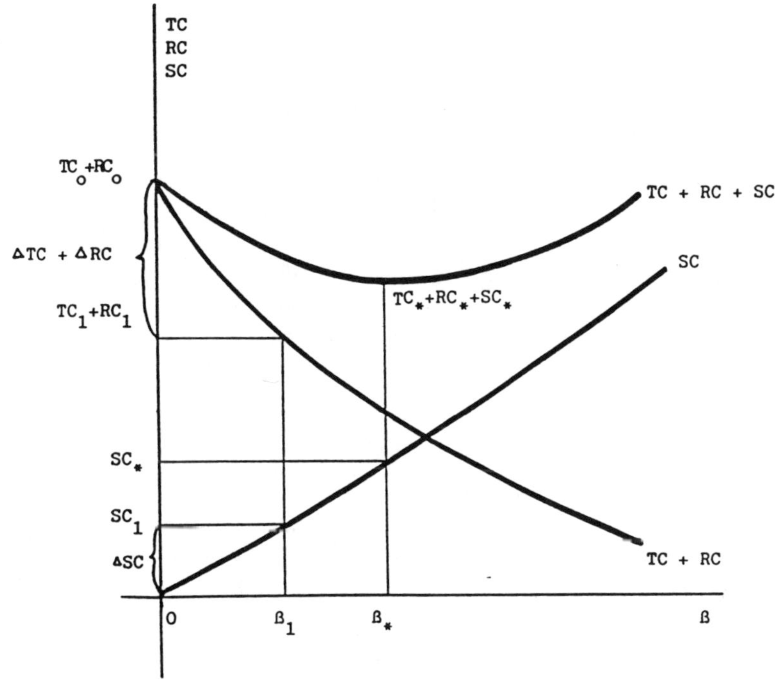

Fig. 2. The optimal design of coordination mechanism.

depicted in Figure 2, whereby β is a measure of complexity of the coordination mechanism. If no coordination mechanism is set up ($\beta = 0$), i.e. the coordination is based on output planning, the transaction and risk costs are $TC_0 + RC_0$. If, on the other hand, a coordination mechanism with the design β_1 is installed, the uncertainty and the transaction and risk costs decline ($\Delta TC + \Delta RC > 0$). However, these transaction and risk cost savings are partly counterbalanced by the set-up costs of the coordination mechanism ($\Delta SC < \Delta TC + \Delta RC$). The design is then optimal, if $\Delta TC + \Delta RC = \Delta SK$; that is the case in β_* (see Figure 2).

In the following section, the concept of coordination efficiency is applied to the question why a vertically integrated firm emerges as coordination mechanism.

III. The Coordination Efficiency of the Vertically Integrated Firm

We assume that the final product is produced in three production stages: In the production stage one the raw material, in the production stage two the intermediate product, and in the production stage three the final good is produced. The question to ask is how the transactions between the production stage two and three are organized. We investigate two designs of vertically integrating coordination mechanisms (CM1, CM2):

(1) CM1 refers to the interfirm organization of transactions, consisting of two independent firms (A, B) which produce the products a and b. CM_a^i and CM_b^i refer

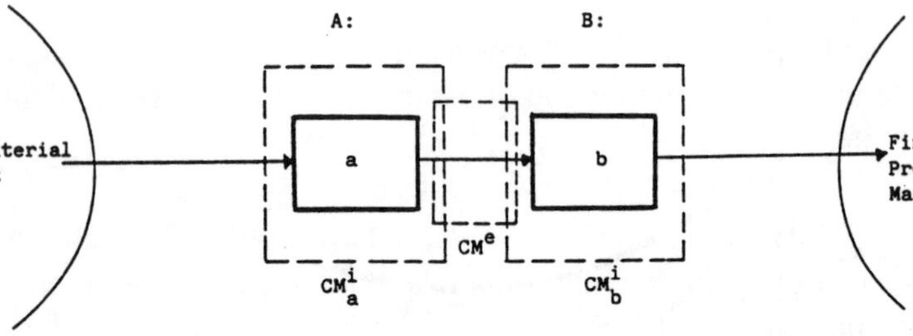

Fig. 3. CM1.

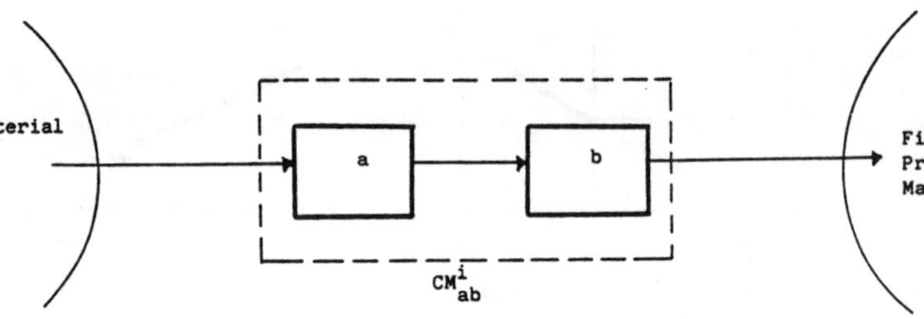

Fig. 4. CM2.

to the internal organization design of A and B and CM^e to the contract design between A and B (see Figure 3).

(2) CM2 is the vertically integrated firm. Hence CM2 refers to the internal organization of the transactions between a and b (CM^i_{ab}) (see Figure 4).

Additionally, in order to explain the evolution of the vertically integrated firm in terms of coordination economies, we assume that economies of scale, scope and learning differences are absent between external and internal coordination. Given this assumption, coordination efficiency means profit maximization or transaction, risk and set-up cost minimization (TC + RC + SC), respectively. Thus coordination efficiency of CM1 is measured by $TC_1+RC_1+SC_1 = (TC^i_a+TC^e_a+SC_a+RC_a)+(TC^i_b+TC^e_b+SC_b+RC_b)$ and of CM2 by $TC_2+RC_2+SC_2 = (TC^i_{ab}+SC_{ab}+RC_{ab})$ (see Figures 3 and 4).

III.1. Determinants of Coordination Efficiency Effects of the Vertically Integrated Firm

Vertical integration has both coordination efficiency increasing effects (transaction and risk cost savings) and coordination efficiency decreasing effects (additional set-up costs).

(A) Coordination efficiency increasing effects

Transaction and risk cost savings result from the lower environmental and behavioral uncertainty and the attenuation of the *ex post* adaptability problem.

(I) Lower environmental and transactional uncertainty: The higher information processing capacity of the internal organization design lowers the environmental and transactional uncertainty (see [M] in Figure 1). This effect is higher, the higher the degree of complexity and change of transactional environment as well as the complexity of transactions is.

(II) Lower behavioral uncertainty: The lower behavioral uncertainty results (1) from the higher degree of goal compatibility (joint profit maximization) (Williamson 1971) between the production stages (see [N] in Figure 1), (2) the attenuation but not elimination of the hold-up problem under asymmetric specific transactions (see [G] in Figure 1) (Eccles and White 1988), and (3) the reduction of information asymmetry due to the higher information processing capacity of the vertically integrated firm (see [F] in Figure 1) (Crocker 1983). This behavioral uncertainty reducing effect is furthermore higher, the higher the asymmetry of transaction specific investments and the complexity and change of transactional environment are.

(III) Attenuation of the ex post adaptability problem: The *ex post* adaptability problem is mitigated because of the higher degree of incentive compatibility and the higher information processing capacity of the internal organization design (see [H] in Figure 1). The higher the degree of transaction specificity and the higher the degree of complexity and change of transactional environment, the higher is the adaptability advantage of the vertically integrated firm.

These coordination efficiency increasing effects are furthermore higher, the higher the potential volume of transactions at the final product market is (Anderson and Schmittlein 1984, p. 388).

(B) Coordination efficiency decreasing effects

On the other hand, the coordination efficiency increasing effects are at least partly compensated by higher set-up costs of the internal organization design. This is due to the higher degree of complexity and/or cognitive and/or incentive compatibility of the internal organization design (as information structure with an embedded motivation structure) see [J], [K], [L] in Figure 1).

III.2. Analysis of transaction and risk cost savings of the vertically integrated firm

In the following, we investigate the transaction and risk cost savings of the vertically integrated firm in detail. Given a certain degree of complexity and change of transactional environment and a certain potential volume of transactions the following hypothesis is examined:

> The vertically integrated firm emerges more (less) likely, the more asymmetric (symmetric) the interfirm transactions are.

III.2.1. Transaction and risk cost savings under symmetric non-specific transactions

Given symmetric non-specific transactions the following transaction and risk cost savings arise:

(A) Transaction cost savings

(I) Environmental and transactional uncertainty:

- Due to the higher information processing capacity of the vertically integrated firm, the environmental and transactional uncertainty and hence the transaction costs as expenses (information, decision, bargaining, control costs) decrease.
- Additionally, the higher information processing capacity of the vertically integrated firm leads to lower information loss and hence to lower transaction costs as opportunity costs of the information flow. Because of the internal coordination of transactions between the two production stages, the firm can better adjust the production and inventory capacity to the consumer demand which lowers the inventory costs and stimulates the demand (Hayes and Wheelwright 1984, p. 288).

(II) Behavioral uncertainty:

- The higher degree of goal compatibility between the production stage two and three leads to lower behavioral uncertainty and hence to lower transaction costs as disincentive and control costs due to information selection and manipulation.
- This disincentive and control cost reducing effect is enhanced by the positive interaction effect between environmental and behavioral uncertainty. Lower environmental uncertainty due to the higher information processing capacity leads to lower behavioral uncertainty because opportunistic behavior can be more easily detected.

		Transaction Specificity		
		Nonspecific	Specific	
			asymmetric	symmetric
Transaction and Risk Costs	CM1	$(TC_1^o + RC_1^o)$	$(TC_1^1 + RC_1^1) > (TC_1^o + RC_1^o)$	$(TC_1^2 + RC_1^2) < (TC_1^1 + RC_1^1)$
	CM2	$(TC_2^o + RC_2^o) < (TC_1^o + RC_1^o)$	$(TC_2^1 + RC_2^1) < (TC_1^1 + RC_1^1)$	$(TC_2^2 + RC_2^2) < (TC_1^2 + RC_1^2)$
TC- and RC- Savings of CM2		$(\Delta TC^o + \Delta RC^o) > 0$	$(\Delta TC^1 + \Delta RC^1) > (\Delta TC^o + \Delta RC^o)$	$(\Delta TC^2 + \Delta RC^2) < (\Delta TC^1 + \Delta RC^1)$

Fig. 5. Transaction and risk costs of CM1 and CM2.

(B) Risk cost savings

- The lower environmental and behavioral uncertainty reduces the risk premium included in the transfer price of the intermediate product a and in the supply price of the final product b.

As a result, given symmetric non-specific transactions, vertical integration has the following transaction and risk cost savings, i.e. $(\Delta TC^0 + \Delta RC^0) > 0$ (see Figure 5):

Lower risk costs and transaction costs as expenses and opportunity costs due to lower environmental and behavioral uncertainty.

In the following, we investigate the higher transaction and risk cost savings of the vertically integrated firm in the case of asymmetric specific transactions.

III.2.2. Transaction and risk cost savings under asymmetric specific transactions

Given asymmetric specific transactions additional transaction and risk cost savings arise:

(A) Higher transaction cost savings

(I) Environmental uncertainty: The transaction and risk cost savings due to lower environmental and transactional uncertainty are approximately as high as in the case of symmetric non-specific transactions.

(II) Behavioral uncertainty: In addition to the higher degree of goal compatibility and the positive interaction effect between environmental and behavioral uncertainty, the attenuation of the hold-up problem results in higher transaction cost savings than under symmetric nonspecific transactions:

- Since the transactions between production stage one and two are internally coordinated, common ownership attenuates the 'hold-up' problem, that is, "the possibility of opportunistic behavior being used to exploit the quasi-rents" (Rubin 1990, p. 9), given asymmetric specific transactions. This leads to lower disincentive cost (lost quasi-rents) and lower control and bargaining costs as expenses, compared with the interfirm coordination design.

(III) Ex post adaptability problem:

- Since, given high transaction specificity, the exit barriers (adjustment costs as lost quasi-rents and additional adjustment expenses) are high, the higher information processing capacity and higher incentive compatibility of the vertically integrated firm attenuates the *ex post* adaptability problem. This lowers the adjustment costs as expenses and opportunity costs of adjustment measures.

(B) Higher risk cost savings

- Due to the higher behavioral uncertainty reduction and the attenuation of the *ex post* adaptability problem, the risk cost savings, which result from the lower risk premium included in the transfer price of the intermediate product a and in the supply price of the final product b, are higher than in the case of symmetric non-specific transactions.

In sum, compared with symmetric non-specific transactions, vertical integration has the following additional transaction and firsk cost savings, i.e. $(\Delta TC^0 + \Delta RC^0) < (\Delta TC^1 + \Delta RC^1)$ (see Figure 5): Higher risk costs and transaction cost savings due to the higher behavioral uncertainty reducing effect and the attenuation of the *ex post* adaptability problem. Herefore, given the potential volume of transactions and the complexity and change of transactional environment, the evolution of the vertically integrated firm is more likely, the higher and more asymmetric the transaction specific investment are.

III.2.3. Transaction and risk cost savings under symmetric specific transactions

Given idiosyncratic transactions, vertical integration leads to lower behavioral uncertainty reduction and hence to lower transaction and risk cost savings than in the case of asymmetric transactions. This is due to the incentive effect of the bilaterally dependent interfirm transactions.

(A) Lower transaction cost savings

(I) Environmental uncertainty: The transaction and risk cost savings are roughly the same as under asymmetric specific transactions.

(II) Behavioral uncertainty:

- Given symmetric specific transactions, the interaction effect between transaction specificity and behavioral uncertainty is negative (incentive effect of bilateral dependency). In this bilaterally dependent situation, where both parties behave cooperatively, no *ex ante* and *ex post* opportunism problem (adverse selection and hold-up problem) exists (Casson 1990, p. 166). Thus no transaction cost savings (control, decision and disincentive costs) arise due to the attenuation of the opportunism problem by vertical integration.
- Moreover, in the case of symmetric specific interfirm transactions, the interaction effect between environmental and behavioral uncertainty is also negative. Hence no additional transaction cost savings (lower disincentive, control, decision costs) due to the behavioral uncertainty reducing effect of the higher information processing capacity of the internal organization design arise.

(II) Ex post adaptability problem:

- Cooperative behavior due to bilateral dependence improves the adaptability of the interfirm coordination design and thus reduces the transaction cost advantage of the vertically integrated firm, compared with asymmetric transactions.

(B) Lower risk cost savings

- The risk cost savings at the intermediate and final good market are lower than in the case of asymmetric specific transactions, because of the lower behavioral uncertainty reduction and the lower *ex post* adaptability advantage of the internal organization design.

Consequently, compared with asymmetric specific transactions, vertical integration has lower transaction and risk cost savings because of the incentive effect of bilaterally dependent interfirm transactions (Thorelli 1986, p. 46), i.e. $(\Delta TC^1 + \Delta RC^1) > (\Delta TC^2 + \Delta RC^2)$ (see Figure 5).

To sum up, the transaction and risk cost savings of the vertically integrated firm result from

(I) the environmental and transactional uncertainty reducing effect of the higher information processing capacity of the internal organization design,

(II) the behavioral uncertainty reducing effect, due to

(IIa) the higher degree of goal compatibility between the production stages,

(IIb) the positive interaction effect between environmental and behavioral uncertainty, as well as

(IIc) the attenuation of the 'hold-up' problem, and

(III) the attenuation of the *ex post* adaptability problem.

The actual extent of transaction and risk cost savings depends on the characteristics of transactions:

(a) Given symmetric nonspecific transactions the transaction and risk cost savings result from I, IIa and IIb.

(b) Given asymmetric specific transactions the transaction and risk cost savings result from I, IIa, IIb, IIc and III.

(c) Given symmetric specific (idiosyncratic) transactions the transaction and risk cost savings result from I, IIa and III.

As a result, we may conclude: Given the complexity and change of transactional environment and the potential volume of transactions, the intrafirm coordination mechanism (unified governance) will emerge more likely, the higher and more asymmetric the transaction specific investments are; conversely, the interfirm coordination mechanism (bilateral governance) will evolve more likely, the higher and more symmetric the transaction specific investments are.

Finally, we show that this result is partly incompatible with the Williamsonian governance structure approach.

IV. Re-analysis of the Williamsonian Governance Structure Approach

The central argument of the Williamsonian governance structure approach (Williamson 1985, 1986; see also Klein, Crawford and Alchian 1978) is summarized in hypothesis 1:

Hypothesis 1

> The higher the transaction specific investments, the more likely unified goverance structures (i.e. internal organization) arise, because high transaction specific investments result in bilateral monopoly (i.e. dependence) that fosters opportunistic behavior (Williamson 1991, p. 279, p. 282)

According to our results, which are compatible with others (Stinchcombe 1985; Eccles and Bradach 1989; Walker and Poppo 1991; Cook and Emerson 1984;

Imai 1987–88; Reddy and Rao 1990; Larson 1992), the Williamsonian argument is incomplete because Williamson does not differentiate between symmetric and asymmetric transactions. The revised version of the governance structure approach is summarized in hypotheses 2 and 3:

Hypothesis 2: Asymmetric specific transactions

> The higher and more asymmetric the transaction specific investments, the more likely unified governance structures (i.e. vertical integration) emerge, because high transactions specific investments of one transactor result in unilateral dependence that fosters opportunistic behavior of the other transactor.

Hypothesis 3: Symmetric specific transactions

> The higher the transaction specific investments, the more likely a bilateral governance structure (i.e. interfirm coordination design) arises, because high transaction specific investments of both transactors result in bilateral dependence that fosters cooperative behavior of both transactors.

Consequently, in the case of recurrent transactions the Williamsonian governance structure approach must be revised as follows (see Figure 6):

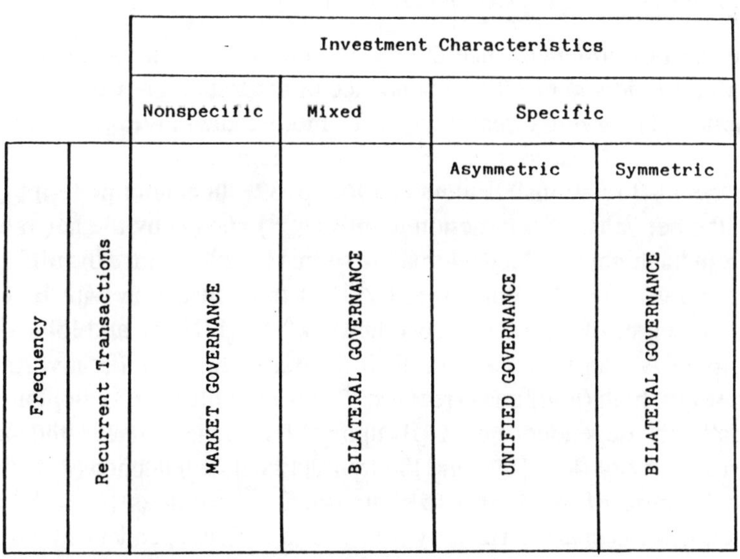

Fig. 6. Transaction specificity and governance structure.

V. Concluding Remarks

The aim of this paper was to explain the evolution of the vertically integrated firm in terms of coordination economies. First we developed the concept of coordination efficiency, which is defined by the sum of transaction, risk and set-up costs of the coordination design. The transaction and risk costs are positively related to uncertainty (environmental, behavioral, transactional), transaction specifity, transaction frequency, and the potential volume of transactions. The set-up costs of the coordination design are determined by the complexity, as well as incentive and cognitive compatibility of the coordination design. Second, this concept was applied to the question of the evolution of the vertically integrated firm as coordination mechanism. Thereby we showed that the vertically integrated firm evolves the more (less) likely, the more asymmetric (symmetric) the interfirm transactions are. Finally, this result was compared with the Williamsonian governance structure approach which overestimates the likelihood of the evolution of the vertically integrated firm, since Williamson does not differentiate between symmetric and asymmetric specific transactions.

Appendix: Transaction Specificity and Transactional Dependence

The purpose of this Appendix is to investigate the relationship between transaction specificity and transactional dependence. First we define transactional dependence in economic terms and second we relate the different transactional characteristics to the different degrees of transactional dependence.

1. Definition of Transactional Dependence

According to the power/dependence theory of Emerson (1962, 1972) and Cook (1977), Cook and Emerson (1978), dependence of the transacor A upon B (d^{AB}) is a joint function (1) varying directly with "A's motivational investments in goals mediated by B", and (2) varying inversely "with the availability of those goals to A outside the A–B relations" (Emerson 1962, p. 32). In economic terms (1) is measured by the net value of transaction with B (g^{AB}) and (2) by the net value of transaction from the highest valued alternative source C (g^{AC}). Since the difference between g^{AB} and g^{AC}, i.e. A's quasi-rent (q^{AB}) of the transaction with B, varies directly with the degree of transaction specificity ($k^A > 0$) (Heide and John 1988), k^A is a measure of A's dependence upon B. If the transaction specific investments of A are high (low), high (low) quasi-rents (q^{AB}) result, which can be exploited by B. Consequently, the dependence of A [B] upon B [A] is measured by the degree of transaction specificity (k^A) [k^B], and the transactional dependence (d) between A and B by the ratio of the transactors' transaction specifities ($d = k^A/k^B$). Bilateral dependence is characterized by $d = 1$, bilateral independence by $d = 0$, and unilateral dependence by $d \gtrless 1$. Furthermore, the strength of transactional dependence can be represented by the degree of transactional cohesion (c) (Emerson

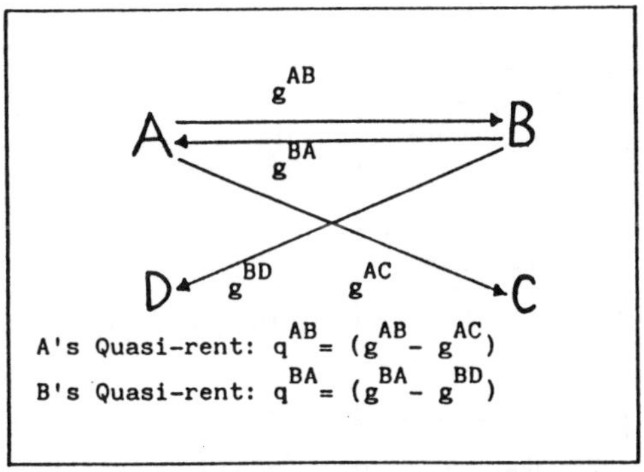

Fig. 7. Transaction specificity and quasi-rents.

1962, p. 34), which is defined as the average of k^A and k^B, i.e. $c = (k^A + k^B)/2$. The higher the transactional cohesion (c), the higher is the mutual dependence.

2. CHARACTERISTICS OF TRANSACTIONAL RELATIONS

Now we investigate the transactional dependence under the different transactional relations.

(1) Idiosyncratic transactions (symmetric specific transactions)

In this case both transactors undertake high transaction specific investments (k^A and k^B are high). Hence both transactors' quasi-rents, which can be appropriated by the other, are equal, i.e. $q^{AB} = (g^{AB} - g^{AC}) = (g^{BA} - g^{BD}) = q^{BA}$ (see Figure 7). Therefore, A and B's adjustment costs are high (high lost quasi-rents and transaction costs as expenses), resulting in high bilaterial dependence (c = high; $d = 1$).

(2) Symmetric non-specific transactions

In this case neither transactor undertakes transaction specific investments ($k^A = k^B = 0$). Hence both transactors' quasi-rents are equal to zero, i.e. $q^{AB} = (g^{AB} - g^{AC}) = q^{BA} = (g^{BA} - g^{BD}) = 0$. Therefore, A and B's adjustment costs are low (no lost quasi-rents and low transaction costs as expenses), which implies bilateral independence ($d = 0$).

(3) Asymmetric transactions

An asymmetric transaction exists if A and B undertake different transaction specific investments resulting in $k^A > k^B$ and $d > 1$ or $k^A < k^B$ and $d < 1$.

If A undertakes high and B low transaction specific investments, B's quasi-rent is lower than A's, i.e. $q^{AB} = (g^{AB} - g^{AC}) > q^{BA} = (g^{BA} - g^{BD})$. On the other

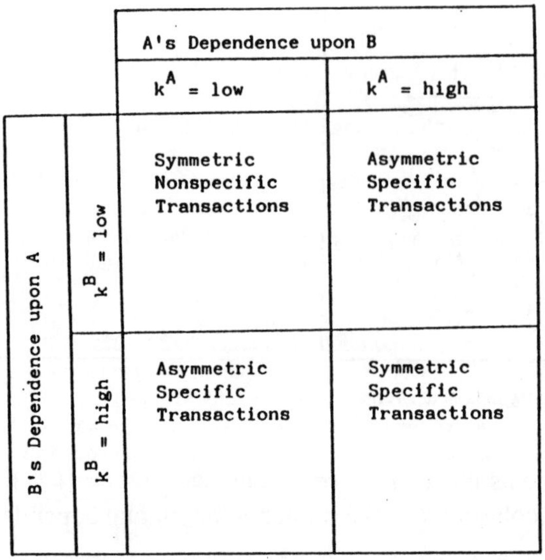

Fig. 8. Transaction specificity and transactional dependence.

hand, if B undertakes high and A low transaction specific investments, A's quasi-rent is lower than B's, i.e. $q^{BA} = (g^{BA} - g^{BD}) > q^{AB} = (g^{AB} - g^{AC})$. Therefore, high quasi-rents of A and low quasi-rents of B, that are appropriable by the other transactor, result in A's [B's] adjustment cost disadvantage [advantage], i.e. in high [low] lost quasi-rents and transaction costs as expenses, and hence in A's [B's] high [low] dependence upon B [A] ($d > 1$).

In sum, symmetric specific transactions are characterized by high bilateral dependence ($d = 1$; k^A and k^B are high), symmetric non-specific transactions by bilateral independence ($d = 0$; k^A and $k^B = 0$), and asymmetric specific transactions by unilateral dependence ($d > 1, k^A > k^B$; or $d < 1, k^A < k^B$) (see Figure 8).

References

Anderson, E. and D.C. Schmittlein (1984) 'Integration of the Sales Force: An Empirical Examination', *Rand Journal of Economics*, **15**, 385–395.

Baligh, H.H. and R.M. Burton (1982) 'The Movable Boundaries between Organizations and Markets', *International Journal of Policy Analysis and Information Systems*, **6**, 435–449.

Barney, J.P. and W.G. Ouchi (1986) *Organizational Economics*, San Francisco.

Bradach, J.L. and R.G. Eccles (1989) 'Price, Authority, and Trust, *Annual Review of Sociology*, **15**, 97–118.

Butler, R. and M.G. Carney (1983) 'Managing Markets: Implications for the Make-Buy Decision', *Journal of Management Studies*, **20**, 213–231.

Casson, M. (1990) *Enterprise and Competitiveness*, Oxford.

Charny, D. (1990) 'Nonlegal Sanctions in Commercial Relations', *Harvard Law Review*, **104**, 373–467.

Cook, K.S. (1977) 'Exchange and Power in Networks of Interorganizational Relations', *Sociological Quarterly*, **18**, 62–82.

Cook, K.S. and R.M. Emerson (1978) 'Power, Equity and Commitment in Exchange Networks', *American Sociological Review*, **43**, 721–739.
Cook, K.S. and R.M. Emerson (1984) 'Exchange Networks and the Analysis of Complex Organizations', *Research in Sociology of Organizations*, **3**, 1–30.
Crocker, K.J. (1983) 'Vertical Integration and the Strategic Use of Private Information', *Bell Journal of Economics*, **14**, 236–248.
Eccles, R.G. and H.C. White (1988) 'Price and Authority in Inter-Profit Center Transactions', *American Journal of Sociology*, **94**, Supplement, S17–S51.
Emerson, R.M. (1962) 'Power-Dependence Relations', *American Sociological Review*, **27**, 31–41.
Emerson, R.M. (1972) 'Exchange Theory', in J. Berger, M. Zelditch and B. Anderson, eds, *Sociological Theories in Progress*. New York, 38–87.
Geanakoplos, J. and P. Milgrom (1991) 'A Theory of Hierarchies Based on Limited Managerial Attention', *Journal of the Japanese and International Economics*, **5**, 205–225.
Heide, J.B. and G. John (1988) 'The Role of Dependence Balancing in Safeguarding Transaction-Specific Assets in Conventional Channels', *Journal of Marketing*, **52**, 20–35.
Hayes, R.H. and S.C. Wheelwright (1984) *Restoring Our Competitive Edge*. New York.
Imai, K. (1987–88) 'The Corporate Network in Japan', *Japanese Economic Studies*, **XVI**, 3–37.
Klein, B., R.G. Crawford, and A.A. Alchian (1978) 'Vertical Integration, Appropriable Rents, and the Competitive Contracting Process', *Journal of Law and Economics*, **21**, 297–326.
Jarillo, J.C. and J.E. Ricart (1987) 'Sustaining Networks', *Interfaces*, **17**, 82–91.
Johanson, J. and L.-G. Mattsson (1987) 'Interorganizational Relations in Industrial Systems: A Network Approach Compared with the Transaction-Cost Approach', *International Studies of Management and Organization*, **XVII**, 34–48.
Larson, A. (1992) 'Network Dyads in Entrepreneurial Settings: A Study of Governance of Exchange Relationships', *Administrative Science Quarterly*, **37**, 76–104.
Lawler, E.E. (1982) 'Increasing Worker Involvement to Enhance Organizational Effectiveness', in P.S. Goodmand and Ass., eds, *Change in Organizations*. San Francisco, 280–315.
Leblebici, H. (1985) 'Transactions and Organizational Forms: A Reanalysis', *Organization Studies*, **6**, 97–115.
Lavington, F. (1925) 'An Approach to the Theory of Business Risk', *Economic Journal*, June, 186–199.
Macneil, I.R. (1986) 'Exchange Revisited: Individual Utility and Social Solidarity', *Ethics*, **96**, 567–593.
Malone, T.W., J. Yates, and R.I. Benjamin (1987) 'Electronic Markets and Electronic Hierarchies', *Communications of ACM*, **30**, 485–497.
Mann, D.P. and J.P. Wissink (1984) 'Inside vs. Outside Production: A Contracting Approach to Vertical Integration', *Discussion Paper 170*, University of Pennsylvania, June.
Masten, S.E., J.W. Meehan, and E.A. Snyder (1991) 'The Costs of Organization', *Journal of Law, Economics, & Organization*, **7**, 1–25.
Perry, M.K. (1989) 'Vertical Integration: Determinants and Effects', in *Handbook of Industrial Organization*, R. Schmalensee, R.D. Willig eds, Vol. 1, Amsterdam, 183–255.
Presott, E.C. and M. Visscher (1980) 'Organization Capital', *Journal of Political Economy*, **88**, 446–461.
Radner, R. (1970) 'Problems in the Theory of Markets under Uncertainty', *American Economic Review*, **60**, 454–460.
Radner, R. (1991) 'The Organization of Decentralized Information Processing', mimeo, November.
Reddy, N.M. and M.V. Rao (1990) 'The Industrial Market as an Interfirm Organization', *Journal of Management Studies*, **27**, 43–59.
Rubin, P.H. (1990) *Managing Business Transactions*. New York.
Shove, G.F. (1930) 'The Representative Firm and Increasing Returns', *Economic Journal*, **XL**, 94–116.
Stinchcombe, A.L. (1985) 'Contracts as Hierarchical Documents' in A.L. Stinchcombe and A.C. Heimer, *Organization Theory and Project Management*. Oslo, 121–171.
Stuckey, J.A. (1983) *Vertical Integration and Joint Ventures in the Aluminium Industry*. Cambridge, Mass.

Thorelli, H.B. (1986) 'Networks: Between Markets and Hierarchies', *Strategic Management Journal*, **7**, 37–51.

Tirole, J. (1988) *The Theory of Industrial Organization*, Cambridge.

Van de Ven, A.H. and R. Drazin (1985) 'The Concept of Fit in Contingency Theory', *Research in Organizational Behavior*, **7**, 333–365.

Walker, G. and L. Poppo (1991) 'Profit Centers, Single Source Suppliers, and Transaction Costs', *Administrative Science Quarterly*, **36**, 66–87.

Williamson, O.E. (1971) 'The Vertical Integration of Production: Market Failure Considerations', *American Economic Review*, **61**, 112–123.

Williamson, O.E. (1975) *Markets and Hierarchies*. New York.

Williamson, O.E. (1985) *The Economic Institutions of Capitalism*. New York.

Williamson, O.E. (1986) *Economic Organization*. New York.

Williamson, O.E. (1989) 'Transaction Cost Economics', in Handbook of Industrial Organization, R. Schmalensee and R.D. Willig eds, Vol. 1, Amsterdam, 136–182.

Williamson, O.E. (1991) 'Comparative Economic Organization: The Analysis of Discrete Structural Alternatives', *Administrative Science Quarterly*, **36**, 269–296.

Windsperger, J. (1991a) 'Transaktionskosten und Informationsstruktur', in L.J. Heinrich, G. Pomberger and R. Schauer hrg, *Die Informationswirtschaft im Unternehmen*. Linz, 201–219.

Windsperger, J. (1991b) 'The Meaning of Adjustment Costs in the Theory of the Firm', *Zeitschrift für Wirtschafts- und Sozialwissenschaften*, **111**, 425–435.

Windsperger, J. (1992) 'A Theoretical Foundation of the Learning Curve', *Jahrbücher für Nationalökonomie und Statistik*, **209**, 223–230.

Young, A.A. (1928) 'Increasing Returns and Economic Progress', *Economic Journal*, **38**, 527–542.

III. DETERMINANTS OF PERFORMANCE

K. Aiginger and J. Finsinger (eds.), Applied Industrial Organization, 133–149.

Why Did UK Manufacturing Profitability Rise Over the 1980s?

JONATHAN HASKEL*
Department of Economics, Queen Mary and Westfield College, University of London, U.K.

Abstract. Profitability in UK manufacturing collapsed in the early 1980s, but then recovered to 1970s levels. To account for the changes in profits we propose a series of extensions of the widely-used Cowling and Waterson (1976) model. Our extensions incorporate demand shocks, varying competition and collusion, and the role of unions. The resulting model encompasses Cowling/Waterson, the Kreps and Scheinkman (1983) varying competition model and the Green and Porter (1984) and Rotemberg and Saloner (1986) varying collusion models. Using a panel of 53 UK industries, 1973–1986 we estimate the encompassing model by generalised methods of moments/instrumental variables. Our major findings are: (a) there is no substantial contribution to changes in aggregate profitability from the batting average effect of movements between sectors; (b) the collapse of profits in the early 1980s was mainly driven by the collapse in demand; (c) the fall in union density in the 1980s has increased profitability despite a fall in concentration. We also find tentative evidence suggesting that collusion is pro-cyclical as in Green and Porter (1984).

Key words: Profitability, competition, unions.

JEL codes: J51, L11, L60.

1. Introduction

No matter how it is measured, UK manufacturing profitability rose strongly in the mid-1980s. Figures for return on capital (Eltis, 1990), price-cost margins (Haskel and Kay, 1990) or return to new investment (Sentence and McKenzie, 1992) all show a marked rise following the collapse in profits in the early 1980s. The purpose of this paper is to investigate why.

Of course, the determination of industry profitability has been the central preoccupation of empirical industrial economics for almost forty years. The thrust of the literature is to test whether increased concentration raises profits, and most studies find a positive, if small, correlation (Schmalensee, 1989). Yet concentration in UK manufacturing has *fallen* during the 1980s. It is this interesting fact that motivates our current investigation. If concentration has tended to reduce profits then what has raised them? Or, are we to conclude that forty years of empirical research has produced the wrong sign?

For alternative explanations of the profits boom, we need turn no further than the popular discussion, which is replete with conjecture. Among the factors suggested have been increased productivity, reduced union power and increased demand (see e.g. Walton, 1991). Although such variables have appeared frequently in empirical studies, their effect is often not robust, see *inter alia* Schmalensee (1989), Geroski (1988) for surveys. For example, using UK manufacturing data, Cowling and Waterson (1976) find no effect of unions on profits, whereas Conyon and Machin (1991) discover a significant negative effect.

Perhaps a more serious problem is that to interpret these correlations we require a satisfactory theory. The traditional framework, set out in Cowling and Waterson (1976), postulates that profit rates depend on concentration, the elasticity of demand and the industry conjectural variation. There is no role for unions or productivity for example, unless they work indirectly through the elasticity of demand say.

In this paper then we have two aims. First, we provide a theoretical framework that can rationalise many of the variables that are often included in profit rate studies. We set out a sequence of models of many of the informal arguments that are often heard to explain increased profitability; increased demand, weaker unions, increased productivity for example. In effect, this gives a series of generalisations of the influential Cowling/Waterson profit rate equation.

Second, we put our model to the test to see what explains the increase in profits over the 1980s. To do this we use a panel data set of 53 three digit UK industries 1973–1986. Our estimation procedure uses generalised method of moments/instrumental variables estimation and we provide a full range of diagnostic tests to check our specifications. To anticipate our results, we find that the collapse in profits at the start of the 1980s is associated with the fall in demand, whilst much of the increase since then has come from reduced union power. We als find tentative evidence tha collusion is pro-cyclical and this lends support to the Green and Porter model of varying collusion.

The plan of this paper is as follows. In Section 2 we review some facts about profitability and its correlates. Using disaggregated industry data, we test whether changes in profitability can be explained by the "batting average" hypothesis whereby value added moves to more profitable sectors. In Section 3 we outline the Cowling and Waterson theory and discuss whether it can account for increases in profitability. In Section 4 we extend the model to incorporate the effects of demand, productivity and unions. In Section 5 we present our estimates and robustness checks. Section 6 summarises and concludes.

2. The Basic Facts

Table I sets out some key data for 1976–86. Profits fell precipitously during the deep recession of the early 1980s, but since then have risen substantially.[1] By contrast, after also falling in the early 1980s concentration has carried on falling. As is well known, unionisation has fallen and unemployment has risen. The data then reveals two interesting facts to be explained. First, profitability collapsed in the early 1980s. Second, profitability then rose strongly to 1970s levels, although concentration was much lower than the 1970s.

TABLE I. Key variables (%)

Year	Price cost margin	Concentration	Unemployment	Union density
1976	0.36	0.42	0.05	0.62
1977	0.37	0.42	0.05	0.63
1978	0.36	0.42	0.05	0.65
1979	0.35	0.42	0.05	0.67
1980	0.30	0.39	0.07	0.68
1981	0.31	0.38	0.11	0.73
1982	0.33	0.37	0.12	0.62
1983	0.35	0.36	0.11	0.61
1984	0.36	0.34	0.09	0.59
1985	0.37	0.34	0.08	0.57
1986	0.38	0.35	0.07	0.56

Note: Price-cost margin is gross value added less wage bill upon gross value added. Concentration is five firm concentration ratio by sales, multiplied by one less the share of imports in home sales. Unemployment is average industry unemployment. Union density average of proportion of employees in the industry unionised. Calculations on basis of panel of 53 three digit industries, see data appendix.

To explore this further we make use of disaggregated data. An attractive explanation of the changes in profits is the "batting average" hypothesis. If the less profitable sectors have declined, leaving the only the best performers, then the average may have risen. To investigate this we first note that the average manufacturing profit rate is an average of profit rates in each sector weighted by the share of value added of each sector. Algebraically, $\pi_M = \Sigma \pi_I v_I$, where π is value added less wage bill over value added, v value added and subscript M denotes manufacturing and I industry. Differentiating gives

$$\dot{\pi}_M = \Sigma \dot{\pi}_I f_I + \Sigma \frac{\pi_I}{\pi_M} \frac{dv_I}{dt} \tag{1}$$

where f_I is the share of profits for each industry in the total and a dot above a variable denotes a proportional rate of change. The first term of (1) says that average profits rise due to increases in each sector (the sectoral growth effect), whilst the second says that the average rises if value added moves to sectors of above average profitability (the batting average effect).

Table II sets out the decomposition of Equation (1) for 1976–1986, and shows clearly that the contribution of the batting average effect is insignificant even in the large shakeout of the 1980–81. To understand the 1980s we have therefore to account for the increases in the different sectors.

3. The Cowling/Waterson Model

Firm i produces a homogeneous good according to a value added production function $Y_i = U^{\gamma} N_i^b K_i^{1-b}$, where Y is output, N is employment, K is capital, and

TABLE II. Decomposition of growth in aggregate profit rate according to: $\dot{\pi}_M = \Sigma \dot{\pi}_I f_I + \Sigma \frac{\pi_I}{\pi_M} \frac{dv_I}{dt}$

Year	Growth in agg profit rate	Sectoral growth effect	Batting average effect
1975	-22.34	-22.22	-5.87
1976	9.57	8.31	0.22
1977	1.64	0.62	-0.22
1978	-3.18	-3.39	0.24
1979	-3.86	-4.38	0.01
1980	-13.93	-16.69	0.43
1981	3.20	1.92	0.93
1982	6.33	4.66	1.21
1983	8.02	6.29	0.44
1984	3.26	3.29	-0.52
1985	2.32	2.17	-0.16
1986	4.03	3.23	-0.12

Note: The numbers do not always round up since the table is constructed by a discrete time approximation to the small changes in the equation. Calculations on basis of panel of 53 three digit industries, see data appendix.

U is utilisation. The demand curve facing each firm in the industry has elasticity η. The firm chooses N_i, to maximise profits Π_i

$$\Pi_i = P_j Y_i - W_j N_i - r_j K_i \tag{2}$$

subject to the production function, demand curve and conjectured responses of other firms. W_j is the labour cost to the firm assumed common across the industry. Following the convention that K and the number of firms are predetermined in the short run, this yields the mark-up condition

$$\frac{P - MC}{P} = \frac{s_i}{\eta}(1 + \theta_i) \tag{3}$$

where s_i is the market share of firm i and θ the conjectural variation. Assuming that $MC = AVC$, multiplying both sides by market share and summing gives the Cowling/Waterson equation

$$\frac{\pi}{PY} = \frac{H}{\eta}(1 + \mu) \tag{4}$$

where $\pi_i = \Pi_i + rK_i$, i.e. revenue less variable cost, H the Herfindahl index of concentration, and μ is the output-weighted conjectural variation.

Equation (4) reveals that there are three mechanisms that might account for increased profit rates; an increase in H, a fall in η or a rise in μ. The following points are worth noting. First, (4) rules out a number of possible candidates for the increase in profits over the 1980s. Profits cannot have risen following a weakening of union power of an increase in productivity. If weakened unions mean lower wages for example the firm merely reduces prices, and profits remain the same. Similarly an increase in utilisation simply lowers marginal cost and hence prices leaving profits the same.

Second, it may be felt that we are relying too rigidly on the theory. However, (4) conveniently summarises a number of popular static oligopoly models as well as the competitive case. It is therefore rather general. Whilst it does not consider an explicit dynamic game, these types models have proved difficult to implement econometrically; the main strength of (4) is as an empirical vehicle. Furthermore we obviously need some theory to interpret observed correlations. Third, (4) is derived for a given number of firms and demand may well affect entry and exit. So, subsequent discussion should be understood as profits for given market structure.

So, can Equation (4) explain the rise in profitability over the 1980s? As Table I shows concentration adjusted by competition from abroad has been falling (see Lyons, 1981, for a rationalisation of this adjustment). Data for the Herfindahl index is unfortunately not available for all these years, but Davies *et al.* (1992) show a fall in the market shares of all the top five firms in a sample of 54 industries, 1979–1986. Bils (1985) and Weitzman (1982) present models where η varies counter-cyclically due to customer attachment and increased variety of products, but without direct data on η a downward movement in the elasticity of demand remains a matter of conjecture. Lastly, μ would have to have risen in the 1980s i.e. firms became more Cournot-like. There is no direct evidence on this.

4. Extensions of the Cowling-Waterson Model

PROFIT RATES AND DEMAND

To introduce demand more directly we follow the recent new-Keynesian models that have stressed the role of demand shocks in price/employment equations, see Blanchard and Fischer (1989) for a survey. Suppose that demand is linear of the form $P = \theta - \delta Y$ where θ is a random variable and the firm sets prices on the basis of expected θ, θ^e. Then (4) becomes

$$\frac{\pi}{PY} = \frac{H}{\eta}(1+\lambda) + \sigma \tag{5}$$

where $\sigma = (\theta - \theta^e)/\theta$ which is a proportional upward demand shock. This is simply a generalisation of the Cowling/Waterson condition. If $\theta = \theta^e$, $\sigma = 0$, and then (5) becomes (4). Positive demand shocks imply that $\theta > \theta^e$ and so $\sigma > 0$ and hence upward demand shocks raise profits.[2]

PROFIT RATES AND CONJECTURAL VARIATIONS

There are two ways to model varying μ; as varying with the type of competition or the degree of collusion. Since μ reflects whether firms are Bertrand or

Cournot competitors then it varies according to the type of competition. Kreps and Scheinkman (1983) view the difference between Cournot and Bertrand competition as depending on production capacity. In Bertrand price competition (with homogeneous goods) undercutting firms acquire the whole market. Firms can only serve this market if unconstrained by capacity. By contrast, if capacity is constrained, firms produce as much as they can leaving the price to be determined in the marketplace; Cournot competition. Since capacity constraints increased over the 1980s (Haskel and Martin, 1992b), profits might have risen if firms became more Cournot-like.

Haskel and Martin (1992b) model the essential insight of Kreps/Scheinkman using the consistent conjectures duopoly model of Bresnehan (1981).[3] Consistent conjectures sets the slope of the reaction function equal to the conjectural variation. Differentiation of (3), aggregating over the industry and assuming the demand curve is linear of slope –1 gives the industry consistent conjecture

$$\mu_i = -1 + \left(\sqrt{\left(\frac{c^2}{4} + c \right)} - \frac{c}{2} \right) \tag{6}$$

where c is the output-weighted sum of the slopes of the individual firms marginal cost curves, and $-1 < \mu < 0$. Capacity constraints appear through c. With no capacity constraints $c = 0$, and so from (6), $\mu = -1$. This is of course Bertrand competition where firms cut prices aggressively since they can serve extra customers at zero marginal cost; from (4), profits are zero. By contrast when capacity is binding $c = \infty$ and so μ is zero. This is the Cournot case; from (4) profits depend upon market concentration. If for simplicity we write a linearised version of (6) as $\mu = -1 + b_1 + b_2\sigma$ where we have assumed that capacity constraints are worsened in times of high demand we have, substituting into (5)

$$\frac{\pi}{PY} = \alpha_1 H + \alpha_2 H * \sigma + \sigma \tag{7}$$

where $\alpha_i = b_i/\eta, i = 1, 2$. Under this theory then, if capacity constraints have risen over the 1980s then competition has become Cournot-like. This explains the rise in profits, which would be expected to be greatest in more concentrated industries.

The second approach to modelling μ is to assume that it reflects the extent of collusion, in which case μ may change if collusion is cyclical. To capture this empirically, we follow Clarke and Davies (1982) and suppose that $\mu = \phi(1/H - 1)$ where ϕ reflects the degree of collusion; if $\phi = 1$ then there is complete collusion. Substituting into (5) gives

$$\frac{\pi}{PY} = \frac{\phi + H(1 - \phi)}{\eta} + \sigma \tag{8}$$

The main approaches to varying collusion are due to Green and Porter (1984) and Rotemberg and Saloner (1986) which are based on time-varying collusion in the presence of uncertainty and imperfect information. As noted by Domowitz,

Hubbard and Petersen (1987), the Green/Porter model predicts that collusion is pro-cyclical while the Rotemberg/Saloner model predicts it is anti-cyclical. We therefore write

$$\phi = a_1 H + a_2 \sigma \tag{9}$$

which simply says that collusion depends on concentration, and varies over the cycle. The Green/Porter model predicts that $a_2 > 0$ and Rotemberg/Saloner that $a_2 < 0$. We would expect that $a_1 > 0$ if say collusion is easier with fewer firms. Substituting (9) into (8) gives

$$\frac{\pi}{PY} = \beta_1 H - \beta_2 H * \sigma + \beta_3 \sigma - \beta_4 H^2 \tag{10}$$

where $\beta_1 = (1 + a_1)/\eta$, $\beta_2 = a_2/\eta$, $\beta_3 = a_2/\eta + 1$, $\beta_4 = a_1/\eta$. Note that (10) encompasses (7), (5) and (4). With regard to (7) it has the testable predictions that the Kreps/Scheinkman model implies the absence of H^2. THe Cowling/Waterson model with demand shocks (5) implies that $\beta_2 = \beta_4 = 0$; and the simple Cowling/Waterson model (4) implies that $\beta_2 = \beta_4 = \beta_3 = 0$. Finally, the signs on σ depend upon how collusion varies over the cycle.

PROFIT RATES AND PRODUCTIVITY

The substantial increase in UK productivity over the 1980s has been extensively noted (Layard and Nickell, 1989; Muellbauer, 1989). It is clear from (4) that productivity cannot raise profit rates. Any increase in output per head will simply lead firms to alter their prices.[4] So the pro-cyclicality of productivity arising from increased utilisation for example, cannot, as the equation stands, explain the cyclical fluctuation in profits.

Much of the macro discussion of productivity centres on the role of overhead labour at the firm (see Layard and Nickell, 1989 for example). To see the effect of overhead labour on profits we follow Haskel and Martin (1992a). Suppose that there are two types of labour which we shall call overhead and productive labour, N_0 and N_p. The production function takes the form (from now on we drop the subscript i for notational convenience)

$$Y = U^{\gamma} N_P^{\alpha_1} N_o^{\alpha_2} K^{1-\alpha} \tag{11}$$

from which we note that those industries who have had the biggest increase in N_P have had the biggest rises in productivity. Profits are now

$$\Pi = PY - WN_P - WN_O - rK \tag{12}$$

where we have assumed for simplicity that both types of labour are paid the same. We assume that N_O is predetermined being the outcome of a previous bargain between firms and workers that we model below. Maximisation of (12) with respect to N_P yields an analogous expression to (8)

$$\frac{\pi}{PY} = \left(\frac{\phi + H(1-\phi)}{\eta} + \sigma\right)\left(1 + \frac{N_o}{N_p}\right) - \frac{N_o}{N_p} + \sigma \tag{13}$$

which shows that an increase in N_p raises π/PY. So, those industries where TFP rose the most would have the biggest rise in profits.

What is the intuition for this result? Overhead labour is like a quasi-fixed labour cost to the firm. The firm chooses N_P to establish a mark-up that depends on monopoly power in the usual way. The econometrician observes a profit rate which includes the wage bill of the N_o workers. So, the presence of overhead labour derives a wedge between the firm's mark-up and its profit rate. An increase in N_O raises this wedge and so reduces the profit rate.

Profit rates and unions

It is often argued that weakened unions lower wages and so margins. Clearly from (4) this is untrue since a reduction in the wage lowers marginal cost and hence mark-ups. We must therefore consider another avenue. Following from the discussion of productivity above if we think of N_O as related to crew sizes and manning levels etc., in the UK it is natural to suppose that it is the subject of a bargain between firms and workers; direct survey evidence on bargaining scope strongly supports this view (Millward and Stevens, 1986).[5] To model this we follow Haskel and Martin (1992a). Suppose union utility, U is of the standard Stone-Geary form (Pencavel, 1984)

$$U = \left(\frac{W}{p} - \left(\frac{W}{p}\right)^*\right)\left(\frac{N_O}{N_P} - \left(\frac{N_O}{N_P}\right)^*\right) \tag{14}$$

where $U_1, U_2 > 0$, so that unions prefer higher wages and more on-the-job leisure, and wages are deflated by economy-wide prices p. Both w and N_0 are given by the outcome of the Nash product

$$\max_{W,N_O} U^\lambda \cdot \pi^{1-\lambda} \tag{15}$$

where λ is the bargaining power of the workers and (15) is evaluated at employment given by (3). Using (12) and (14), maximising (15) with respect to N_O, subject to (3), and rearranging gives

$$\frac{N_O}{N_P} = (1-\lambda)\left(\frac{N_O}{N_P}\right)^* + \lambda\left(\frac{1}{\alpha(1-M)} - 1\right). \tag{16}$$

If we suppose that $(N_O/N_P)^*$, the reservation overhead labour ratio, depends (negatively) on the industry unemployment rate, we can linearise (16) to obtain

$$\frac{N_O}{N_P} = a_4 + a_5 M + a_6 \lambda + a_7 \sigma. \tag{17}$$

This expression has a plausible intuition. Increased monopoly power raises the profitability of firms and so the ability of workers to negotiate easier manning levels. Increased union power also raises overhead labour. But, increased unemployment lowers the outside options for unions and so makes them less able to demand high overhead labour.[6]

Equations (17) and (13) make clear the effects of unions on profits. From (17), a reduction in union power λ reduces N_O/N_P, and from (13) this increases profit rates. Substituting (17) into (13) and using (10) gives

$$\frac{\pi}{PY} = \gamma_0 + \gamma_1 H + \gamma_2 H * \sigma + \gamma_3 \sigma + \gamma_4 H^2 + \gamma_5 H^3 + \gamma_6 H * \lambda + \gamma_7 H * \sigma^2$$

$$+\gamma_8 H * \sigma * \lambda + \gamma_9 H^2 * \lambda + \gamma_{10} H^2 * \sigma + \gamma_{11} \lambda + \gamma_{12} \lambda * \sigma + \gamma_{13} \sigma^2 \quad (18)$$

where $\gamma_1 = \beta_1 + \beta_1 a_4$, $\gamma_2 = -\beta_2 + a_7\beta_1 + \beta_3 a_5 - \beta_2 a_4$, $\gamma_3 = \beta_3 - a_7 + \beta_3 a_4$, $\gamma_4 = -\beta_4 + a_5\beta_1 - \beta_4 a_4$, $\gamma_5 = -a_5\beta_4$, $\gamma_6 = \beta_1 a_6$, $\gamma_7 = -\beta_2 a_7$, $\gamma_8 = -\beta_2 a_6$, $\gamma_9 = -\beta_4 a_6$, $\gamma_{10} = -\beta_4 a_7 - \beta_2 a_5$, $\gamma_{11} = a_6$, $\gamma_{12} = a_6\beta_3$, $\gamma_{13} = a_7\beta_3$. Once again (18) encompasses previous Equations (10), (7), (5) and (4).

5. Estimation and Results

In this section we estimate our encompassing Equation (18). We shall see what theory is favoured by the data and use the estimates to decompose the increase in profits in the 1980s into its constituent causes.

To estimate (18) we use a panel data set of UK manufacturing industries, taken from the UK Census of Production, where industries are defined at a three digit level. Our panel consists of 53 industries, 1973 to 1986. Details and definitions are discussed in the data appendix. The panel nature of the data enables us to control for unobserved heterogeneity between industries and partial adjustment. Our data therefore differs from many of the studies in the UK that are cross-section (see Clarke, 1986, or Hay and Morris, 1990, for a survey).

The specification of the regression dependent variable raises a number of issues discussed at some length in Conyon and Machin (1991) and Haskel and Martin (1991). The omission of raw materials from (2) assumes that the gross output production function is separable in value added and raw materials, which is quite standard in macro price equations, see inter alia Bruno and Sachs (1985) or Layard and Nickell (1986). Hence PY in the numerator and denominator of (18) is value added. The wage bill is defined as wages and salaries costs plus employers' national insurance contributions since this is part of wage costs to the firm. Hence our dependent variable is value added less wages and salaries less employers' taxes, divided by value added.

Concerning the independent variables we have no data on the Herfindahl index and so for H we use the five-firm concentration ratio by sales, multiplied by the one less the share of imports in home sales. To measure σ we use industry unemployment, which is derived from the responses of the active searchers in the Labour Force Survey to the question relating to their last job. Naturally unemployment has a secular element in it, but this should be removed in part by the time dummies. Furthermore, the active search element is less susceptible to the vagaries of benefit administration that contaminate the headline unemployment figures. Measures such as industry sales growth present formidable instrumentation problems. We include time dummies in our equations to pick up demand effects, common mismeasurement and the like.[7]

As for estimation methodology, comparison of the pooled and fixed effects estimates for similar equations in Domwitz *et al.* (1986a,b) and Levy (1986) suggests that unobserved heterogeneity between industries is a serious problem. To eliminate this we take first differences of (18), which is computationally convenient and removes much of the potential collinearity in (18). However, this induces a $MA(1)$ error (which we test for) and so to instrument the endogenous right-hand-side variables we use instruments dated $t-2$. Our generalised method of moments instrumentation procedure is designed to use all the valid available instruments and works as follows. If the first period is t, in period $t+2$ available valid instruments are dated t, whilst in period $t+3$ they are dated t and $t+1$, and so on. The instrument set therefore expands as we run through the data, see Arellano and Bond (1989). We report heteroscedastic-robust test statistics for instrument validity and serial correlation, and heteroscedastic-robust one-step t-statistics, since Monte-Carlo evidence suggests the two-step standard errors are biased downwards (see Arellano and Bond, 1991).

Our first set of results are set out in Table III. In the first column we report a regression of Equation (18). In general the regression co-efficients are rather poorly determined which is not surprising in a model that is almost certainly over-parameterised. Removing the insignificant variables leads to column 2. The m_2 statistic reveals that there is no evidence of second-order serial correlation. The time dummies are jointly significant. The length of the panel meant that the two-step Sargan test was unavailable, and so we have reported the one-step although we should note that Monte-Carlo evidence suggests that it substantially overrejects instrument validity (Arellano and Bond, 1991).

The major implications of our results are the following. First, we may reject a number of the theories set out in Section III.[8] The significance of the interactive effects suggests that the simple Cowling and Waterson model or the augmented demand model are insufficient. The Kreps and Scheinkman model implied the absence of H^2 and so its significance suggests that this model can be rejected. The significance of the union effect in interacted form suggests that overhead labour and collusion considerations are important.

Second, we may use the pattern of significance of our results to examine the remaining theories. Unfortunately we are unable to recover the co-efficients unambiguously.[9] Inspection of the significant parameters reveals two possibilities:

TABLE III. Profitability regressions – estimates of first difference of Equation (18) (dependent variable π/PY).

	(1)	(2)
H	0.22	
	(2.26)	
$H * \sigma$	–0.10	–0.008
	(2.23)	(3.00)
σ	1.80	
	(1.22)	
H^2	–0.12	0.28
	(1.38)	(2.86)
H^3	0.06	
	(1.02)	
$H * UNION$	–0.12	
	(1.67)	
$H * \sigma^2$	–0.37	
	(1.70)	
$H * UNION * \sigma$	0.007	0.001
	(2.32)	(3.59)
$H^2 * UNION$	–0.007	–0.004
	(1.20)	(3.09)
$H^2 * \sigma$	0.34	
	(1.67)	
$UNION$	0.04	
	(1.24)	
$UNION * \sigma$	–0.02	–0.003
	(1.55)	(3.82)
σ^2	–0.05	
	(0.36)	
$m_1[N(0.1)]$	–2.49	–2.45
$m_2[N(0.1)]$	–1.00	–0.65
Jt signif of time dums	45.43	53.94
(χ^2)	(11)	(11)
Sargan (χ^2)	95.22	145.9
	(55)	(63)

Notes:
(i) Absolute t statistics in brackets. Those reported are heteroscedastic-robust one-step estimates from DPD package. See Arellano and Bond (1988).
(ii) For all equations there are 53 industries 1976–1986.
(iii) All equations include constant and time dummies. H is measured by five firm sales concentration ratio, σ by log unemployment and $UNION$ by industry union density. Coefficients on terms in H are actual coefficients $*10^{-2}$.
(iv) m_1 and m_2 are the Arellano-Bond (1988) one-step heteroscedastic robust test against first and second-order serial correlation, and Sargan is their instrument validity test. We expect an m_1 error from first differencing, m_2 checks there is no correlation between the differenced errors and their second lag (necessary condition for undifferenced errors to be white noise); Sargan is valid if this is not rejected.
(v) All estimates first differences. Instruments are six lags on terms in H_{it} from $t-2$ back, variables dated $t-2$ for variables with H included, and variables dated t otherwise.

TABLE IV. Accounting for the rise in profitability 1980 to 1986 (calculated on basis of regression in column 2 of Table III)

Actual change in profits, 1980–1986	0.090
Predicted change due to change in:	
$H * sigma$	0.037
H^2	–0.087
$H * UNION * \sigma$	–0.141
$H^2 * UNION$	0.180
$UNION * \sigma$	0.051
Time dummies	0.019
Total predicted change in profits	0.059

(a) $a_6 > 0$, and so $\beta_4 > 0$, and $\beta_2, \beta_3 < 0$, or

(b) $a_6 < 0$, and so $\beta_4 < 0$, and $\beta_2, \beta_3 > 0$.

The condition that $a_6 < 0$ implies that unions lower the amount of overhead labour, and this seems to contradict most of the available evidence on unions and productivity (Metcalf, 1990).[10] We shall therefore assume that condition (a) holds. In turn, $\beta_4 > 0$ implies that collusion is more likely in concentrated industries, which seems plausible. $\beta_2, \beta_3 < 0$ imply that collusion is pro-cyclical (recall that we have measured σ by unemployment). This supports the Green and Porter (1984) model, and is inconsistent with Rotemberg and Saloner (1986).

Third we may use our estimates to explain the causes of the increase in profits over the 1980s. In Table IV we set out a decomposition of the change from 1980 to 1986. As the table shows, the main contributor was the fall in $H^2 * UNION$. This interactive term arises from the joint effects of unions bargaining with concentrated firms being closer to monopolies. The fall in unionisation means that unions were less able to impose higher manning levels on firms and so profits raised. The H^2 term picks up the effect, implicit in (10), that the marginal effect of ϕ on the profit rate rises as H falls. Recall that we noted above the apparent paradox that concentration is now lower than the 1970s but profitability is about the same. Our results suggest that the key offsetting factor was the decline in unionisation. So our results are consistent with the recent literature suggesting that the decline in unionisation has raised productivity (Layard and Nickell, 1989; Gregg, Machin and Metcalf, 1991).

As for the rapid fall in profits in the early 1980s a similar decomposition for 1979–1982 was dominated by the increase in unemployment that meant a substantial rise in $H * \sigma$ and $\lambda * \sigma$. Hence the collapse in profits in the early 1980s was driven by the collapse in demand. The economic mechanism that our model suggests is that since collusion is pro-cyclical it became more difficult in the early 1980s.

Finally as a check of robustness we added the capital/output ratio, instrumented by itself lagged twice. It was positively signed but insignificant leaving the other variables unaffected. We added a lagged dependent variable to allow for partial adjustment of the sort explored in the persistence of profits literature (see Levy, 1986, Geroski and Jacquemin, 1986, and Mueller, 1990 for example). The coefficient was 0.08 but with t statistic of 1.2. The other variables were unaffected.

6. Conclusion

In this paper we have examined changes in UK manufacturing profitability over the 1970s and 1980s. The major facts to be explained are twofold. First, profits fell sharply in the early 1980s. Second, concentration in UK manufacturing is now lower than in the 1970s yet profitability is about the same. We have begun by exploring the contribution of the batting average effect, whereby value added moves to sectors of above average profitability. Our first finding is that this has had a small impact. This suggests that we need to understand changes in profits in each sector. To do this we have proceeded as follows.

First, we have extended the basic Cowling/Waterson model to include varying collusion, demand shocks, and the role of unions. We have proposed an encompassing equation where the models of Cowling and Waterson (1976), Clarke and Davies (1983), Kreps and Scheinkman (1983), Green and Porter (1983) and Rotemberg and Saloner (1986) are special cases. Second, we have estimated the model on a panel of fifty three UK manufacturing industries, 1976–1986. Our estimation procedure uses generalised method of moments/instrumental variables estimation. Our major findings are:

(a) the collapse of profits in the early 1980s was due to the severe fall in demand;

(b) the decline of unions in the 1980s has increased profitability.

Somewhat more tentatively, we would conclude that collusion is pro-cyclical, supporting the Green and Porter (1983) model.

We should stress a number of caveats concerning our work. First, our equations are based on linearised versions of models that do not have the rich, but often restrictive, detail of many game-theoretic models. We must rely on the belief that the equations capture the key thrust of the results. Second, to discriminate between the Green/Porter and Rotemberg/Saloner models we were forced to assume that unions impose higher manning levels on the firm. Whilst this is in line with the bulk of the evidence, our support for Green and Porter does depend on this assumption. Lastly, as is usual in empirical work we are forced by data availability to proxy theoretical variables such as union bargaining power and demand by union density and unemployment, and relegate a number of unobservables into the fixed effects.

Overall however, we believe that the most important conclusion is that the simple Cowling/Waterson model is inadequate to explain the fluctuations in profitability over the cycle. Developing further theory is vital if we are to put a structural interpretations on the kind of industry panel equations that are increasingly being estimated.

Data Appendix

The data has been compiled by Ian Small of Queen Mary and Westfield College, University of London. The main source is the Census of Production, Annual Report, Summary Volume.

DATA DEFINITIONS AND SOURCES

Gross value added
Gross value added, from Annual Report.

Employment
Total employment, from Annual Report.

Wages
Wages, salaries and employers national insurance contributions, from Annual Report.

Sales
Value of industry sales, from Annual Report.

Five-firm concentration ratio
Measured on the basis of sales. From Annual Report.

Exports
Value of exports, from Quarterly Returns.

Imports
Value of imports, from Quarterly Returns.

Union density
Union density estimates were obtained on a 2-digit basis from Martin Wall of the London School of Economics, and scaled to be consistent with the density figures in Bain and Price (1980).

Unemployment
2-digit unemployment rates were generated by the LFS, from Mark Walsh of the LSE.

Capital Stock
Two digit capital stock data from the Blue Book.

Notes

* For very useful comments I thank Josef Falkinger, Paul Geroski and David Audretsch. I thank Chris Martin for letting me use much of our joint work and Ian Small for the data.

1. Profits are measured by value added less wage bill over value added to be congruent with the empirical work; see discussion below.
2. With a linear demand curve η is pro-cyclical which would explain the fall in profits in the 1980s. Without direct evidence on η this hypothesis is untestable.
3. Of course, the notion of consistent conjectures has been strongly criticised, see e.g. Shapiro (1989). Here we use it here simply to present the essential idea.
4. To see this the left hand side can be written as $1 - p/(w/b(y/n))$ in which case any rise in y/n simply causes a fall in p.
5. To the event that overhead labour is affected by shirking, efficiency wage considerations (Shapiro and Stiglitz, 1986) may be important, so that N_O/N_P would be affected by wages at the firm relative to the outside. Given the stability of the industry wage structure (Haskel and Martin, 1990) we think it unlikely that this would account for the 1980s profit increase.
6. The second way that it is suggested that unions affect profits is via the efficient bargains hypothesis that assumes both wages and employment are bargained over simultaneously (Leontief, 1946). Price-cost margins then turn out to depend on union and monopoly power. The major problem with this view is that it is inconsistent with the direct evidence of what labour contracts actually contain; typically in the UK unions do not bargain over employment (see Oswald, 1987), and Oswald and Turnbull, 1985).
7. As we report below the inclusion of the capital/output ratio does not affect our results. We should note in passing that our theory does not predict the inclusion of the capital/output ratio as is often done in an attempt to "correct" margins to reflect market power. Whether the profits/sales ratio is a sensible measure of market power is important but our aim here is solely to test the theory. It is also sometimes argued that there was faster capital/labour substitution over the 1980s but there seems no reason to suppose that the capital/output ratio measures the increased rate of substitution. Finally, the equation is derived for a given number of firms. If capital is a barrier to entry then the number of firms is reduced and so H falls, so there is no need to include capital separately.
8. Although we should emphasise that we are of course testing our parameterisations of the theories involved.
9. Unscrambling proceeded as follows: the insignificance of $H\lambda$ suggested $\beta_1 = 0$ or $a_6 = 0$, but the significance of $H^2\lambda$ suggested that $\beta_4 \neq 0$, and $a_6 \neq 0$, so together $\beta_1 = 0$. Likewise, $a_5 = a_7 = 0$ which suggests that N_O/N_P is unaffected by H or σ. There were no inconsistencies in the implied restrictions except that the insignificance of λ implies that a_6 is equal to zero. However, from (13) this result is solely due to the absence of a constant in (10), which might otherwise appear as a result of a risk premium and/or linearisation.
10. In our framework this can only arise if unions have a preference for *less* on-the-job leisure. Freeman and Medoff (1984) argue that the presence of a union "voice" may raise productivity by aiding participation.

References

Arellano, M. and Bond, S. (1988) 'Dynamic Panel Data Estimation Using DPD – A Guide for Users', Institute for Fiscal Studies, Working Paper, September.

Arellano, M. and Bond, S. (1991) 'Some Tests of Specification for Panel Data: Monte Carlo Evidence and an application to Employment Equations', *Review of Economic Studies*, March.

Bain, G. and Price, R. (1980) *Profiles of Union Growth*, Oxford: Blackwell.

Bils, M. (1985) 'Essays on the Cyclical Behaviour of Price and Marginal Cost', Ph.D dissertation, MIT.

Binmore, K., Rubinstein, A., and Wolinsky, A. (1986) 'The Nash Bargaining Solution in Economic Modelling', *Rand Journal of Economics* **17**, 2, Summer.

Blanchard, O. and Fischer, S. (1989) *Lectures on Macroeconomics*, MIT Press.

Bresnahan, T. (1981) 'Duopoly Models with Consistent Conjectures', *American Economic Review* **71**, 934–945.

Bruno, M. and Sachs, J. (1985) *The Economics of Worldwide Stagflation*, Oxford: Basil Blackwell.

Clarke, R. and Davies (1982) 'Market Structure and Price-Cost Margins', *Economica* **49**, 277–287.

Conyon, M. and Machin, S. (1991) 'The Determination of Profit Margins in UK Manufacturing', *Journal of Industrial Economics* **34**, 369–382.

Cowling, K. and Waterson, M. (1976) 'Price-Cost Margins and Market Structure', *Economica* **43**, 267–274.

Domowitz, I., Hubbard, R., and Petersen, B. (1986a) 'Business Cycles and the Relationship Between Concentration and Price-Cost Margins', *Rand Journal of Economics* **17**, 1–17.

Domowitz, I., Hubbard, R., and Petersen, B. (1986b) 'The Intertemporal Stability of the Concentration Margins Relationship', *Journal of Industrial Economics* **35**, 13–34.

Domowitz, I., Hubbard, R., and Petersen, B. (1987) 'Oligopoly Supergames: Some Empirical Evidence on Margins and Prices', *Journal of Industrial Economics* **37**.

Eltis, W. (1990) 'British Industrial Policy for the 1990s', in T. Congdon *et al.*, *The State of the Economoy*, London: IEA.

Freeman, R. and Medoff, J. (1984) *What do Unions Do?*, New York: Basil Books.

Geroski, P. (1988) 'Competition Policy and the Structure-Performance Paradigm', in Davies, S. and Lyons, B. (Eds.), *Economics of Industrial Organisation*, Longman.

Geroski, P. and Jacquemin, A. (1988) 'The Persistence of Profits: A European Comparison', *Economic Journal* **98**, 375–389.

Green, E. and Porter, R. (1984) 'Noncooperative Collusion Under Imperfect Price Information', *Econometrica* **52**, 87–100.

Gregg, P., Machin, S., and Metcalf, D. (1991) 'Signals and Cycles', UCL Discussion Paper, 91–15.

Haskel, J. and Kay, J.A. (1990) 'Competitive Advantage in UK Manufacturing', *Economic Outlook*, June, Gower.

Haskel, J. and Martin, C. (1991) 'Non-Competitive Wage Determination, Firms and the Inter-industry Wage Structure', Queen Mary College, Department of Economics Paper 235.

Haskel, J. and Martin, C. (1992a) 'Margins, Concentration, Unions and the Business Cycle: Theory and Evidence for Britain', Queen Mary College, Department of Economics Working Paper, and forthcoming in *International Journal of Industrial Organization*.

Haskel, J. and Martin, C. (1992b) 'Capacity and Competition: Empirical Evidence on UK Panel Data', Queen Mary College, Department of Economics Paper 251.

Kreps, D. and Scheinkman, J. (1983) 'Quantity Pre-Commitment and Bertrand Competition Yield Cournot Outcomes', *Rand Journal of Economics* **14**, 326–337.

Layard, R. and Nickell, S. (1986) 'Unemployment in Britain', *Economica*, Supplement, 87, pp. S121–170.

Layard, R. and Nickell, S. (1989) 'The Thatcher Miracle', *American Economic Review* **79**, 215–219.

Levy, D. (1986) 'The Speed of the Invisible Hand', *International Journal of Industrial Organisation* **5**, 79–92.

Leontief, W. (1946) 'The Pure Theory of the Guaranteed Wage Contract', *Journal of Political Economy* **54**, 76–79.

Lyons, B. (1981) 'Price-Cost Margins, Market Structure and International Trade', in D. Currie, D. Peel and W. Peters (Eds.), *Microeconomic Analysis*, London: Croom Helm.

Milward, N. and Stevens, M. (1986) *British Workplace Industrial Relations, 1980–1984*, Gower.

Muellbauer, J. (1988) 'The Assessment: Productivity and Competitiveness in UK Manufacturing', *Oxford Review of Economic Policy* **2**, 1–25.

Mueller, D. (Ed.) (1990) *The Dynamics of Company Profits: An International Comparison*, Cambridge University Press.

Oswald, A. (1987) 'Efficient Contracts Are on the Labour Demand Curve: Theory and Facts', Centre for Labour Economics Discussion Paper 284.

Oswald, A. and Turnbull, P. (1985) 'Pay and Employment Determination in Britain: What are Labour Contracts Really Like', *Oxford Review of Economic Policy* **1**, 80–97.

Pencavel, J. (1984) 'The Trade-off Between Wages and Employment in Union Objectives', *Quarterly Journal of Economics* **99**, 215–232.

Rotemberg, J. and Saloner, G. (1986) 'A Supergame-Theoretic Model of Price Wars During Booms', *American Economic Review*, 390–407.
Schmalensee, R. (1989) 'Inter-Industry Studies of Structure and Performance', in R. Schmalensee and R. Willig (Eds.), *Handbook of Industrial Organisation*, Vol. II, North Holland.
Sentance, A. and McKenzie, D. (1992) 'Exploding the Myth of Low UK Profitability', *CBI Economic Situation Report*, London: CBI.
Shapiro, C. (1989) 'Theories of Oligopoly Behaviour', in R. Schmalensee and R. Willig (Eds.), *Handbook of Industrial Organisation*, Vol. II, North Holland.
Shapiro, C. and Stiglitz, J. (1984) 'Equilibrium Unemployment as a Worker Discipline Device', *American Economic Review* **74**, 433–444.
Walton, D. (1991) 'Profits: After the Fall', *Goldman Sachs UK Economic Analyst*, London: Goldman Sachs.
Weitzman, M. (1982) 'Increasing Returns and the Foundations of Unemployment', *Economic Journal* **92**, 787–804.

K. Aiginger and J. Finsinger (eds.), Applied Industrial Organization, 151–165.

Collusion, Concentration and Profits*

An Empirical Confrontation of an Old Story and a Supergame Implication

KARL AIGINGER
University of Linz and Austrian Institute of Economic Research, Vienna, Austria

Abstract. The paper confronts the hypothesis of a positive profitability concentration relationship ('the old story') with a robust prediction of supergame models ('the new story'). In supergames the feasibility of collusion (and to some degree also actual profits) depends on relative profitability of defection versus that of collusion. The determinants for this evaluation – the time discount proper, riskiness of markets, exit probability and lags – can be summarized as 'relevant time discount'. Cross section empirical evidence (97 sectors, 886 firms) is more in line with the supergame prediction. The evidence depends on the variables chosen to proxy the 'relevant time discount'. Its value is limited as any evidence for game theoretical models supplied by cross section aggregate data. We followed Sutton (1991) to test robust predictions and Schmalensee (1989) to investigate the robustness of the results.

JEL codes: L11, C72.

Key words: Concentration, profits, volatility of demand, supergames.

1. Plan of the Paper

The positive relationship between profit margins and concentration is one of the oldest stories in industrial organization. Non cooperative game theory however does not predict a simple relation between profits and concentration, but rather different results depending on the action space, the horizon and interactions of firms.

In supergames we find a set of related parameters which crucially determine the feasibility of collusion: the time discount rate proper, the length of detection and punishment lags, exit probability and uncertainty about the market conditions. We summarize these variables into a wider concept of a 'relevant time discount rate', which weigths the advantages of defection (in one period) relative to the advantages of continued collusion. The *feasibility* of collusion and the 'relevant time discount rate' are predicted to be negatively related. This could lead to an empirically observable (negative) relation between actual profits and proxies for

* I would like to thank Gerhard Clemenz, Sepp Falkinger, Paul A. Geroski, Georg Kirchsteiger, Dennis C. Mueller, Manfred Neumann, Robert Porter for helpful comments and suggestions. Part of the research was done during my sabbatical at M.I.T. Special thanks to Dagmar Guttmann and Traude Novak who gave assistance in providing the data and reading various drafts of the manuscript.

this set of variables. Due to the well known multiplicity of equilibria in supergames there is no one to one relationship between a supergame result and an empirically testable prediction. The proxies determine the feasibility of collusion, something like an 'upper bound' to equilibrium profits.

We use cross section data to test first the hypothesis of a positive profitability – concentration relation ('the old story') and secondly that of a negative relation between profits and proxies for the 'relevant time discount rate' ('the new story').

The limits of cross section data to test theories are well discussed in the literature, testing implications of game theory with aggregate data adds some more problems. Game theoretical concepts can 'often be mapped into empirical categories in a rather loose and informal way' (Sutton, 1991, p. 6). Many researchers focus analysis therefore on a very specific market ('ultra micro' approach). We follow Sutton that it may be worth 'to find some (necessarily weak) predictions that are robust in the sense that they hold across a wide class of models' (Sutton, 1991, p. 7). However we do not claim to test game theoretical models but to confront concentration as determinant of profits with variables hinted at in a specific class of supergames. Even this humble approach heavily relies on the available proxies for the relevant time discount.

The paper is structured as follows. The next section repeats the arguments for a positive profitability-concentration relationship and the limits of cross section studies. In Section 3 the conditions for collusion as derived in supergames are presented and summarized into the concept of the 'relevant time discount factor' (to prevent confusion remind that game theory formulate the crucial conditions for collusion using discount *factors* i.e. the inverse of discount *rates*). Section 4 describes the data used to test the old profit concentration story and introduces four proxies for the relevant time discount rate. The evidence for 97 three digit industries and a set of 896 firms for Austrian manufacturing is presented in Section 5. Section 6 summarizes the results, its limits and prospects. The appendix follows the 'Schmalensee postulate' for cross section studies (Schmalensee, 1989) to test the robustness of the findings.

2. The Original Story

The traditional foundation for the positive concentration profitability relationship relies on micro economic theory with collusion presumptions added. The competitive firm earns normal profits only, the monopoly accumulates extra profits,[1] in between these extreme models collusion is easier the fewer firms are in the market and the higher barriers of entry are.[2]

The implied direction of causality in Bain's argument was never uncontested. Demsetz (1974) argued that efficient firms increase their market shares so that markets may look concentrated as a result of efficiency rather than collusion. The collusion and the efficiency hypothesis can be discriminated empirically,[3] the policy consequences are different. The implied forecast for the concentration-profitability relation is however the same. Among the standard theories[4] which do not forecast a positive profit concentation relationship we want to mention rent dissipation hypothesis (Posner, 1975) and x-inefficiency theory (Frantz, 1988).

The empirical evidence on the relation had once been impressive (see Weiss, 1974). It became mixed as additional 'structural' variables were added, some papers find even negative coefficients if market shares are added.[5] A recent review by Salinger (1990) found instable coefficients of concentration over time (in the majority of years they are positive).

Today cross section studies on the profitability concentration relation belong to the most contemptuous research areas. A part of the argument against profitability-concentration studies applies to cross section studies in general (no structural form, direction of causality), another part to the empirical implementations (measurement of concentration, profits, marginal costs, see Fisher and McGowan, 1983; Bresnahan, 1989; Schmalensee, 1989).

3. Supergames and the Relevant Time Discount Factor

Supergames[6] is the class of non cooperative games in which an identical static game is infinitely repeated. Its relevance is sometimes questioned since 'anything' can happen (there is a multiplicity of equilibrial). We believe however that there is some structure in the supergames which may lead to an empirically testable prediction.

The crucial role for the feasibility of collusion is played by the discount rate. It determines the weight of the presence (in which defection is considered) versus that of the future (in which punishment would follow). At first this seems to be a rather trivial result. But many adaptions of this model to real world circumstances can be derived just by upblowing or downsizing the discount rate proper by some transformation (or some variable) and thus shifting the border line between feasibility and non feasibility of collusion.

In the starting model n firms are engaged in a price game of infinite horizon. The discount *factor* is δ, the inverse of the discount rate. Larger δ can be interpreted as patience. We start with collusion (at the monopoly price). If one firm defects cooperation is halted and price is set at marginal costs forever.

The profits of collusion is the future profit stream V_c, this is monopoly profit divided by the number of firms and adequately discounted. The profits from defection V_d is the one period monopoly profit π^m and then zero profits forever. Equation (1) compares the profits under defection versus collusion and equation (2) gives the condition for the sustainability of collusion.

$$V_d = \pi^m < (1 + \delta + \delta^2 + \ldots)\pi^m/n = \pi^m/[n(1-\delta)] = V_c \qquad (1)$$

$$\delta > (n-1)/n \qquad (2)$$

Collusion will happen when the discount factor is larger than $(n-1)/n$. In case of 100 firms δ has to be higher than 0.99 to facilitate collusion, for $n = 3$ only higher than 2/3. This makes collusion more probably the smaller the number of firms and (under certain assumptions) for less concentration.[7]

Incorporating detection lags or a period between detection and punishment is just an easy modification. If detection or start of punishment takes two periods the defector enjoys monopoly profits for two periods, see LHS of equation (3). The critical value facilitating collusion is the square root of that in the starting model, so collusion becomes harder to sustain (equation (4)). This could be seen as a first step of transforming a proper discount factor into a wider concept. More generally the sustainability of collusion decreases with the number of periods elapsing between defection and punishment.

$$\pi^m(1+\delta) < (1+\delta+\delta^2\ldots)\,\pi^m/n = (1-\delta)\,\pi^m/[n(1-\delta)] \tag{3}$$

$$\delta > \sqrt{(n-1)/n} \tag{4}$$

If the riskiness of the markets imply that the horizon of the game is uncertain (exit is possible), the relevant benchmark to sustain collusion is the discount factor proper multiplied by the probability to survive σ. Again collusion becomes harder to achieve, see equation (5).[8]

$$\delta^{\text{rel}} = \delta^{\text{prop}} \cdot \sigma \qquad\qquad \sigma = \text{probability of survival} \tag{5}$$

Green and Porter (1984) present a model of quantity competition and Tirole (1989) its modification for price competition. Firms do not observe their rivals' prices but infer them from own demand. Low own demand may be due to weak market condition or to defection of the partner. The discount factor needed to sustain collusion increases with the degree of uncertainty. For a given probability α of no demand and $(1-\alpha)$ for demand, the discount factor necessary for collusion increases in α. For $\alpha = 1/4$ and for two firms, it is 2/3 (compare this to $\delta > 1/2$ in the starting model for $n = 2$). For certain demand or its perfect predictability we return to the condition in equation (2).

All these factors like time discount proper, length of detection and punishment lag, demand uncertainty, exit probability can be summarized into a concept of the 'relevant time discount factor', δ^{rel}. The smaller this time discount factor the less the probability of collusion.

Let us formalize this set of additional determinants[9] of the feasibility of collusion and its components in equation (6).

$$\delta^{\text{rel}} = f(\delta^{\text{prop}}, \tau, \alpha, \sigma) \tag{6}$$

The components of this 'relevant time discount factor' are empirically closely related. Time discount factor proper is defined as $\delta = \mathrm{e}^{-rt}$, where r is the instantaneous rate of interest and t is real time between periods and depends on the length of the period. And if detection takes time it is somewhat arbitrary either to define a longer period (thus changing δ^{prop}) or to say detection takes two periods ($\tau = 2$).

Another constituant element of the discount factor is risk and the amount of 'risk adjustment' will probably vary with demand uncertainty α and probability of survival σ. And detection and punishment lags will not be exogeneous, but depend on uncertainty of markets and the patience of participants.

To sum up the most robust implication of supergames is the following: the feasibility of collusion depends positively on the discount factor (and therefore negatively on the discount rate and its components time discount rate proper, risk, lags, exit probability). Of course there are modifications depending on the game played (Bertrand reversion versus Cournot reversion), on the sophistication of the punishment structure (two or three tier strategies) and whether we allow strategic interactions (signalling, reputation). And changing the scope for collusion does not mean that profits should be linearily related to indicators for 'the relevant time discount'. We have to keep in mind that many outcomes different from collusion are also equilibria in supergames. But at least the models suggest to look for such indicators as a preliminary test.

Predicting a negative influence of risk and uncertainty on profits sounds natural as seen from the supergame and collusion perspective. However portfolio theory would suggest that in equilibrium risky markets[10] need higher 'target rates of profits' (because of higher risk premia). If target rates of profits are higher (due to risk) and actual rates are lower (due to less collusion), exit and entry must be blockaded in some way (as the empirical literature on the persistence of profit differences tells). The predicted negative impact on profits of proxies for uncertainty (and relevant discount rate in general) is an interesting and refutable implication of supergames.

4. Transfer into an Empirical Model

The step between the theoretical prediction and empirical testing is a large one. This is true (and well described in literature) for the old positive concentration margin story and maybe even more for the implied negative relation between profits and 'relevant time discount rate'.

We follow traditional lines to test the old story. Profit is the net profit margin (PCN), concentration is the share in value added by the largest four firms in 1983 (CR_4). Indicators on employment per plant (*SIZE*), heterogeneity (*PROD*), market openess (EXP, $OPEN$) and capital intensity (INV) are added to correct for structural factors other than concentration.

To test the relationship suggested in the supergames we proxied the 'relevant time discount rate' by time volatility of production ($VOLPROD$) and exports ($VOLEXP$) and by the unpredictability of production and exports. ($NPRED$-$PROD$, $NPREDEXP$). The first set is calculated as standard deviation of the annual growth rate of production and exports in each of the 97 industries (1980–87), the second group as the standard error of the loglinear regression of production respective exports on time again for the 97 sectors.

The economic rational for $VOLPROD$ and $VOLEXP$ is that heavy fluctuations of demand will endanger tacit collusion due to information lags, noisiness of information etc. Markets with large fluctuations will also be those with uncertain future and higher exit probability. Export data are used since the volatility of the export market may indicate fuzziness of information and riskiness better than the domestic market in a small open economy like Austria. Even more important than fluctuations will be their unpredictable part. We apply the 'naive forceast' of a time trend to proxy the predictable part and assert that the remaining variance of production and exports is unpredictable ($NPREDPROD$ respective $NPREDEXP$). All four variables are supposed to proxy the 'relevant time discount *rate*', so we expect them to be negatively related to profits.

Still there is a large difference between the concept of 'relevant time discount rate' and our empirical variables, but at least we get some information whether it is worth to continue on the line suggested by this model class.

5. The Empirical Evidence

In the 'plain vanilla equation' (the term was used by Salinger, 1990) *concentration* is – if anything – negatively related to profits. The negative coefficient is significant according to the usual t-test, but this should not be interpreted rigorously because of the specification problems in this simple equation. The coefficient is strikingly robust (always between 0.15 and 0.17) if *structural variables* like export ratio (*EXQ*), market openess (*OPEN*), or capital intensity (*INVEST*) are added. The coefficient of determination is low (adjusted $R^2 = 0.07$ to 0.09, Table I).

The rather robust negative influence of concentration vanishes if we add a size variable (*SIZE* is employment per plant). In this case the coefficient for concentration becomes insignificant, the t-value for *SIZE* is larger than that of concentration, both coefficients are insignificant probably due to multicollinearity (the adjusted coefficient of determination rises after including *SIZE*). This suggests that concentration maybe is a proxy for size and that profits and size are negatively related. This puts the old Demsetz hypothesis upside down, that concentration is the consequence of successful growth of market shares and that concentration may follow from efficiency. It is more in line with organizational slacks or X-inefficiency raising with size as proposed by Leibenstein (1966) and Frantz (1988). The significance of the negative influence is not so strong that we want to push this point without further investigation.

The indicators on volatility and unpredictability all have the expected negative sign. In the single equations three of the four regression coefficients are significant. The coefficient of determination for the markets is 0.13 respective 0.14, which is quite high for cross section studies and nearly double as high as that for concentration. The sign is negative as suggested by the models indicating higher profits for stable and predictable markets. The results are robust to modifications in the profit concept, to changes of the year of investigation, and to the inclusion of additional

TABLE I. Profit margins and concentration – the old story plus structural variables (t-value in parenthesis below coefficient).

CR_4	EXP	$OPEN$	$PROD$	$SIZE$	$INVEST$	R^2	STE
−0.16						0.074	15.1
(−2.83)							
−0.15	−0.007					0.071	15.2
(−2.77)	(−0.21)						
−0.15		−0.008				0.076	15.2
(−2.72)		(−0.78)					
−0.16			−0.01			0.071	15.2
(−2.81)			(−0.32)				
−0.08				−0.02		0.095	15.0
(−1.11)				(−1.62)			
−0.16					0.76	0.087	15.1
(−2.95)					(1.35)		

Dependent variable: $PCM = (S–W–D–M)/(S–M)$; average 1980–1987, 97 3 digit sectors in Austrian manufacturing.
S = sales
W = payroll
D = depreciation
M = material
CR_4 = share of value added in 4 largest firms, 1983
EXP = export in % of production
$OPEN$ = export plus import (= openess) in % of production
$PROD$ = number of 4-digit industries in 3-digit industries
$SIZE$ = employment per plant
$INVEST$ = investment in relation to total costs
STE = standard error of residuum
R^2 = coefficient of determination (adjusted)

variables (see appendix).

If concentration, size and volatility (or unpredictability) are put into the same equation volatility and unpredictability dominate. Concentration sometimes influences profits in an inplausible negative way, but if size is added this influence is no longer significant. Volatility and unpredictability of export markets are the best determinant in equations explaining up to 20% of the variance in net profit margins.

The micro data set (886 firms) confirms the robustness of the results. If anything concentration (whether concentration rates or market shares or Herfindahls are used) decrease profits, but size is more important (in the anti Demsetz way). Market volatility decreases profits and is the strongest single variable. Again the robustness of the findings was tested by changing the profit concept, time period and adding structural variables.

TABLE II. Profit margins, volatility, non-predictability – proxies for the 'relevant time discount rate', (t-value in parenthesis below coefficient).

VARPROD	*VAREXP*	*NPREDPROD*	*NPREDEXP*	CR_4	*SIZE*	R^2	*STE*
−0.66						0.084	15.1
(−2.94)							
	−0.44					0.126	14.7
	(−3.77)						
		−9.86				0.003	15.7
		(−0.59)					
			−50.02			0.140	14.6
			(−4.00)				
−0.54				−0.13		0.122	14.8
(−2.40)				(−2.27)			
	−0.40			−0.13		0.173	14.3
	(−3.48)			(−2.47)			
−0.54				−0.05	−0.02	0.141	14.6
(−2.40)				(−0.71)	(−1.63)		
	−0.41			−0.05	−0.02	0.196	14.1
	(−3.57)			(−0.72)	(−1.81)		
			−43.90	−0.06	−0.02	0.195	14.2
			(−3.55)	(−0.83)	(−1.51)		

Dependent variable: *PCM* = *(S-W-D-M)/(S-M)*; average 1980–1987, 97 3-digit sectors in Austrian manufacturing.
S = sales; W = payroll; D = depreciation; M = material.
VARPROD = standard deviation of production growth 1980–1987
VAREXP = standard deviation of export growth 1980–1987
NPREDPROD = standard error of 'naive trend forecast' of production
NPREDEXP = standard error of 'naive trend forecast' of exports
CR_4 = share of value added in 4 largest firms, 1983
SIZE = employment per plant

6. Caveats, Conclusions, Further Research

The old story of a positive concentration – margin relation is not supported by the data. If anything the relation is negative, but concentration seems to be a proxy for size (which is related negatively to profits as proposed by X-inefficiency theory, Frantz, 1988).

Supergames predict – for a given number of firms – the feasibility of collusion to decrease with time discount rate, market uncertainty, exit probability, detection and punishment lags. This set of related factors – the 'relevant time discount *rate*' – is proxied by variables on the volatility and unpredictability of demand in the empirical part. These variable successfully explain a certain part of the cross section profit variance, with the correct signs and robust coefficients. Data are more consistent with the supergame prediction of less collusion in volatile markets than

TABLE III. Robustness test: Concentration and gross profit margins (t-value in parenthesis below coefficient).

CR_4	EXP	$OPEN$	$SIZE$	$ENERG$	$INVEST$	R^2	STE
−0.12						0.070	11.6
(−2.74)							
−0.11	−0.04					0.094	11.4
(−2.53)	(−1.74)						
−0.10		−0.02				0.115	11.3
(−2.52)		(−2.34)					
−0.11			−0.007			0.068	11.6
(−2.71)			(−0.52)				
−0.14				0.83		0.147	11.1
(−3.45)				(3.05)			
−0.13					1.45	0.174	10.9
(−3.19)					(3.57)		

Dependent variable: $PCM\text{–}GROSS = (S-W-M)/(S-M)$;
average 1980–1987, 97 3-digit sectors
in Austrian manufacturing.
S = sales; W = payroll; M = material.
CR_4 = share of value added in 4 largest firms, 1983
EXP = export in % of production
$OPEN$ = export plus import (= openess) in % of production
$SIZE$ = employment per plant
$ENERG$ = share of energy costs of total costs
$INVEST$ = investment in relation to total costs
STE = standard error of residuum
R^2 = coefficient of determination (adjusted)

with the portfolio theory demanding higher profits in riskier markets. This result hints at considerable mobility barriers for capital in Austria.

We do not claim to test supergame models. Their variety is too large, many outcomes may be equilibria, model assumptions and real world circumstances are too different. But we find that empirical data are more in line with some proxies for riskiness and volatility in a way predicted by supergames than with the older story of a positive relationship between concentration and margins. More work need to be done (preferable with the micro data set or with panel data) to bridge the gap between the theory of supergames and empirical data, but it seems to be a 'stylized fact' that volatility and unpredictability depress real world profits. The channel may or may not be that modelled in supergames. The suggestion to test these determinants however came from non cooperative game theory.

TABLE IV. Robustness test: Gross profit margins and proxies for the discount rate (t-value in parenthesis below coefficient).

CR_4	$VARPROD$	$VAREXP$	$(SIZE)$	$(VALADD)$	R^2	STE
−0.09	−0.45				0.127	11.2
(−2.14)	(−2.62)					
−0.10		−0.24			0.130	11.2
(−2.42)		(−2.68)				
−0.02		−0.25	−0.02		0.176	10.9
(−0.30)		(−2.82)	(−2.44)			
−0.18		−0.31		0.07	0.425	9.1
(−5.00)		(−4.17)		(7.06)		

Dependent variable: $PCM\text{–}GROSS = (S\text{–}W\text{–}M)/(S\text{–}M)$;
average 1980–1987, 97 3-digit sectors
in Austrian manufacturing.
S = sales; W = payroll; M = material.
CR_4 = share of value added in 4 largest firms, 1983
VARPROD = standard deviation of production growth 1980–1987
VAREXP = standard deviation of export growth 1980–1987
SIZE = employment per plant
VALADD = value added per employee

Appendix: On the Robustness of the Findings[11]

In assessing the problems and merits of inter-industry studies Schmalensee (1989) emphasized that cross section evidence should be robust. Even then it may not be an adequate test of specific theories, but it helps to formulate stylized facts, which could be used as starting points for more theoretical reasoning.

We tested this robustness by calculating a variety of concept for most variables. For *profit margin* we calculated gross and net margins, we used sales in the denominator instead of net value added, we calculated them for a single year (1983) and for the whole period (1980–87). Correlation between the ratios is rather high. For concentration we calculated CR_4 and CR_8, we used shares of value added. Data are available for 1976, 1983, 1988. The correlation between all these data is more than 0.90.

For the functional relation we used linear regressions, semi logarithmic, non parametric methods. We excluded several basic sectors (oil, mining) and eliminated outliers.

The main findings – negative impact on margins by concentration and size, with the latter as stronger determinant and negative impact on profits by volatility and nonpredictability of demand – remained statistically significant for the impressive majority of all these variations.

We had also the possibility to use a recently available data panel (firm data for 886 manufacturing firms) to check whether the simultaneous inclusion of concen-

TABLE V. Robustness test: Concentration, (net) profit margins 1983, volatility (*t*-value in parenthesis below coefficient).

CR_4	*PLANTS*	*SIZE*	*VARPROD*	*VAREXP*	*VALADD*	R^2	*STE*
			−0.86			0.090	18.4
			(−3.14)				
				−0.50		0.108	18.2
				(−3.46)			
−0.23						0.107	18.2
(−3.45)							
−0.23	−0.002					0.103	18.3
(−3.17)	(−0.17)						
−0.16		−0.02				0.118	18.2
(−1.78)		(−1.29)					
−0.29					0.06	0.175	17.6
(−4.33)					(2.90)		
−0.19			−0.68			0.157	17.7
(−2.87)			(−2.50)				
−0.20				−0.44		0.186	17.4
(−3.12)				(−3.14)			
−0.12		−0.02		−0.45		0.198	17.3
(−1.46)		(−1.43)		(−3.19)			
−0.27				−0.50	0.07	0.276	16.5
(−4.24)				(−3.75)	(3.54)		

Dependent variable: *PCM = (S–W–M)/(S–M)*; 97 3-digit sectors in Austrian manufacturing, 1983.
S = sales; *W* = payroll; *M* = material.
CR_4 = share of value added in 4 largest firms, 1983
PLANTS = number of plants in 3-digit sector
SIZE = employment per plant
VARPROD = standard deviation of production growth 1980–1987
VAREXP = standard deviation of export growth 1980–1987
VALADD = value added per employee

tration and market shares or of Herfindahls and market shares did matter. If two of the three variables are combined usually both have a negative coefficient. Again *SIZE* can capture much of the negative impact of market shares and concentration.

The influence of volatility is stronger than that of market shares, Herfindahls, concentration rates and size.

Notes

1. This is the essence of the story for the long run equilibrium. If however entry (or exit) is blockaded, competition could give positive and negative profits. Even monopoly could go with negative profits (due to fixed costs or strategic considerations) in the short run. Theoretical predictions are more robust about the price cost margin, than about profits as such.

TABLE VI. Robustness test: Microdata (886 firms) 1983 (t-value in parenthesis below coefficient).

CR_4	MS	$HERF$	$VARPROD$	$VAREXP$	EXP	INV	$VALADD$	R^2	STE
	−0.173		−1.169		0.021	−0.335	0.497	0.400	15.2
	(−1.670)		(−6.974)		(1.357)	(−4.447)	(18.25)		
		−0.033	−1.284		0.023	−0.335	0.500	0.399	15.2
		(−0.541)	(−6.889)		(1.413)	(−4.424)	(18.137)		
−0.01			1.230			−0.331	0.498	0.399	15.2
(−0.032)			−5.380)			(−4.337)	(18.164)		
	−0.371			−0.906	0.022	−0.311	0.556	0.408	15.1
	(−3.704)			(−7.660)	(1.400)	(−4.142)	(17.795)		
		−0.178		−0.899		−0.280	0.557	0.406	15.1
		(−3.375)		(−7.595)		(−3.704)	(17.744)		
−0.082				−0.757		−0.285	0.552	0.402	15.2
(−2.512)				(−5.832)		(−3.758)	(17.555)		

MS = Market share of firm in 2-digit industry
$HERF$ = Herfindahl Index for 2-digit industry
CR_4 = share of largest firms, 1983
EXP = Export/sales ratio
INV = Investment/sales ratio
$VARPROD$ = standard deviation of production growth 1980–1987 in 2-digit industry
$VAREXP$ = standard deviation of export growth 1980–1987 in 2-digit industry

2. Bain (1956), Stigler (1964). As Paul A. Geroski pointed out in the discussion of this paper Bain's main interest was to determine some critical value for concentration which could be used in antitrust policy.
3. Schmalensee (1987), Harris (1988). Weiss (1989) proposes to use price instead of profit margin as dependent variable, partly with the argument to incorporate Demsetz' position.
4. The term 'standard theories' indicates non game theoretical theories in this context. Of course Bertrand models do not forecast a positive relationship between profits and concentration (at least for homogeneous markets). Cournot models do forecast a positive relationship with demand elasticity as additional determinant of profit margin.
5. An insignificant – and sometimes even negative – coefficient is found for concentration on profits especially if market share and concentration rates are used. See Ravenscraft (1983), Martin (1983). See Neumann, Boebel and Haid (1985) for a model (Cournot plus fringe) where a negative concentration rate may be theoretically justified, or Adelman and Stangle (1985) for a critique of single equations including market shares and concentration. Negative coefficients are also found in studies on banking profits and concentration, see Gilbert (1984).
6. For an overview see Shapiro, 1989 or Tirole, 1989.
7. Remind that any discount factor depends on a proper time discount and the length of the period $\delta = e^{-rt}$, where r is the instantaneous rate of interest and t is real time. Which discount factor is considered as realistic of course depends on the time period considered. If the time period is a week even 0.99 could be realistic, if the relevant time period is a year this is totally implausible.
8. Rotemberg and Saloner (1986) show that it is hard to sustain collusion facing demand fluctuations, especially in phase of high demand. The advantage of defection may be that high in booms, that the patience needed for collusion may not be attained. Staiger and Wolak (1992) investigated the relationship between collusion, business conditions, uncertain demand and capacity contraints recently. Other models show that the price stickyness facilitates collusion, since in 'any Markov perfect equilibrium, profits are bounded away from the competitive profits' (Tirole, 1989, p. 256).
9. We disregard the importance of the number of firms since the 'old story' put so much emphasis

on this point and concentrate on the 'innovations' presented by the supergame literature. The number of firms may be a bridge between the old and the new story.
10. More exactly firms facing undiversifiable risk.
11. The micro data set for 886 firms became recently available. See: Aiginger, K., Ch. Gartner, and F. Partsch (1991), *Empirische Industrie- und Außenhandelsökonomie*, unpublished.

References

Adelman, M.A. and B.E. Stangle (1985), 'Profitability and Market Share', in F.M. Fisher (ed.), *Antitrust and Regulation*, Cambridge, London: MIT Press.
Aiginger, K. (1987), *Production and Decision Theory under Uncertainty*, Blackwell.
Aiginger, K. (1989), 'The Optimal Reaction of Production and Investment on Uncertainty', in M. Funke (ed.), *Factors in Business Investment*, Augsburg: Springer.
Bain, J.S. (1951), 'Relation of Profit Rate on Industry Concentration: American Manufacturing, 1936–1940', *Quarterly Journal of Economics* **65**, 293–324.
Bain, J.S. (1956), 'Barriers to New Competition', Cambridge: Harvard Press.
Blair, J. (1972), *Economic Concentration*, New York: Hartcourt.
Baum, C. (1978), 'Systematische Fehler bei der Darstellung der Unternehmenskonzentration durch Konzentrationskoeffizient auf Basis Industriestatistischer Daten', *Jahrbuch für Nationalökonomie und Statistik* **193 (1)**, 30–53.
Blanchard, O.J. (1986), *Discussion on Hart 1986*, see Hall.
Bradburd, R.M. and A.M. Over (1982), 'Organizational Costs, 'sticky' Equilibria and Critical Levels of Concentration', *Review of Economics and Statistics* **64**, 50–58.
Bresnahan, T.F. (1981), 'Duopoly Models with Consistent Conjectures', *American Economic Review* **71**, 934–994.
Bresnahan, T.F. (1989), 'Empirical Studies of Industries with Market Power', in R. Schmalensee and R.D. Willig (eds.), *Handbook of Industrial Organization*, Amsterdam, New York: Elsevier Publishers.
Bulow, J., J. Geanakopolos, and D. Klemperer (1985), 'Multimarket Oligopoly, Strategic Substitutes and Complements', *Journal of Political Economy*, 488–511.
Buzzel, R.D. and B.T. Gale (1982), *The PIMS Principles: Linking Strategy to Performance*, New York, Free Press.
Caves, R.E. and D.R. Barton (1990), 'Efficiency in U.S. Manufacturing', Cambridge, London: MIT Press.
Cheng, L. (1985), 'Comparing Bertrand and Cournot Equilibria: A Geometric Approach', *Rand Journal of Economics* **16**, 146–152.
Cowling, K. and M. Waterson (1976), 'Price Cost Margins and Market Structure', *Economica* **38**, 378–394.
Curry, B. and K.D. George (1963), 'Industrial Concentration: A Survey', *Journal of Industrial Economics* (March).
Davis, S., P. Geroski, and D. Vlassopoulos (1990), *How Concentrated are Markets in the U.K.?*, mimeo, Lille.
Demsetz, H. (1973), 'Industry Structure, Market Rivalry, and Public Policy', *Journal of Law and Economics* **16**, 1–10.
Demsetz, H. (1974), 'Two Systems of Belief about Monopoly', in H.J. Goldschmid, H.M. Mann, and J.F. Weston (eds.), *Industrial Concentration: The New Learning*, Boston: Little, Brown & Company.
Dixit, A.K. (1980), 'The Role of Investment in Entry Deterrence', *Economic Journal* **90**, 95–106.
Domowitz, I., G. Hubbard, and B.C. Petersen (1987), 'Oligopoly Supergames: Some Empirical Evidence on Prices and Margins', *Journal of Industrial Economics* **35**, 379–398.
Fisher, F.M. and J.J. McGowan (1983), 'On the Misuse of Accounting Rates of Return to Infer Monopoly Profits', *American Economic Review* **73 (1)**, 82–97.
Frantz, R.S. (1988), *X-Efficiency: Theory, Evidence and Applications*, Boston: Kluwer.
Fudenberg, D. and E. Maskin (1986), 'The Folk Theorem in Repeated Games with Discounting and Incomplete Information', *Econometrica* **54**, 533–554.

Gale, B.T. (1972), 'Market Share and the Rate of Return', *Review of Economics and Statistics* **54**, 421–423.

Gale, B.T. and B.S. Branch (1982), 'Concentration versus Market Share', *Antitrust Bulletin*, 83–106.

Geroski, P.A., 'Specification and Testing the Profits-Concentration Relationship: Some Experiment for the U.K.', *Economica* **48**, 279–288.

Geroski, P.A. (1987), *Competition and Innovation*, Report prepared for the E.C. Commission, Brussels.

Geroski, P.A. (1990), 'Innovation and the Evolution of Market Structure', *The Journal of Industrial Economics* **38** (March), 299–314.

Geroski, P.A. and A. Jacquemin (1988), 'The Persistence of Profits: A European Comparison', *Economic Journal* **98**, 375–389.

Gilbert, R.A. (1984), 'Bank Structure and Competition', *Journal of Money, Credit and Banking* **16 (4)**, 617–660.

Gort, M. and R. Singamsetti (1976), 'Concentration and Profit Rates: New Evidence on an Old Issue', *Explorations in Economic Research* **3**, 1–20.

Grabowski, H.G. and D.C. Mueller (1978), 'Industrial Research and Development, Intangible Capital Stocks, and Firm Profit Rates', *Bell Journal of Economics* **9**, 328–343.

Green, E.J. and R.H. Porter (1984), 'Non-Cooperative Collusion under Imperfect Price Information', *Econometrica* **52**, 87–100.

Hall, R.E. (1986), 'Market Structure and Macroeconomic Fluctuations', *Brookings Papers on Economic Activity* **2**, 285–322.

Hall, R.E. (1988), 'The Relation between Price and Marginal Cost in U.S. Industry', *Journal of Political Economy* **96 (5)**, 921–947.

Harris, F. (1988), 'Testable Competing Hypotheses from the Structure Performance Theory: Efficient Structure versus Market Power', *Journal of Industrial Economics* **36**, 267–280.

Hirschey, M. (1985), 'Market Structure and Market Value', *Journal of Business* **58**, 89–98.

Jacquemin, A. (1990), 'Horizontal Concentration and European Merger Policy', *European Economic Review* **34**, 539–550.

Jacquemin, A., P. Buigues, and F. Ilzkovitz (1989), 'Horizontal Mergers and Competition Policy in the European Community', *European Economy* **40** (May).

Jacquemin, A., E. de Ghellinck, and C. Huveneers, 'Concentration and Profitability in a Small, Open Economy', *Journal of Industrial Economics* **29**, 131–144.

Jacquemin, A. and H.W. De Jong (1977), *European Industrial Organization*, New York: Wiley.

Kreps, D. and J. Scheinkman (1983), 'Quantity Precommittment and Bertand Competition Yield Cournot Outcomes', *Bell Journal of Economics* **14**, 326–337.

Leibenstein, H. (1966), 'Allocative Efficiency versus X-Efficiency', *American Economic Review* **56**, 392–415.

Martin, S. (1983), *Market, Firm and Economic Performance*, New York: Salomon Brothers Center.

Maskin, E. (1986), 'The Existence of Equilibrium with Price Setting Firms', *American Economic Review* **76**, 382–386.

Maskin, E. and J. Tirole (1987), 'A Theory of Dynamic Oligopoly III; Cournot Competition', *European Economic Review* **31**, 947–968.

Maskin, E. and J. Tirole (1988A), 'A Theory of Dynamic Oligopoly I', *Econometrica* **56**, 549–569.

Maskin, E. and J. Tirole (1988B), 'A Theory of Dynamic Oligopoly II', *Econometrica* **56**, 571–599.

Neumann, M. (1980), 'Marktmacht und Kosteninflation', *Jahrbuch für Nationalökonomie und Statistik* **195**, 477f.

Neumann, M. (1990), 'Industrial Policy and Competition Policy', *European Economic Review* **34**, 562–567.

Neumann, M., I. Boebel, and A. Haid (1983), 'Business Cycle and Industrial Market Power', *Journal of Industrial Economics* **32**, 187–195.

Neumann, M. and A. Haid (1985), 'Concentration and Economic Performance', in J. Schwalbach (ed.), *Industry Structure and Performance*, Berlin: WZB Edition Sigma.

Neumann, M., I. Boebel, and A. Haid (1985), 'Domestic Concentration, Foreign Trade and Economic Performance', *International Journal of Industrial Organization* **3**, 1–19.

Ordover, J. and W. Baumol (1988), 'Antitrust Policy and High Technology Industries', *Oxford Review*

of Economic Policy **4**.
Perry, M. (1982), 'Oligopoly and Consistent Conjectural Variation', *Bell Journal*, 197–205.
Phillips, A. (1976), 'A Critique of Empirical Studies of Relations between Market Structure and Profitability', *Journal of Industrial Economics* **24**, 241–249.
Porter, R. (1983A), 'Optimal Cartel Trigger Price Strategies', *Journal of Economic Theory* **29**, 313–338.
Porter, R. (1983B), 'A Study of Cartel Stability: The Joint Executive Comittee 1980–86', *Rand Journal of Economics* **14**, 301–314.
Posner, R. (1975), 'The Social Costs of Monopoly and Regulation', *Journal of Political Economy* **83**, 807–827.
Ravenscraft, D.J. (1983), 'Structure Profit Relationships at the Line of Business and the Industry Level', *Review of Economics and Statistics*, pp. 22–31.
Rotemberg, J. and G. Saloner (1986), 'A Supergame Theoretic Model of Business Cycles and Price War during Booms', *American Economic Review*, 390–407.
Salinger, M. (1990), 'The Concentration-Margins Relationship Reconsidered', Brookings Papers: Microeconomics, pp. 287–335.
Scherer, F.M. (1969), 'Market Structure and the Stability of Investment', *American Economic Review* **59**, 72–79.
Schmalensee, R. (1985), 'Do Markets Differ Much?', *American Economic Review* **75**, 341–351.
Schmalensee, R. (1987), 'Collusion versus Differential Efficiency: Testing Alternative Hypothesis', *Journal of Industrial Economics* **35**, 399–425.
Schmalensee, R. (1989), 'Interindustry Studies of Structure and Performance', in R. Schmalensee and R.D. Willig (eds.), *Handbook of Industrial Organization, II*, Amsterdam, New York: Elsevier Publishers.
Shaked, A. and J. Sutton (1982), 'Relaxing Price Competition through Product Differentiation', *Review of Economic Studies* **49**, 131–146.
Shaked, A. and J. Sutton (1990), 'Multiproduct Firms and Market Structure', *Rand Journal of Economics* **21**, 45–62.
Shapiro, C. (1989), 'Theories of Oligopoly Behavior', in R. Schmalensee and R.D. Willig (eds.), *Handbook of Industrial Organization*, Amsterdam, New York: Elsevier Publishers.
Singh, N. and X. Vives (1984), 'Price and Quantity Competition in a Differentiated Duopoly', *Rand Journal of Economics* **15**, 546–554.
Spence, M. (1977), 'Entry, Capacity, Investment and Oligopolistic Pricing', *Bell Journal*, 534–544.
Staiger, R.W. and F.A. Wolak (1992), 'Collusive Pricing with Capacity Constraints in Presence of Demand Uncertainty', *Rand Journal of Economics* **23 (2)**, 203–220.
Stigler, G. (1964), 'A Theory of Oligopoly', *Journal of Political Economy*, 44–61.
Sutton, J. (1991), *Sunk Costs and Market Structure*, Cambridge, London: MIT Press.
Tirole, J. (1989), *The Theory of Industrial Organization*, Cambridge, London: MIT Press.
Vives, X. (1985), 'On the Efficiency of Cournot and Bertrand Competition with Product Differentiation', *Journal of Economic Theory* **36 (1)**, 166–175.
Waterson, M. (1980), 'Price Cost Margin and Successive Market Power', *Quarterly Journal of Economics* **94**, 135–150.
Waterson, M. (1990), 'Product Differentiation and Profitability: An Asymmetric Model', *Journal of Industrial Economics* **39**, 113–130.
Weiss, C.R. (1993), *Preisrigidität und Marktstruktur*, Europäische Hochschulschriften, Vol. 1448, Frankfurt am Main, Peter Lang.
Weiss, L.W. (1974), 'The Concentration – Profits Relationship and Antitrust', in H.J. Goldschmid, H.M. Mann, and J.F. Weston (eds.), *Industrial Concentration: The New Learning*, Boston: Little, Brown & Company.
Weiss, L.W. (1989), *Concentration and Price*, Cambridge, London: MIT Press.

K. Aiginger and J. Finsinger (eds.), Applied Industrial Organization, 167–186.

Structure-Performance in Banking: An Application to a Typical Universal Banking System

PETER MOOSLECHNER and YVONNE SCHNITZER*
Austrian Institute of Economic Research, Wien, Austria

Abstract. While the structure-performance-approach is a standard tool of analysis for banking markets in the US there are only a few studies in this tradition for European countries. Based on two large newly compiled micro-databases for Austrian banks this paper makes an attempt to illustrate some elements of the structure-performance-relationship in banking under typical universal banking conditions. One important feature in this context is an explicit treatment of market delineation, the construction of a relevant market for each individual bank. The results of cross-section as well as pooled time-series estimates are rather mixed: Whereas cross-section regressions show almost no significant influence of market share and concentration on bank profitability both variables turned out to have a significant impact in pooled time-series estimates. Moreover, the impact of market structure on performance depends crucially on the set of control variables included.

JEL-codes: G2, L1, L8

Key words: Structure-performance, universal banking, market delineation, bank profitability

I. Introduction

This paper deals with banking markets in an industrial economics context. Two observations constitute the beginning of our work on this subject: An astonishing lack in banking studies in an industrial economics tradition for Europe and the possible connection between market structure and low profitability in Austrian banking.

While the structure-performance-paragdigm of industrial economics is accepted as a standard tool of analysis for banking markets in the US[1] there are only a few studies in this tradition for European countries, for example Bourke (1989), Conti (1992) and Steinherr and Huveneers (1992a).[2] Several reasons may contribute to this rather surprising situation. Although European banking markets are far from uniform (Bröker 1989; Porta 1990; OECD 1992) the structure of most banking markets in Europe – perhaps with the notable exception of the United Kingdom – is very different from that in the United States. This is not only because segmentation between commercial and investment banking is less pronounced but also because there are large shareholdings of banks in non-financial companies, substantial ownership of industry by banks and the importance of "integrated banks" as opposed to bank holding companies. However, two basic structural elements constitute the main distinctions between the banking system in the US and Europe, in particular in an empirical analysis of market structure and performance:

(1) Contrary to the US "universal banking" is a major feature of the banking system in many European countries. European banks are allowed to engage themselves in nearly all kinds of banking business without special permission. There is no clear-cut distinction between commercial banking and the securities markets in many countries as it is valid since the Glass-Steagall-Act of 1933 for the US.
(2) In a similar manner "nationwide banking" is characteristic for the strategic market orientation of large European banks compared to substantial restrictions on interstate banking in the US. There exists at least one important group of banks in each European country – in general the commercial banks – that is not restricted in its geographical scope of business.[3]

In general, both features make it much more difficult than in the US to define, delimit and analyse relevant banking markets and to identify their participants under Eurpean conditions. In addition, the availability of the necessary bank-by-bank database for applying estimates of the structure-performance-paradigm is poor for European banking markets.

The second observation is that in Austria, a country with a pronounced universal banking system, the number of banks is very large, bank branch density is very high and, at the same time, bank profitability is among the lowest of all OECD-countries. This automatically leads to the question if market structure can explain – at least in part – the poor profitability in Austrian banking and if some sort of competitive behaviour can be identified under conditions of universal banking that may be responsible for this result.

Last but no least in preparing for the integration of financial markets within a single European banking market for several reasons a worldwide tendency in favour of universal banking has emerged (Steinherr and Huveneers, 1992b). From the point of view of a traditional universal banking structure the advantages of this model seem to be overemphasized.

Based on these observations the paper tries to overcome some of the European deficiencies in an empirical application of the structure-performance-hypothesis to the Austrian banking system. The Austrian banking system can be seen as a very typical representative of the universal banking model.[4] The standard Austrian bank is universal in business and can act nationwide. Likewise market entry is open to potential domestic and foreign applicants. Altogether there are many points that seem to characterize the Austrian banking system as a highly contestable environment.

The paper starts by illustrating some features in the development of market structure in Section II that may have been important in changing the competitive environment of Austrian banking. The empirical estimates presented in Sections III and V are based on two – new developed – micro-databases that contain selected balance sheet items for a large cross section of banks and time series data of 13 large banks for a period from 1974 to 1990. Section IV briefly describes the data of the cross section database and, in particular, reviews the explicit treatment of market delineation. As it will be shown, market delineation is one of the central issues in this analysis. Some conclusions, caveats and remaining questions are discussed in the last section.

Following the intentions of Schmalensee (1985) the approach utilized throughout this paper is fundamentally descriptive. To make it clear at the very beginning, what we try to get is a first serious illustration of possible structure-performance-relationships under conditions of pronounced universal banking as a starting point for further discussion and research. We do not claim to give a "final explanation" at this stage of our work.

II. Features of Market Structure and Competition

Although the number of banks on the Austrian banking market is very large the market is dominated by a small group of large banks and banking groups that do business nationwide. This would normally be labeled an oligopolistic market structure but there are indicators that the market has moved significantly towards increased competition or contestability over the last ten to fifteen years. Without doubt these factors are of central importance in interpreting market structure and the results of any structure-performance-analysis (Baumol, 1991).

(1) Since the mid-seventies the legal and administrative barriers to enter the Austrian banking market or specific parts of it have been removed step by step. First the restrictions on branching were abolished, second the typical banking firm was allowed to do all kinds of banking business and finally the liberalisation of international capital movements opened up the market for international competition. As far as the national market is concerned this led to an increase in market share for a small group of large banks that were able to expand their business nationwide. The main result of this process was the development of some sort of two tier market: one part of the market driven by the – potential – competition of and within this group of large banks and a second part of the market consisting of many very small banks of only limited and local importance.

(2) The extent of this change in market structure is illustrated by substantially increasing entry rates of the five largest universal banks in regional markets.[5] Table I shows entry rates for the biggest five universal banks headquartered in Vienna[6] on a state level. Entry to the banking market of a state or province can happen by branching or by acquisition. The (relative) entry rates displayed measure the increase in bank offices of these 5 large Viennese banks as a percentage of the overall increase in bank offices in the same area. While on their home market Vienna the market share of the 5 banks in new bank offices

TABLE I. Market entry rates* of 5 large Vienna-based banks by state

	1970/65	1975/70	1980/75	1985/80	1990/85
Niederösterreich	25.9	7.1	16.9	31.9	63.2
Burgenland	0.0	12.5	20.3	84.6	14.3
Steiermark	6.8	17.2	15.7	11.9	58.5
Kärnten	0.0	6.8	12.1	26.3	412.5
Oberösterreich	4.8	6.4	7.9	9.0	27.8
Salzburg	5.6	6.9	11.7	20.8	14.8
Tirol	0.0	(.1	6.7	3.5	20.6
Vorarlberg	8.3	16.7	13.6	11.1	35.0
8 States	7.0	9.0	12.7	17.8	47.5
Vienna	68.0	71.0	62.9	56.2	41.7
Austria	19.3	21.2	18.3	25.5	46.0

* "Market Entry Rates" are defined as the increase of bank offices by these 5 Viennese banks in a regional market through new branches or by acquisition as a percentage of the total increase in banking offices. These "relative" entry rates may exceed 100% because of the acquisition of existing branch networks.
Source: Austrian National Bank, own calculations.

has diminished over the last 15 years, they have significantly expanded their branch networks to all other regional markets. In the period 1985 to 1990 nearly half of all new branches outside Vienna were established by the group of five. For example the data for Kärnten in this period show the effect of an acquisition of a large regional branch network by a Vienna-based bank.

(3) In an international comparison of bank profitability the Austrian banking market is the least profitable within all OECD-countries in terms of total net income. Profitability has been diminishing since the late seventies. At least this profit situation does not contradict an assumption that some sort of competitive pressure is present.

(4) Finally the level of exit rates in Austrian banking seems rather high (Table a result that can be interpreted as an indicator of contestability. Exit rates are measured as the decrease in the number of banking headquarters in percentage rates. With the notable exception of Vienna these rates are high and they have risen further throughout the eighties. The somewhat lower exit rates for Vienna are biased by the fact that Vienna – as the main financial center of Austria – has attracted a number of new established – specialized – banks that compensate for the exit of traditional banking headquarters. Unfortunately the data available do not allow to calculate these two effects separatly.

TABLE II. Market exit rates* of banks by state

	1970/65	1975/70	1980/75	1985/80	1990/85
Niederösterreich	15.6	30.4	24.6	24.9	5.3
Burgenland	0.0	0.0	2.1	46.4	6.7
Steiermark	5.8	10.4	6.9	42.8	6.8
Kärnten	0.5	1.6	4.5	47.4	13.3
Oberösterreich	1.6	4.4	3.5	5.1	9.1
Salzburg	0.0	0.0	2.2	0.0	6.9
Tirol	1.0	14.2	13.0	6.8	3.6
Vorarlberg	6.8	7.3	19.7	21.3	0.0
8 States	5.2	13.4	10.7	24.7	7.0
Vienna	1.6	1.6	−14.5	− 5.6	2.7
Austria	6.6	13.0	9.8	23.3	6.7

* "Market Exit Rates" are defined as the decrease in the number of banking headquarters in percentage rates.
Source: Austrian National Bank, own calculations.

III. Cross-section Regressions

The first step in getting some insights in structure-performance-relationships under universal banking conditions is based on cross-section estimates. The data stem from a newly compiled bank database covering 956 observations of Austrian banks for the years 1988 and 1989.[7] The estimation method used follows the mainstream of structure-performance-regressions in the literature, postulating a linear relationship between an indicator of bank profitability, market share and market concentration. In order to control for systematic differences in bank-specific factors and "real" market conditions a set of control variables is added. These control variables capture the balance sheet structure and the cost situation of the bank, the geographic range of business (number of relevant markets) and some demand side variables (population, share of agricultural production) of the markets relevant to an individual bank. Finally dummy variables account for different types of banks.

The theoretical background of this approach suggests that there is a causal link between market structure, bank conduct and performance. More specifically it has been argued that banks may earn collusive profits in concentrated markets. Contemporary approaches of structure-performance emphasize an alternative "efficient-structure"-hypothesis (Demsetz, 1973). It postulates a positive relationship between bank profitability and market structure that can be attributed to gains made in market share by more efficient banks. This would suggest that firm-specific efficiency seems to be the dominant variable in explaining bank profitability.

According to Weiss (1974) it is essential for the correct estimation of structure-performance "... that one takes both market share and concentration into account at the same time". The studies by Smirlock (1985) for banking markets and by Ravenscraft (1983) for other industries are examples of empirical work along these lines of research. Usually market share and profitability are strongly correlated whereas concentration becomes insignificant and/or negative in regressions including market share.

Our cross-section regressions fit very well compared to those of studies for US-banking.[8] The overall significance is much better, especially when net interest income is used as a measure of bank profitability (Table III). But market structure seems to be of only very limited importance in this relationship. The only significant influence of market share can be deducted in the regressions explaining net interest income. Unfortunately the sign of the coefficient is negative and therefore in contradiction to expectations according to the "efficient-structure"-hypothesis. There is no significant impact of market concentration on bank profitability independent of whether it is measured by net interest income, return on equity or total net income (= return on total assets).

In contrast to market structure the set of control variables included performs well.[9] The most important negative influence on total net income and return on equity can be identified for the cost variables. It turned out that typical for a good performance of an Austrian bank are a high share of savings deposits and of loans to non-banks.

One of the most interesting aspects of the estimates concerns the stability of results, a question hardly discussed in the literature. As can be seen from the spectrum of t-values reported in Table IV the results are very sensitive to variations in the set of explanatory variables included.

Two examples may illustrate the importance of this fact:

* The (missing) significance of market concentration is connected to the type of "real" market analysed. Excluding the share of agricultural production – a variable meant to catch some demand side factors – from the regression leads to a significant negative impact of concentration on profitability. On the other hand the inclusion of a market share variable does not change the influence of concentration.
* The coefficient of the market share variable varies with the balance sheet structure and the type of the bank. Including indicators of balance sheet structure to the equation attributes a positive sign to the market share variable, whereas the type of bank dummies produce a severe negative market share impact.

These illustrations lead to the conclusion that the stability of results according to the specification of the regressions should be of central importance in structure-performance analysis. As our results have shown one must be concerned that concentration and market share may be only proxies for some other variables that affect a bank's profitability and unless those "other" variables are adequately controlled for, the estimated effect of the market structure variables may capture

TABLE III. Summary of cross-section regression results (t-statistics in parenthesis)

Explanatory variables	Net interest income*	total net income*	rate of return on equity
Loans to non-banks*	0.0151	0.0132	0.2375
	(12.04)	(10.68)	(10.43)
Savings deposits*	0.0094	0.0049	0.0887
	(8.91)	(4.75)	(4.64)
Equity capital*	0.0585	0.0875	-1.4378
	(5.84)	(8.88)	(7.93)
Total wage costs*	0.8671	-0.1631	-3.6078
	(14.54)	(2.78)	(3.34)
Expenses on materials*	0.5759	-0.4695	-8.4232
	(7.69)	(6.37)	(6.21)
"Raiffeisenbank"	0.0008	-0.0011	-0.0081
	(1.00)	(1.31)	(0.51)
"Volksbank"	0.0044	0.0019	0.0280
	(5.01)	(2.26)	(1.75)
"Sparkasse"	0.0046	0.0010	-0.0037
	(5.28)	(1.17)	(0.23)
"Hypothekenbank"	0.0065	0.0026	0.0248
	(4.38)	(1.75)	(0.92)
Population per district	-0.0000	-0.0000	-0.0000
	(1.25)	(1.52)	(1.98)
Share of industrial production	0.0057	0.0049	0.0766
	(4.50)	(3.92)	(3.32)
Share of agricultural prod.	0.0219	0.0053	0.1118
	(7.85)	(1.93)	(2.21)
Number of markets	-0.0001	-0.0000	-0.0002
	(1.39)	(0.96)	(0.17)
Herfindahl index	0.0023	0.0015	0.0433
	(1.32)	(0.86)	(1.39)
Market share	-0.0077	-0.0013	-0.0141
	(5.68)	(0.97)	(0.57)
R^2	0.75	0.33	0.25
SEE	0.0038	0.0037	0.0688
Observations	956	956	956

* Percentage of balance sheet totals

much more than the effect of concentration or market share. As an example, our results reflect the possibility for concentration to be a proxy for a bank's location – especially whether it is situated in smaller rural markets versus in larger urban ones.

TABLE IV. Change in market structure impact of profitability with regard to alternative sets of explanatory variables

Set of Explanatory Variables	A Complete model			B Agriculture excluded	C Balance sheet structure		
Performance Indicator	E1	E2	E3	E4	E5	E6	E7
Net interest income							
Herfindahl*	–0.91		1.32	–2.28	–3.29		–3.81
Market share*		–5.60	–5.68	–3.48		1.18	2.26
R2	0.74	0.75	0.75	0.73	0.51	0.50	0.51
Total net income							
Herfindahl*	0.53		0.86	0.01	0.02		–0.74
Market share*		–0.69	–0.96	–0.43		2.45	2.56
R2	0.32	0.32	0.32	0.32	0.19	0.20	0.20
Return on Equity							
Herfindahl*	1.26		1.39	0.47	1.17		0.87
Market share*		–0.04	–0.57	0.05		1.14	0.83
R2	0.23	0.23	0.23	0.23	0.14	0.14	0.14

	D Cost variables			E Bank-type			F Demand factors		
	E8	E9	E10	E11	E12	E13	E14	E15	E16
Net interest income									
Herfindahl*	–2.43		–2.04	–5.07		–3.19	–2.16		–0.61
Market share*		–1.57	–0.89		–6.22	–4.79		–4.79	–4.30
R2	0.53	0.53	0.53	0.33	0.34	0.34	0.21	0.23	0.23
Total net income									
Herfindahl*	0.42		0.05	–0.41		–0.16	0.22		0.16
Market share*		1.25	1.17		–0.77	–0.67		0.19	0.13
R2	0.00	0.00	0.00	0.09	0.09	0.09	0.07	0.07	0.07
Return on Equity									
Herfindahl*	0.81		1.09	0.04		0.28	0.92		1.56
Market share*		–0.79	–1.08		–9.68	–0.73		–1.63	–2.07
R2	0.00	0.00	0.00	0.03	0.03	0.03	0.05	0.05	0.05

* t-values; Number of observations = 956
Alternative sets of explanatory variables:
A: Complete set of explanatory variables as in Table IV.
B: Share of agricultural production excluded.
C: Loans to Non-banks, Savings Deposits, Equity Capital.
D: Total Wage Costs, Expenses on Materials.
E: Raiffeisenbank, Sparkasse, Hypothekenbank, Volksbank, Number of Markets.
F: Population, Agricultural Production, Industrial Production.

But one can also question the exogeneity of concentration as well as other variables used in bank-structure-performance regressions. Thus, market structure may excert influence on banks' portfolio selection with the effect that the coefficient of concentration is biased towards zero since some of the influence of market structure is being captured in the variables controlling for the bank's balance-sheet structure.

Unfortunately the studies published so far on this subject mostly neglect these problems. For this reason it is not very clear to what extent the positive relationship between concentration and bank profitability obtained in most banking studies follows from a specific choice of control variables.

Altogether the cross-section results show almost no significant influence of market structure on performance. Bank profitability under Austrian universal banking conditions is mainly connected with balance sheet structure, "real" market conditions and the type of the bank.

IV. Market Delineation: Some Definitions and Descriptive Statistics on a Cross-section Database of Austrian Banks

There are two major attempts in this paper to give some new and different insights compared to common interpretations of banking structure in Austria so far:

(1) For the first time empirical estimates in Austrian banking are based on a database of individual bank data, large banks as well as small ones, with many observations that give a more or less complete representation of total market structure.

(2) There is an explicit treatment of market delineation – the construction of a relevant market area for each individual bank – to determine relevant market shares for each bank and adequate concentration ratios for each market.

The cross-section database compiled consists of 956 observations for banks in the years 1988 and 1989. Included are universal banks only: 545 rural cooperative banks, 210 savings banks, 151 popular cooperative banks, 11 mortgage banks and 39 commercial banks. Balance sheet totals for banks included in the sample range from 429,5 billion AS to 235 million AS.

One of the major problems dealt with in empirical applications of the structure-performance approach is how to measure market structure. Market structure is usually approximated by market share and market concentration. But it is extremely difficult to define a meaningful (relevant) market area and a reasonable measure of concentration in an universal banking system with nationwide banking, because banks are operating in many different product and geographical markets. For the purpose of the present study differences in market structure by banking products are neglected, only one market share per bank – derived from balance sheet totals – is calculated. Geographically a district (Bezirk) is treated as a banking market[10],

TABLE V. Means of variables for 956 banks by type of geographic orientation

	Local banks	Regional banks	National banks	All banks
Variables				
Net interest income*	3.54	2.30	1.50	3.43
Total net income*	1.06	0.71	0.38	1.03
Savings deposits*	78.73	30.47	18.11	74.85
Loans to non-banks*	55.27	41.39	45.33	54.33
Equity captital*	5.91	5.22	4.62	5.84
Total wage costs*	1.17	0.85	0.66	1.14
Total operating expenses*	1.96	1.42	1.09	1.91
Population per district (in thousands)	130.7	225.8	595.4	146.7
Share of agricultural production (in %)	8.47	4.42	2.91	8.14
Share of industrial production (in %)	33.55	30.04	30.57	33.30
Number of markets	1	5	21	2
Market share (in %)	0.12	0.17	0.10	0.12
Herfindahl index	0.18	0.18	0.10	0.18
Observations	885	48	23	956

* Percentages of balance sheet totals

although the demand for banking services without doubt is not restricted by district borders.

Based on this concept each bank has a relevant market of its own, ranging from at least one district for a local bank to nationwide active banks with many districts served.[11] The number of districts relevant to an individual bank is determined by its branching network. Because there are, in general, no balance sheet data available for bank branches, market structure is measured empirically within the relevant market of each bank separately, including the balance sheet totals of all banks headquartered in one of the districts of the relevant markets.[12] Competition from nationwide and regional active banks is captured by the number of branches of these banks in the relevant market area but turned out to be insignificant.

This market delineation process formed the basis for connecting bank-specific variables to relevant banking markets and allocating "real" characteristics of these markets (the districts) to individual banks. Certainly this must be seen as a first and special attempt to geographically delineate markets in banking and of course many improvements are necessary. Nevertheless the descriptive statistics reported in Tables V to VII point out some interesting characteristics of banking market structure.

TABLE VI. Means of variables for 956 banks by market shares

	Market share ranges					
	0–10%	10–20%	20–30%	30–40%	40–50%	>50%
Variables						
Net interest income*	1.92	1.90	1.57	1.49	2.34	2.46
Total net income*	10.0	11.5	10.7	10.5	13.6	11.2
Savings deposits*	31.25	25.37	20.50	14.07	34.48	39.60
Loans to non-banks*	48.28	47.12	35.96	33.11	40.39	51.25
Equity capital*	5.55	5.30	5.14	4.81	6.17	7.68
Total wage costs*	0.70	0.78	0.56	0.50	0.84	0.89
Total operating expenses*	1.18	1.28	0.94	0.89	1.41	1.45
Population per District (in thsd.)	209.1	76.2	126.4	146.4	82.6	49.8
Share of agricultural production (in %)	7.07	1.68	8.10	7.95	6.04	6.44
Share of industrial production (in %)	33.36	32.19	34.93	34.98	36.04	30.25
Number of markets	2	2	1	1	1	1
Local banks	483	243	81	49	21	13
Regional banks	18	8	5	2	0	0
National banks	15	2	0	0	0	0
All banks = observations	519	253	90	55	23	16

* Percentage of balance sheet totals

Taking the distinction of banks according to their geographic range of operation as an example (Table V) the means of variables show large differences for the three groups of banks defined: By far the largest group of banks in Austria and in the database are local banks. The average number of districts a bank is operating in rises from 1 district for local banks to 21 districts for nationwide banks. The relevant number of inhabitants per district is positively correlated with the size of the bank, rising significantly from local to national orientation, whereas the share of agricultural production in districts served decreases.

Savings deposits constitute a clear lower share of liabilities for national banks and the same is true for equity capital. Above all the profitability of local and regional banks exceeds that of banks with nationwide business and the same holds for market concentration measured by the Herfindahl index in the relevant market area.

More details on interesting patterns of market structure in banking are reported in Tables VI and VII where the variables are arranged by market share and by market concentration respectively.

TABLE VII. Means of variables for 956 banks by concentration ranges

	Concentration ranges (Herfindahl index)				
	.0–.10	.10–.20	.20–.30	.30–.40	> .40
Variables					
Net interest income*	1.77	2.65	1.43	2.38	2.38
Total net income*	0.51	0.80	0.54	0.68	0.82
Savings deposits*	25.03	48.11	15.19	37.77	48.10
Loans to non-banks*	48.31	41.58	37.28	44.57	46.89
Equity capital*	5.44	5.80	4.82	6.36	7.43
Total wage costs*	0.70	0.91	0.47	0.91	0.88
Total operating expenses*	1.17	1.51	0.83	1.53	1.40
Population per district (in thsd.)	198.8	116.9	298.8	135.3	67.6
Share of agricultural production (in %)	10.01	9.55	6.22	4.53	3.21
Share of industrial production (in %)	30.91	33.57	34.69	30.67	41.11
Number of markets	5	1	1	1	1
Local banks	115	438	226	94	17
Regional banks	8	19	1	7	2
National banks	16	0	2	0	0
All banks = observations	139	460	237	101	19

* Percentage of balance sheet totals

V. Results of Pooled Time Series Estimates

The second approach to illustrate some elements of the structure-performance-relationship under universal banking conditions uses pooled time series data. For 13 large Austrian banks annual data have been compiled for the period 1974 to 1990 generating a pooled database with 221 observations.

Different from the cross-section calculations presented above the "real" characteristics of the relevant banking market structure (population, production shares, etc.) could not be captured in time series form. The dataset covers mainly firm specific variables coming out of the balance sheet and the income statement of the 13 banks analysed.[13] It is completed by 4 variables measuring the market share of each bank and market concentration (Herfindahl index[14]). Each of the two market structure variables is calculated in two different ways, applying two different concepts of the relevant market: on the one hand the indicators measure market structure within the group of 13 banks and on the other hand vis-a-vis the whole banking system. The calculation of the Herfindahl index for the whole banking system uses the one-bank-assumption for the rest of the banking system, treating all banks not included explicitly as one bank with one market share.

Three dummy variables are added to control for the influence of (a) substantial changes in banking laws in the years 1979 and 1986, (b) the distinction between banks doing business nationwide and banks acting on regional markets only and (c) the special role of three large banks as "Spitzeninstitute", as some sort of centralized banking institutions for a group of smaller banks.

In a rather descriptive manner the regressions "explain" (1) net interest income and (2) total net income of banks by a set of variables out of the firm specific and dummy variables described (Regressions E1 and E4 in Tables VIII and IX; see Table X for a list of variables and their definitions).

In a second step these estimates are extended by including the market share and the concentration variables respectively. Contrary to the pure cross section estimates these results indicate a significant and simultaneous influence of market share and concentration on performance. Measured within the group of 13 banks both market share and concentration show a positive impact on performance, with a significant but very small influence of market share. In contrast market concentration has a much greater influence, exceeding that of most other variables in the equation. The importance of market share and concentration on performance is much more substantial in respect to net interest income than to total net income. But in part the influence of these two variables in the total net income equation is captured by the net interest income variable that gives the most important "explanation" of total net income of all variables. Including both market structure variables simultaneously improves the significance of both coefficients and of the estimation as a whole.

The most interesting aspect of the regressions seems to be a change in sign for the market concentration variable if a Herfindahl index for the whole banking system is applied. Whereas the parameters of the market share variables are nearly unchanged, market concentration now shows a significant negative influence on performance.

An economic explanation for this result has to be looked for in the relation between competition within the group of 13 large banks and competition between this group and the rest of the banking system. Taking the results as they are, this would lead to an interpretation that increased market concentration within the group of 13 banks increases their performance while increased concentration coming from outside reduces their profitability.[15]

Altogether the results may lead to a conclusion that an increase in market share is not a highly successful strategy to improve banking performance. The effects of an increase in market concentration on profitability depend crucially on the special circumstances of the concentration process.

TABLE VIII. Summary of OLS-regression-results for net interest income (t-statistics in parenthesis)

Explanatory variable	E1	E2	E3
Total interest costs*	–0.0990	–0.1162	–0.0727
	(6.17)	(7.28)	(4.63)
Total wage costs per employee	0.0129	0.0152	0.0223
	(3.99)	(4.78)	(12.33)
Bonds as assets*	0.0178	0.0202	0.0135
	(4.78)	(5.35)	(4.47)
Savings deposits*	0.0223	0.0218	0.0217
	(11.64)	(11.58)	(5.91)
Dummy banking law	–0.0020	–0.0017	–0.0007
	(2.94)	(3.24)	(1.42)
Dummy regional banks	0.0050	0.0060	0.0060
	(9.07)	(9.74)	(10.01)
Dummy "Spitzeninstitute"	–0.0030	–0.0036	–0.0036
	(5.09)	(5.55)	(5.80)
Market share: 13 Banks		0.0001	
		(2.16)	
Herfindahl index: 13 banks		0.0895	
		(3.93)	
Market share: banking system			0.0002
			(2.06)
Herfindahl index: banking system			–0.0814
			(5.56)
R2	0.82	0.84	0.85
F-value	142.88	122,73	132,26
Statistics of scaled residuals			
Mean	0.000	0.000	0.000
S.D.	0.984	0.979	0.979

* Percentage of balance sheet totals

VI. Some Conclusions, Caveats and Questions

As usual in research in general and in economics in particular the analysis of a certain problem leads to new puzzles, new questions and multiple needs of further research. The main purpose of this paper was an attempt to give an illustration of some elements of the structure-performance-approach under typical universal banking conditions. Using new developed micro-databases for Austrian banks the results of cross-section and pooled time-series estimates are rather mixed.

Cross-section regressions show almost no significant influence of market share and market concentration variables on indicators of bank profitability while pooled time-series calculations for 13 large banks produce significant impacts for both

TABLE IX. Summary of OLS-regression-results for total net income (t-statistics in parenthesis)

Explanatory variable	E4	E5	E6
Net interest income*	0.8113	0.8301	0.8053
	(23.65)	(24.42)	(23.98)
Total operating costs*	–0.6810	–0.7204	–0.7042
	(17.15)	(17.90)	(17.80)
Loans to non-banks*	0.0048	0.0034	0.0036
	(5.25)	(3.47)	(3.72)
Savings deposits*	–0.0055	–0.0042	–0.0040
	(5.21)	(3.71)	(3.45)
Bonds as liabilities*	–0.0116	–0.0091	–0.0098
	(8.00)	(5.71)	(6.19)
Equity capital*	0.0493	0.0503	0.0373
	(5.17)	(5.41)	(3.62)
Dummy banking law	–0.0008	–0.0008	–0.0006
	(7.45)	(8.14)	(4.19)
Dummy regional banks	0.0013	0.0016	0.0019
	'(5.96)	(6.45)	(6.79)
Dummy "Spitzeninstitute"	–0.0014	–0.0015	-0.0014
	(5.42)	(5.89)	(5.75)
Market share: 13 banks		0.0000	
		(2.42)	
Herfindahl index: 13 banks		0.0225	
		(3.09)	
Market share: banking system			0.0001
			(2.60)
Herfindahl index: banking system			–0.0157
			(2.62)
R2	0.91	0.92	0.92
F-value	239.56	208.80	206.04
Statistics of scaled residuals			
Mean	0.000	0.000	0.000
S.D.	0.979	0.975	0.975

* Percentage of balance sheet totals

variables. An increase in market share may lead to a positive but very small impact on performance while significant positive as well as negative coefficients have been obtained for market concentration.

The most important negative influences on profitability measured in rates of return can be identified for cost variables. Lack of cost efficiency and above average intensity of competition may contribute to these results. In contrast a high share of

TABLE X. List of variables

	Cross section	Pooled time series
Performance indicators:		
Net interest income/Balance sheet totals	*	*
Total net income/Balance sheet totals	*	*
Rate of return on equity (Total net income/Equity capital)	*	
Balance sheet structure:		
Loans to non-banks/Balance sheet totals	*	*
Bonds as assets/Balance sheet totals		*
Savings deposits/Balance sheet totals	*	*
Bonds as liabilities/Balance sheet totals		*
Equity capital/Balance sheet totals	*	*
Cost variables:		
Total wage costs/Balance sheet totals	*	
Total wage costs per employee		*
Expenses on materials/Balance sheet totals	*	
Total interest costs/Balance sheet totals		*
Total operating costs/Balance sheet totals		*
"Real" market structure (Demand factors):		
Population per district	*	
Share of agricultural production	*	
Share of industrial production	*	
Market structure:		
Number of Markets (in which the bank is operating one or more branches)	*	
Market share (individual market share in each banks own relevant market)	*	
Market share: 13 Banks (market share within the group of 13 large banks)		*
Market share: Banking system (market share vis-a-vis the balance sheet totals of the whole banking system)		*
Herfindahl index (individual Herfindahl index for each relevant market)	*	
Herfindahl index: 13 banks (Herfindahl index within the group of 13 large banks)		*
Herfindahl index: Banking system (Herfindahl index vis-a-vis the balance sheet totals of the whole banking system)		*
Dummy variables:		
"Raiffeisenbank" (Rural credit co-operatives)	*	
"Volksbank" (Popular credit co-operatives)	*	
"Sparkasse" (Savings banks)	*	
"Hypothekenbank" (Mortgage banks)	*	
Banking law (major changes in banking laws 1979 and 1986)		*
Regional banks (banks with regional geographic orientation)		*
"Spitzeninstitute" (centralized banking institutions with special functions for a group of smaller banks)		*

savings deposits and of loans to non-banks are typical for a good performance of a bank.

First of all these results point to the fact that it is rather difficult to apply the standard US-approach of structure-performance to European universal and nationwide banking conditions. Very poor data availability and servere problems in geographical market delineation limit the empirical possibilities. Beyond that our experiences with cross-section estimates doubt the stability of US-results, a feature hardly discussed in the literature. As our results show the sign, magnitude and significance of market share and concentration variables in an "explanation" of bank profitability depends crucially on the set of control variables included that control for differences between banks in balance sheet composition and differences in the "real" market structure of different geographical markets.

Although there are no clear-cut conclusions, the results emphasize the necessity of further research in geographical delineation for banking markets to overcome the basic deficiencies of applying the standard structure-performance-model to universal banking.

Better market delineation means that one has to deal with the following questions in particular: What is the relevant geographic market of a bank and what are indicators that can be used to delimit this market area in a more sophisticated way? Do these markets, their market structure and the delineation process differ with regard to different types of banking business and bank products? Are there different types of markets leading to substantial differences in bank behaviour? As we have shown some of these questions can perhaps be addressed by distinguishing between different types of banks, for example analysing local, regional and national banks separately.

Beside market structure Berger and Humphrey (1991) have recently shown for a large sample of US-banks that firm-specific inefficiencies dominate over scale and product mix economies in an explanation of observed cost differentials. In so far as cost differences are passed through to profits the explicit treatment of cost inefficiencies could be expected to influence structure-performance-relationships.

Without doubt limited data availability is *the* essential restriction in empirical application as it prevents the construction and use of alternative sets of control variables. Beyond that there are of course considerations to what extent bank balance sheet structure variables are more or less endogenous variables and should be replaced by some other "type of bank's business" variables. Last but not least better data availability would allow to do sequences of cross-section estimates for several years to identify the time-invariant part(s) of market structure-performance-relationships. In econometric perspective an important need would be to check alternative functional forms of estimation.

Finally there are some basic doubts whether the structure-performance-approach as it has been developed for production industries can be applied to banking as a service industry without substantial modifications (Britton, Clark and Ball, 1992).

Notes

* We are indebted to Paul Geroski, Manfred Neumann, Peter Rosner, Fritz Schebeck, Gunther Tichy and two anonymous referees for very helpful comments on an earlier draft of this paper. Any remaining errors and omissions are, of course, our own responsibility.

1. For an overview of emprical studies for the US see Heggestadt (1979), Rhoades (1982), Gilbert (1984) and Weiss (1989). The theoretical application of the structure-performance-approach to banking is discussed in Hannan (1991). A problem left open in the literature so far is the basic question, if a model developed for production industries can be applied to a service industry as banking without substantial modifications (see Britton, Clark and Ball, 1992).
2. It is typical for these studies that the conclusions of their empirical analyses are limited, because their database consists of a small number of very large banks in different countries.
3. Features of geographic market delineation in banking and their consequences are reviewed in Wolken (1984).
4. See Gardener and Molyneux (1990) for an excellent treatment of banking markets in Europe, their essential structural differences and long-term development. Frankel and Montgomery (1991) and OECD (1992) give an up-to-date comparison of banking structure and bank performance in large OECD-countries.
5. For effects of interstate banking and market entry on bank profitability in the US see Morris (1984), Clark (1988) and Chong (1991).
6. The five banks are: Creditanstalt-Bankverein, Länderbank, Zentralsparkasse, Erste Österreichische Sparkasse and BAWAG.
7. See Section IV for a short description of database contents, market delineation and a summary of descriptive statistics.
8. For an overview of empirical results for the US see Heggestadt (1979), Rhoades (1982), Gilbert (1984) and Weiss (1989).
9. See Table X for a list of variables.
10. Treating Vienna as one district 85 Austrian banking markets were represented in our analysis.
11. A bank was treated as a regional bank if it has branches in at least 4 and up to 12 districts.
12. Only for small banks operating in 2 or 3 districts we were able to allocate balance sheet totals to these districts using employment figures.
13. Britton, Clark and Ball (1992) identify four baskets of variables essential for catching the basic intentions of the structure-performance-approach: Basic market conditions, market structure, market conduct and performance.
14. Again the calculations of Herfindahl indices are based on balance sheet totals.
15. In addition the cross-section results presented in Section III point to some more possible explanations for a negative impact of concentration on performance.

References

Amiel, D. and L. Froeb (1991) 'Do Firms Differ Much?', *Journal of Industrial Economics*, **39**, 323–331.

Baumol, W. (1991) 'Determinants of Industry Structure and Contestable Market Theory', in D. Greenaway, M. Bleaney and I. Stewart, eds, *Companion to Contemporary Economic Thought*, London and New York: Routledge.

Baumol, W. and R. Willig (1986) 'Contestability: Developments since the Book', *Oxford Economic Papers*, **38**, Supplement, 9–36.

Berger, A. and D. Humphrey (1991) 'The Dominance of Inefficiencies over Scale and Product Mix Economies in Banking', *Journal of Monetary Economics*, **28**, 117–148.

Berger, A. and T. Hannan (1989) 'The Price-Concentration Relationship in Banking', *Review of Economics and Statistics*, **71**, 291–299.

Bourke, Ph. (1989) 'Concentration and other Determinants of Bank Profitability in Europe, North America and Australia', *Journal of Banking and Finance*, **13**, 65–79.

Britton, L., T. Clark, and D. Ball (1992) 'Modify or Extend? The Application of the Structure Conduct Performance Approach to Service Industries', *The Service Industries Journal*, **12**, 43–43.

Bröker, G. (1989) *Competition in Banking*, Paris: OECD.
Calem, P. and G. Carlino (1991) 'The Concentration/Conduct Relationship in Bank Deposit Markets', *Review of Economics and Statistics*, **73**, 268–276.
Chong, B. (1991) 'The Effects of Interstate Banking on Commercial Banks Risk and Profitability', *Review of Economics and Statistics*, **73**, 78–84.
Clark, J. (1988) 'Entry Barries, Market Concentration and Bank Profitability: A Switching Regression Approach', Federal Reserve Bank of Kansas City, Research Working Paper 88–12.
Conti, V. (1992) 'Profitability in Banking: An International Comparison', in V. Conti and M. Maccarinelli, eds, 'Bank Profitability, Capital Adequacy and Optimal Size in Modern Banking: Three Studies', Research Papers in Banking and Finance, Institute of European Finance, Bangor.
Demsetz, H. (1973) 'Industry Structure, Market Rivalry and Public Policy', *Journal of Law and Economics*, **16**, 1–9.
Domowitz, I., G. Hubbard, and B. Petersen (1985) 'The Intertemporal Stability of the Concentration-Margins-Relationship', Federal Reserve Bank of Kansas City, Research Working Paper 85–09.
Frenkel, A. and J. Montgomery (1991) 'Financial Structure: An International Perspective', *Brookings Papers on Economic Activity*, 257–310.
Gardener, E. and Ph. Molyneux (1990) *Changes in Western European Banking*, London: Unwin Hyman.
Gilbert, R. (1984) 'Studies of Bank Market Structure and Competition: A Review and Evaluation', *Journal of Money, Credit and Banking*, **16**, 617–660.
Hancock, D. (1989) 'Bank Profitability, Deregulation and the Production of Financial Services', Federal Reserve Bank of Kansas City, Research Working Paper 89–16.
Hannan, T. (1991) 'Foundations of the Structure-Conduct-Performance Paradigm in Banking', *Journal of Money, Credit and Banking*, **23**, 68–84.
Heggestad, A. (1979) 'Market Structure, Competition and Performance in Financial Industries: A Survey of Banking Studies' in F. Edwards, ed, *Issues in Financial Regulation*, New York.
Hirtle, B. (1991) 'Factors Affecting the Competitiveness of Internationally Active Financial Institutions', *Federal Reserve Bank of New York Quarterly Review*, **16**, 38–51.
Morris, Ch. (1984) 'The Competitive Effects of Interstate Banking', *Federal Reserve Bank of Kansas City Economic Review*.
OECD (1991) *Bank Profitability*, Paris: OECD.
OECD (1992) *Banks under Stress*, Paris: OECD.
Porta, A. (1990), ed, *The Separation of Industry and Finance and the Specialisation of Financial Institutions*, Milan.
Ravenscraft, D. (1983) 'Structure Profit Relationships at the Line of Business and the Industry Level', *Review of Economics and Statistics*, **65**, 22–31.
Rhoades, St. (1982) 'Structure-Performance Studies in Banking: An Updated Summary and Evaluation', Board of Governors of the Federal Reserve System, Staff Studies 119, Washington.
Rhoades, St. and R. Rutz (1982) 'Market Power and Firm Risk: A Test of the "Quiet-Life Hypothesis"', *Journal of Monetary Economics*, **9**, 73–85.
Salinger, M. (1990) 'The Concentration-Margins Relationship Reconsidered', *Brookings Papers on Economic Activity*, Microeconomics Issue, 287–321.
Schmalensee, R. (1985) 'Do Markets Differ Much?', *American Economic Review*, **75**, 341–351.
Schmalensee, R. (1988) 'Industrial Economics: An Overview', *Economic Journal*, **98**, 643–681.
Smirlock, M. (1985) 'Evidence on the (Non) Relationship between Concentration and Profitability in Banking', *Journal of Money, Credit and Banking*, **17**, 69–83.
Steinherr, A. and Ch. Huveneers (1992a) 'On the Performance of Differently Regulated Financial Institutions: Some Empirical Evidence', IRES, Discussion Paper 9221, Louvain.
Steinherr, A. and Ch. Huveneers (1992b) 'Institutional Competition and Innovation: Universal Banking in the Single European Market', in A. Mullineux, ed, European Banking, Oxford: Blackwell.
Weiss, L. (1974) 'The Concentration-Profits Relationship and Antitrust', in H. Goldschmid, H. Mann and J. Weston, eds, *Industrial Concentration: The New Learning*, Boston: Little Brown.
Weiss, L. (1989) 'A Review of Concentration-Price-Studies in Banking', in L. Weiss, ed, *Concentration and Price*, Cambridge and London: MIT Press.

Wolken, J. (1984) 'Geographic Market Delineation: A Review of the Literature', Board of Governors of the Federal Reserve System, Staff Studies 140, Washington.

K. Aiginger and J. Finsinger (eds.), Applied Industrial Organization, 187–203.

Market Structure and Pricing Behaviour in Austrian Manufacturing

CHRISTOPH R. WEISS*
University of Linz, Austria; Visiting scholar: Department of Economics, Harvard University, Cambridge, U.S.A.

Abstract. The paper provides a formal model of price rigidities which is consistent with the observed difference in pricing across industries. The empirical test for a sample of Austrian manufacturing industries confirms the derived propositions. Concentration, inventoriability, export orientation, and disparities in firm size do not influence the price level directly but are shown to have an impact on the sensitivity of prices to demand and cost changes. Cost (demand) changes are less (more) fully transmitted into prices in concentrated industries.

Key words: Oligopoly model, administered prices, econometric price equations, Austrian manufacturing

JEL codes: D4, L11, L60

I. Introduction

The observation that some sectors of the macroeconomy are characterised by sluggish price adjustment to demand shocks, whereas others exhibit rapid price changes, was first made by Means (1935). Means observed that prices of agricultural products have been falling substantially (63 percent) whereas those of agricultural implements only decreased moderately (6 percent). Sectoral differences in pricing behaviour similar to those identified by Means between 1929 and 1933 for the U.S. economy appear to have been operative between 1979 and 1982 as a consequence of the OPEC oil price shock (see Table I). Actual prices of agricultural implements have been sensitive to this cost shock whereas those of agricultural products remained unchanged.

Although a number of theories have been put forward to explain why prices might be inflexible (for a recent survey see Gordon, 1990), "they do not satisfactorily explain why these factors should be so important for, say, the motor vehicle industry but not for textile products" (Allen, 1988, p. 139f). Although Means himself did not provide a formal model to explain the observed differences in firm behaviour, Means' administered pricing hypothesis directed ones attention to the link between industrial market structure and price flexibility. Early formulations of this hypothesis were rather vague and therefore subject to various interpretations. The original approach pursued by Means identified administered pricing industries according to the observed infrequency of price changes. However, beginning with

TABLE I. Relative flexibility of prices versus output (percentage changes)

	1929–33		1979–82		
	Prices	Outputs	Prices (actual)	(real)	Outputs
Agricultural implements	−6	−80	34	7	−41
Motor vehicles	−16	−80	32	5	−31
Cement	−18	−65	27	0	−25
Iron and steel	−20	−83	20	−7	−45
Auto tires	−33	−70	24	−3	−14
Textile products	−45	−30	21	−6	−5
Food products	−49	−14	13	−14	2
Leather products	−50	−20	4	−23	−15
Petroleum products	−56	−20	71	44	−55
Agricultural products	−63	−6	0	−27	5

Source: Andrews and Rausser (1986, p. 416).
Remarks: Real price changes are nominal changes minus core inflation between 1979 and 1982, which was estimated by GNP implicit deflator at 27% for the U.S. economy.

DePodwin and Selden (1963) and Weiss (1966), the hypothesis was increasingly interpreted in a different way. The typical regression model estimated to test for administered prices includes the concentration ratio (or changes in the concentration ratio) as an additional exogenous variable in the reduced form of the cross-section equation for price:

$$\Delta P_i = \beta_1 \Delta C_i + \beta_2 \Delta D_i + \beta_3 CR_i + \varepsilon_i \quad (1)$$

Changes in prices (ΔP_i) in industry *i* are explained in terms of changes in costs (ΔC_i), demand (ΔD_i), and concentration (CR_i). Clearly, this approach focuses on the extent to which prices change rather than the frequency of change. During the last 30 years, this concept has been subject to numerous empirical tests (Weiss, 1966, Phlips, 1971, 1973, Weston and Lustgarten, 1974, Kelton and Weiss, 1989, Jones and Laudadio, 1990). They have yielded ambiguous and conflicting results. The main difficulty in resolving the administered pricing controversy undoubtedly has been the lack of any formal model providing a link between concentration and pricing behaviour in a profit maximising framework.[1]

A first attempt to provide a theory of price rigidities which is consistent with the observed differences across industries was made by Phlips (1980).[2] Utilising a model of an industry comprised of *n* identical firms he concludes, that cost (demand) changes are more (less) fully transmitted into prices in industries with a large number of firms. In terms of Equation (1) we would therefore expect to find that concentration does not influence the price level directly ($\beta_3 = 0$) but has an impact on the sensitivity of prices to cost- and demand fluctuations by affecting the coefficients of the cost and demand variable (β_1 and β_2) respectively. This approach clearly points to the specification error associated with regression models such as Equation (1), aimed at testing the administered pricing hypothesis.[3] Phlips also provides a first econometric test of (and actually finds some empirical support for) this proposition by comparing the regression coefficients in (1) associated with the cost and demand variables in two subsets, which have been identified as industries with "small" ($\leq 50\%$) and "large" concentration ratios respectively.[4]

The present paper extends the Phlips analysis in theoretical as well as empirical aspects. Firstly, in the case of an industry comprised of identical firms, the concentration ratio exactly mirrors the "number-of-firms" effect. In a more general framework, there are two "causes" of concentration in industries: too few firms and significant disparities in firm size. Utilising a multiple leader-follower model puts us in a position to simultaneously investigate the impact of firm size as well as the number of firms on pricing behaviour. In contrast to earlier papers, where the investigation of scale effects has commonly been neglected, firm size is shown to have a substantial influence on pricing decisions in Austrian manufacturing industries.

Secondly, from an econometric point of view the empirical procedure of testing the model could be improved. Phlips himself (1973) argues that the choice of a threshold above which industries are classified as "concentrated" is arbitrary and could have an impact on the derived conclusions. The use of a critical level of concentration as classification criterion does not allow to capture the continuous relationship between concentration and pricing behaviour. The regression analysis which will be applied in the present paper eliminates the necessity of choosing this concentration cut-off point. Furthermore, regression analysis has the advantage to simultaneously consider the impact of additional factors besides concentration which might influence pricing behaviour.[5]

The paper is organised as follows: Section II describes a simple model which illustrates theoretically the impact of concentration on industries pricing behaviour by distinguishing between the number-of-firms and the firms-size effect. After describing the data utilised in Section III, the estimation procedure as well as the empirical results are presented in Section IV. Finally, Section V contains some concluding remarks.

II. The Model

An approach to model pricing behaviour in industries characterised by disparities in firm size is the multiple leader-follower model proposed by Daughety (1990).[6] Consider an industry comprised of m leader firms and n followers, where the followers maximise their profits on the assumption that rival production is fixed (i.e. Cournot conjectural variation). The leaders recognise this behaviour (i.e. they use the followers' best-response function to decide on a profit maximising output level) but let them play Cournot against other leaders. As will be seen below, this model provides a wide range of potential market structures.

To formalise the above reasoning, let the $n + m$ firms in industry produce a homogenous product at a constant marginal cost c; the leaders' output is $mq_L = Q_L$ and the followers produce $nq_F = Q_F$. Total output in industry Q is sold at price p; for convenience, we assume the inverse demand equation to be linear $p = \alpha - \beta Q$ where $\alpha, \beta > 0$. Now consider the profit maximisation problem of a typical follower firm. If the second-order condition for a profit maximum

$$\frac{\partial^2 \pi_F}{\partial q_F^2} < 0$$

is met, the followers profit π_F is maximised if Equation (2) is satisfied.

$$\frac{\partial \pi_F}{\partial q_F} = p(Q) + q_F \frac{\partial p}{\partial q_F} - c = 0 \tag{2}$$

Under the Cournot assumption, which implies that

$$\frac{\partial p}{\partial q_F} = \frac{\partial p}{\partial Q}\frac{\partial Q}{\partial q}\frac{\partial p}{\partial q_F} = \frac{\partial p}{\partial Q}\frac{\partial Q}{\partial q_F} = -\beta,$$

we can manipulate Equation (2) to obtain the reaction function, which records the typical followers profit maximising responses to the aggregate leaders output decisions.

$$\frac{\partial q_F}{\partial Q_L} - \frac{1}{1+n} \tag{3}$$

The reaction curve is known by the leaders and is incorporated into their profit maximising problem. For a typical leader who assumes that all followers act according to (3) and expects all other leaders not to change their output decisions, the conjectural variation is

$$\frac{\partial p}{\partial q_L} = \frac{\partial p}{\partial Q}\frac{\partial Q}{\partial q_L} = \frac{\partial p}{\partial Q}\left[\frac{\partial Q_L}{\partial q_L} + \frac{\partial Q_F}{\partial q_L}\right] = -\beta\frac{1}{1+n}.$$

Incorporating this and the inverse demand function into the first-order condition for a typical leader firm, which is similar to (2), we obtain the leaders output level

$$q_L = \frac{\alpha - c}{\beta(1+m)},$$

whereas the followers output level can now be written as

$$q_F = \frac{\alpha - c}{\beta(1+m)(1+n)} = \frac{1}{1+n}q_L.$$

Clearly sophistication is rewarding for leaders since $q_F < q_L$ and $\pi_F < \pi_L$ under the assumption of identical marginal costs for leaders and followers. Substituting the equation for q_L and q_F into the inverse demand equation and simplifying, we obtain the following price equation.

$$p = \mu\alpha + \tau c \tag{4}$$

$$\mu = \frac{1}{(1+m)(1+n)} \quad \text{and} \quad \tau = \frac{n+m(1+n)}{(1+m)(1+n)}$$

Market price *p* appears as a linear function of the intercept (α) of the inverse demand curve and marginal cost (*c*). For a given number of firms we would expect to find cost changes to have a larger impact on market price than an increase in demand ($\tau > \mu$). This proposition corresponds to the findings of Godley and Nordhaus (1972) for the British manufacturing industry and will be tested empirically in Section IV. Furthermore, Equation (4) casts doubt upon regression analyses in which the concentration ratio appears as an independent variable in addition to demand and cost variables. By way of contrast, market structure influences the price level by affecting the coefficients of the demand and cost variable.

To investigate this relationship in more detail, we explicitly define the concentration ratio (CR_k), which is typically used as a proxy for market structure in empirical work in terms of our previous analysis:

$$CR_{(k=1)} = \frac{q_L}{mq_L + nq_F} = \frac{1+n}{n+m(1+n)}.^{7}$$

It can be seen easily that an increase in the total number of firms ($n + m$) either by increasing the number of small (n) or large firms (m) respectively decreases $CR_{(k=1)}$ as well as the coefficient of the demand variable (μ) while increasing the coefficient of the cost variable (τ). We therefore would expect a positive correlation between μ and $CR_{(k=1)}$ and a negative one between τ and $CR_{(k=1)}$. This conclusion corresponds to the results of Phlips (1980).

However, concentration also changes if the total number of firms in an industry ($n + m$) is fixed but the share of small and large firms varies ("firm size"). Consider the case of an increase in m which is exactly matched by a decrease in n leaving the total number of firms unchanged. The total changes in τ, μ, and $CR_{(k=1)}$ will then be equal to

$$d\tau = \frac{\partial\tau}{\partial m}dm - \frac{\partial\tau}{\partial n}dn = \frac{n-m}{(1+m)^2(1+n)^2} \quad \text{where } d\tau \begin{cases} <0 \text{ if} & m>n \\ =0 \text{ if} & n=m \\ >0 \text{ else} & \end{cases} \tag{5a}$$

$$d\mu = \frac{\partial\mu}{\partial m}dm - \frac{\partial\mu}{\partial n}dn = \frac{m-n}{(1+m)^2(1+n)^2} \quad \text{where } d\mu \begin{cases} >0 \text{ if} & m>n \\ =0 \text{ if} & n=m \\ <0 \text{ else} & \end{cases} \tag{5b}$$

$$dCR_{(k=1)} = \frac{\partial CR_{(k=1)}}{\partial m}dm - \frac{\partial CR_{(k=1)}}{\partial n}dn = -\frac{(1+n)^2+1}{[n+m(1+n)]^2} < 0 \tag{5c}$$

As long as the share of small firms $n/(n+m)$ is above the threshold level of 50% the above drawn conclusions remain unchanged. However, if this share is initially below the critical level we observe a negative relationship between μ and $CR_{(k=1)}$ and a positive one between τ and $CR_{(k=1)}$. Although it seems not very realistic to assume that the number of leaders is equal to the number of followers (or even $m > n$), the threshold value where the relationship between the coefficients of the price equation and concentration changes depends on the special exogenous modifications considered. If we investigate the merger of two initially small firms to one large firm the critical level now lies between 66.6% and 75%.[8]

Irrespective of the precise level of this switch point the model outlined above leads to 4 propositions which can be tested empirically.

1. For a given market structure cost changes have a larger impact on market price than demand fluctuations.
2. Concentration (*CR*) has an impact on prices by influencing the coefficients of the demand and cost variable (τ and μ, respectively). The impact of *CR* on τ is always opposed to the relationship between *CR* and μ.
3. The impact of concentration on the coefficients of the price equation is non-linear[9] and, furthermore, depends on the size distribution of firms in industry. We would expect to find an interaction effect between concentration and firm size when explaining μ and τ respectively.
4. In industries put together by a relatively small share of big firms we would expect to find a negative (positive) relation between the coefficient of the cost (demand) variable and concentration. However, if the share of big firms increases, the impact of concentration on τ (μ) is expected to be positive (negative).

Of course, concentration and disparities in firm size do not fully characterise market structure. The degree of domestic seller concentration will represent an accurate measure of market structure only in industries isolated from *international competition*. In cases where industries face significant import competition or sell a large share of production to more competitive world markets we would expect prices to be closer to competitive levels. International competition is therefore expected to reduce (increase) the sensitivity of firms to demand (cost) changes. *Barriers to entry*, whether against domestic or international competitors, should have the opposite effect. Furthermore, recent work on pricing in macroeconomics emphasises the role of *inventories*. Inventories enable firms to meet part of any short-run fluctuation in demand by altering inventory holdings, rather than by changing prices. Industries characterised by a large share of inventories to output are expected to report a smaller sensitivity of prices to demand changes.

III. Data

The sample for the price, cost, and demand variables cover 17 two-digit manufacturing industries over the period 1974.Q4 to 1988.Q3: (1) metal ore mining;

(2) other mining; (3) stone and clay; (4) glass; (5) chemicals; (6) paper; (7) paper products; (8) wood products; (9) leather; (10) leather products; (11) textiles; (12) clothing; (13) basic metal industries; (14) machinery; (15) transportation equipment; (16) fabricated metals except machinery; (17) electrical products. These industries account for roughly 76% of total industrial production in Austria. More disaggregated data on prices, demand and cost variables are not available for Austrian manufacturing. The cost variable (C_t) in the price equation has been defined as $C_t = (P_t^M M + P_t^W L + P_t^I R_t)/y_t$ where P_t^M is the material price index, M_t is the volume of materials, P_t^W is a composite index including data on wages and salaries; L_t is employment, P_t^I is the price index for investment goods, R_t is the interest rate, and y_t is output.

The variable D_t is proxied by "excess demand": $D_t = -I_t/(y_t - I_t)$, where I_t is net investment in inventory holdings. The dependent variable in the regression analysis is the wholesale price index. Table A-I in Appendix 1 gives some descriptive statistics.

The four firm concentration index based on employment data in 1983 has been obtained from Aiginger (1990, p. 139). In our sample of 17 industries, CR varies between 94.6% and 5.7%, and it exceeds 20% in 10 industries. Therefore, we conclude that our sample consists mainly of industries that are oligopolistic in nature. The capital-output ratio for various industries has been calculated from Hahn (1990). The relation of the volume of exports (or imports) in industry to its output, the proxy variable for firm size, as well as the ratio of inventory holdings to industries output as a proxy for inventoriability has been obtained from the "WIFO Datenbank" and the "Industriestatistik 1983, 2. Teil". Small firms are defined to have between 0 and 500 employees and large firms employ over 500 people.

IV. Evidence

The theoretical model presented suggests a two-step procedure. The parameter values for μ and τ are first estimated for a sample of 17 Austrian manufacturing industries with quarterly time series data. The original data have been transformed to fourth differences in order to obtain stationarity of the series.[10] In a second step, the estimated parameters are used as dependent variables to investigate the impact of concentration, the degree of asymmetry in firm size, international competition, and inventoriability by means of a cross-section analysis.

1. The Price Equation

The availability of data for several industries over a series of years suggests to pool cross-section and time-series data. The estimation procedure applied is the "Cross-sectionally Heteroskedastic and Timewise Autoregressive Model" discussed in Kmenta (1986). Beside the gains in efficiency of the parameter estimates, pooling furthermore has the advantage to make the decision whether each cross-section unit is characterised by the same parameter values for cost- and demand variables on the basis of statistical testing. The test involves a comparison of the residual sum of squares under the null hypothesis that the equal-coefficient restrictions are correct with an alternative specification (the so-called least square dummy variable model), which allows for industry-specific parameter values by the introduction of binary variables. The resulting error sum of squares are compared by means of an F-test.

The estimation results are shown in Table II.

Three different models have been estimated. In the first column all estimated parameters are assumed to be constant over cross-section units. The second column allows to test the hypothesis that only the slope coefficients are equal for all industries and that the intercept differs (covariance model), and the last column refers to the case in which both, the intercept and the slope coefficients differ.

For industry as a whole Table II reports a significant positive effect of both demand and cost changes on the wholesale price index and a positive but insignificant constant term.[11] On a more disaggregated level, we find that there are significant differences in the estimated intercept as well as slope parameters in the various industries, indicated by the two F-ratios. According to Table II, firms react to cost changes in a more systematic way than to demand fluctuations. Economic theory suggests that profit maximisation implies unambiguously an increase in the optimal price when the marginal cost curve shifts upward whereas the result is not so clear in the case of a demand increase. In the latter one the direction of the price change depends on the shape of the marginal cost curve.[12] Accordingly, the coefficient of variation for μ_i (0.825) is approximately 3 times the calculated coefficient of variation for the τ_i parameters (0.280). A comparison of the beta coefficients for the parameters μ_i and τ_i illustrates the heavy weight attributed to cost factors. In model 2 a standard deviation change in ΔD leads to a 0.06 standard deviation change in ΔP whereas this figure in 0,73 in the case of a standard deviation change in ΔC. If industry-specific parameter values are allowed for, the influence of the cost variable decreases (see model 3), although even now, the beta coefficients for ΔC_i exceeds the beta values for ΔD_i in all industries. This result is consistent with our theoretical expectations and with recent econometric work on pricing behaviour indicating, that both, cost and demand elements are important in price setting.[13]

2. Explaining Price Rigidity

The parameter estimates of μ and τ for the various industries (column three in Table II) now puts us in a position to investigate the impact of concentration, and the degree of asymmetry in firm size on μ and τ by means of a cross- section analysis. It is however important to notice, that the dependent variables are themselves estimates with different standard errors, and therefore the assumption of homoskedasticity need no longer be satisfied. This will be taken into account by

TABLE II. The estimation results of the price equation: $\Delta^4 P_{t,i} = \theta_i + \mu_i \Delta^4 D_{t,i} + \tau_i \Delta^4 C_{t,i} + \varepsilon_{t,i}$ for 17 industries

	Model 1			Model 2			Model 3		
	Param.	(t-value)	/Beta-C./	Param.	(t-value)	/Beta-C./	Param.	(t-value)	/Beta-C./
θ	15.580	(1.83)	/–.–/						
θ_1				60.805	(1.21)	/–.–/	16.409	(0.47)	/–.–/
θ_2				41.575	(0.27)	/–.–/	38.612	(0.45)	/–.–/
θ_3				25.486	(1.45)	/–.–/	50.428	(2.92)	/–.–/
θ_4				13.366	(0.14)	/–.–/	4.123	(0.07)	/–.–/
θ_5				13.863	(0.44)	/–.–/	−6.384	(−0.29)	/–.–/
θ_6				58.029	(0.92)	/–.–/	12.566	(0.91)	/–.–/
θ_7				36.068	(2.09)	/–.–/	27.670	(1.64)	/–.–/
θ_8				30.951	(1.45)	/–.–/	−0.964	(−0.05)	/–.–/
θ_9				−17.835	(−0.08)	/–.–/	−33.401	(−0.19)	/–.–/
θ_{10}				9.107	(0.32)	/–.–/	28.376	(1.07)	/–.–/
θ_{11}				8.676	(0.51)	/–.–/	−14.963	(−0.88)	/–.–/
θ_{12}				15.644	(0.74)	/–.–/	−21.599	(−1.06)	/–.–/
θ_{13}				24.652	(0.40)	/–.–/	33.664	(1.95)	/–.–/
θ_{14}				19.693	(0.85)	/–.–/	19.931	(0.82)	/–.–/
θ_{15}				68.498	(1.82)	/–.–/	69.984	(2.59)	/–.–/
θ_{16}				0.089	(0.01)	/–.–/	−9.328	(−0.67)	/–.–/
θ_{17}				−5.798	(−0.23)	/–.–/	0.282	(0.01)	/–.–/
μ	0.499	(6.91)	/0.056/	0.502	(6.92)	/0.056/			
μ_1							19.085	(14.99)	/0.101/
μ_2							17.123	(7.83)	/0.139/
μ_3							13.815	(8.76)	/0.059/
μ_4							42.832	(22.70)	/0.128/
μ_5							72.986	(13.68)	/0.042/
μ_6							93.528	(12.64)	/0.043/
μ_7							90.577	(8.86)	/0.044/
μ_8							36.032	(17.47)	/0.066/
μ_9							6.516	(2.49)	/0.088/
μ_{10}							75.163	(14.24)	/0.074/
μ_{11}							35.562	(22.53)	/0.077/
μ_{12}							38.204	(13.97)	/0.108/
μ_{13}							36.271	(13.26)	/0.087/
μ_{14}							0.263	(3.84)	/0.027/
μ_{15}							8.231	(10.19)	/0.093/
μ_{16}							34.863	(22.17)	/0.051/
μ_{17}							0.389	(2.54)	/0.015/
τ	62.611	(44.52)	/0.734/	62.024	(43.35)	/0.727/			
τ_1							70.942	(25.63)	/0.197/
τ_2							58.031	(10.16)	/0.221/
τ_3							47.952	(12.82)	/0.111/
τ_4							45.089	(25.54)	/0.177/

TABLE II. *Continued*

	Model 1			Model 2			Model 3		
	Param.	(t-value)	/Beta-C./	Param.	(t-value)	/Beta-C./	Param.	(t-value)	/Beta-C./
τ_5							101.976	(41.79)	/0.152/
τ_6							109.976	(62.96)	/0.261/
τ_7							69.201	(19.44)	/0.105/
τ_8							72.113	(22.72)	/0.114/
τ_9							73.891	(12.30)	/0.547/
τ_{10}							63.545	(16.07)	/0.094/
τ_{11}							92.040	(32.93)	/0.151/
τ_{12}							58.468	(10.37)	/0.113/
τ_{13}							36.411	(14.53)	/0.113/
τ_{14}							61.235	(15.84)	/0.157/
τ_{15}							66.558	(14.37)	/0.156/
τ_{16}							73.182	(35.19)	/0.111/
τ_{17}							57.923	(10.38)	/0.079/
DF		983			967			935	
Buse R^2		0.685			0.690			0.947	
R^2		0.678			0.683			0.947	
SEE		0.969			0.824			0.351	
DW		1.792			1.795			1.600	
RHO		0.076			0.076			0.175	
F value:	Model 2 against model 1: 24,63								
	Model 3 against model 2: 136,98								

Remarks: DF is the number of degrees of freedom. The definition of the Buse R^2 is found in Buse (1973), R^2 stands for the correlation between observed and predicted values. SEE labels the standard error of the estimate, DW is the Durbin-Watson statistic and RHO is the correlation coefficient between errors in two subsequent time periods.

the use of an appropriate weighting scheme, along the lines suggested by Amemiya (1978) and Saxonhouse (1977), which attempts to reduce the influence of those observations with a high standard error and to enhance the influence of observations with a low standard error.[14] Results of the weight least squares regression are reported in Table III.

From the weight least squares estimation explaining the variation in the parameter of the cost variable in the price equation (τ) for various industries we find that our theoretical expectations are widely confirmed. Table III suggests a non-linear impact of concentration (CR_4) as well as an interaction effect with firm size (S).[15] At mean values for the variable S and XR ("Export Ratio") we get $\tau = 73.067 + 0.772CR_4 - 0.023(CR_4)^2$. Figure 1 plots this relationship. The coefficient of the cost variable increases moderately with concentration until $CR4$ exceeds 16.78% and decreases subsequently. For the most part, the relationship between τ and CR_4 is negative which corresponds to our theoretical model. Figure 1 furthermore

TABLE III. Cross-section estimates of equation explaining variation in the parameter estimates of the price equation

Dependent variable		Parameter estimates (t-value)		Parameter estimates (t-value)	
		(τ)		(μ)	
Independent variables	Symbol				
(1) Intercept	INT	46.404	(5.01)	69.825	(4.22)
(2) Concentration	CR	–.–		−1.418	(−3.44)
(3) (Concentration)^2	CR^2	−0.023	(−10.32)	0.048	(4.18)
(4) Share of Big Firms	S	–.–		2.395	(4.11)
(5) Export Ratio	XR	0.562	(2.97)	–.–	
(6) Inventoriability	INV	–.–		−195.810	(−7.33)
(7) (2)*(4)	CR*S	0.026	(8.48)	−0.064	(−4.41)
DF			13		11
R^2 (adj.)			0.589		0.705
SEE			15.964		16.387
BPG-χ^2 (DF)			1.228 (3)		3.089 (5)

Remarks: Numbers in parentheses are absolute t-values, computed from heteroskedasticity-consistent standard errors (see White, 1980). DF is the number of degrees of freedom, R^2 (adj.) is the R^2 adjusted for the degrees of freedom, and SEE labels the standard error of the estimate. BPG is the Breusch-Pagan-Godfrey test. The critical value of the chi-square with 3 (5) degrees of freedom in 6.25 (9.24) at the 90% significance level.

illustrates the impact of asymmetries in firm size. If we compute the relationship between τ and CR_4 at the highest value of S observable in the industry sample (*S(maximum)* = 78,57), the coefficient of the cost variable increases for a given level of seller concentration. In this case τ increases with CR_4 up to a critical level of 44,41%. Utilising the minimum of S instead (*S(minimum)* = 12.14) produces a negative relationship between τ and CR_4 over the whole concentration scale.

Industries strongly engaged in international trade are more inclined to follow costs in determining prices than industries in the protected sector, which supports the common view that the competitive threat arising from international trade stimulates competition. A high export ration (*XR*), indicating that firms have themselves adjusted to the pressures of international competition, increases the coefficient of the cost variable in Table III. However, the relation of total volume of trade (exports and imports) in each industry to its output as well as the import ratio did not exercise an significant impact on τ.[16]

With respect to the estimation equation explaining the sensitivity of prices to demand changes, Table III again suggests a significant non-linear impact of concentration. Furthermore, the interaction term between *CR* and *S* is also statistically different from zero and suggests, that prices are less sensitive to demand changes in industries with a large share of big firms. This corresponds to the hypothesis derived from the theoretical model. Figure 2 plots the relationship at mean values for the

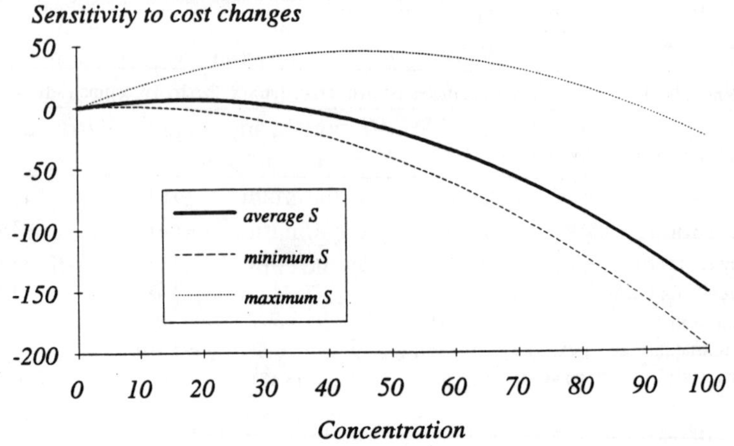

Fig. 1. The relationship between concentration and the sensitivity of prices to cost changes.

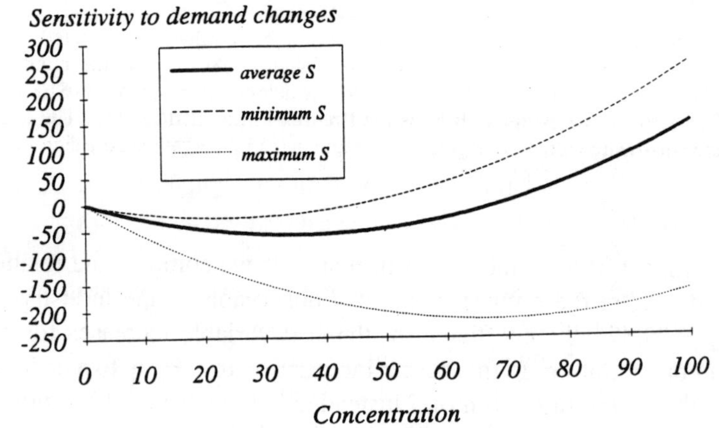

Fig. 2. The relationship between concentration and the sensitivity of prices to demand changes.

variables S and INV ("Inventoriability"): $\mu = 86.881 - 3.318\ CR_4 + 0.048(CR_4)^2$. At mean values of S the coefficient of the demand variable decreases with concentration up to a critical level of 34.56%. In the case of a minimum (maximum) value of S, this threshold value decreases (increases) to 22.86% (67.15%).

For a given value of CR_4 Table III suggests that firm size, despite the negative interaction effect with concentration, has a positive impact on the sensitivity of prices to demand changes. Mills and Schumann (1985) have shown, that small firms use more flexible production technologies than large firms. The increased production flexibility enables them to meet changes in demand by altering production rather than by changing prices. Accordingly, industries overwhelmingly comprised of small firms are c.p. reported with a low coefficient of the demand variable (μ). A similar argument holds for the role of inventories in pricing decisions. In industries where output is inventoriable (i.e. where the costs of storage are low) firms will absorb demand shocks by altering inventory holdings at a given price (c.f. Blinder, 1982). Accordingly, Table III reports a significant negative impact of "Inventoriability" (*INV*) on the sensitivity of prices to demand changes.

In contrast to the first column of Table III the inclusion of the share of exports in industries production did not improve the estimation results. In both equations (column 1 and 2), barriers to entry proxied by the capital-output ratio did not exert an significant impact on the coefficients of the price equation.

V. Summary and Conclusion

Links between the industrial organisation of markets and macroeconomic outcomes are receiving increasing theoretical and empirical attention. In this context, the present paper investigates the relationship between pricing behaviour and structural characteristics of market organisation.

We conclude that there are significant differences in pricing, which can be explained to some extent by industry differences in concentration, export orientation, inventoriability, and disparities in firm size. It should be noted, that the empirical approach chosen in this paper allows other influences on pricing behaviour to be considered simultaneously as well.

Market structure does not influence prices directly but has an impact on the sensitivity of prices to demand and cost changes measured by the parameters of the demand and cost variable in the price equation (μ and τ, respectively). The impact of concentration (*CR*) on both parameters is non-linear and depends on the size distribution of firms in industry. The relationship between *CR* and μ (τ) is positive (negative) in industries put together by a small share of big firms. However, as firm size (*S*) increases, the opposite result is obtained. One therefore has to conclude, that the links between price flexibility and industrial structure are characterised by a complex set of interactions which render the identification of a clear and overriding relationship which has been assumed in the specification of a number of regression models aimed at testing the administered pricing hypothesis.

TABLE AI. Summary statistics of all variables used

Variables	Industry	Mean	Standard deviation	Numbers of Obs.
Price index	metal ore mining	148,540	278,140	58
	other mining	2,996	488,980	
	stone and clay	146,570	142,690	
	glass	32,652	237,950	
	chemicals	34,482	239,850	
	paper	94,565	397,750	
	paper products	63,206	177,120	
	wood products	114,530	128,450	
	leather	166,990	1067,100	
	leather products	107,480	149,580	
	textiles	64,332	243,720	
	clothing	137,060	218,620	
	basic metal	90,213	152,350	
	machinery	105,840	269,690	
	transportation equipment	118,390	214,250	
	fabricated metals	32,262	141,450	
	electrical products	37,265	145,000	
Unit Costs	metal ore mining	1,575	3,782	58
	other mining	−0,493	5,554	
	stone and clay	1,962	2,784	
	glass	0,157	5,764	
	chemicals	0,458	2,154	
	paper	0,812	3,387	
	paper products	0,552	2,162	
	wood products	1,339	1,905	
	leather	2,148	10,648	
	leather products	1,542	1,554	
	textiles	0,900	2,235	
	clothing	1,914	2,127	
	basic metal	1,112	4,429	
	machinery	1,408	3,500	
	transportation equipment	0,852	3,344	
	fabricated metals	0,516	2,173	
	electrical products	0,697	1,893	
Demand	metal ore mining	1,474	7,602	58
	other mining	−0,078	11,914	
	stone and clay	0,246	6,255	

TABLE AI. *Continued*

Variables	Industry	Mean	Standard deviation	Numbers of Obs.
	glass	−0,008	4,391	
	chemicals	0,064	0,843	
	paper	0,017	0,673	
	paper products	0,086	0,708	
	wood products	0,429	2,658	
	leather	1,905	19,702	
	leather products	−0,167	1,437	
	textiles	−0,028	3,160	
	clothing	1,148	4,018	
	basic metal	0,607	3,473	
	machinery	−0,987	150,340	
	transportation equipment	−0,133	16,482	
	fabricated metals	0,205	2,114	
	electrical products	1,261	55,480	
4 Firm Concentration ratio		29,259	21,389	17
Export Ratio		47,444	18,702	17
Share of Big Firms		29,686	17,222	17
Inventoriability		0,276	0,131	17

Notes

* I am indebted to the participants of the Industrial Organization Conference held in Vienna in June 1992 and especially to Helmut Schuster and Karl Aiginger for valuable comments.

1. "... it is not surprising that no clear evidence has emerged from this empirical work, since there is no theoretical reason why the value of the rate of change of prices would be directly influenced by market structure variables" (Encaoua and Geroski, 1986, p. 52).
2. More recently, Allen (1988) shows that a theory of price adjustment where product quality in unobservable and reputation matters may be consistent with these observations as well.
3. Furthermore, this model allows to explain, why concentration affects the flexibility to cost- and demand changes differently (see Table I). The typical regression model (1) does not take this into account.
4. Phlips adopted a concentration ratio of 50% as critical level for Belgium and the Netherlands and a lower figure (40%) for France, since larger countries typically have smaller concentration ratios. Bradburd and Caves (1987) is a more recent example following this approach.
5. In an excellent survey on the impact of industrial organisation on macroeconomics Carlton (1989) observes that "one possible reason why macroeconomics has not paid more attention to industrial organisation is that much of industrial organisation seems fixated on answering how the behaviour of markets differ as industry concentration changes" (p. 911). Especially in the case of a small and open economy (Belgium, The Netherlands, and Austria) the existence of strong international competition is likely to dilute the market power of domestic firms measured by the rate of concentration.
6. Alternatively, one can imagine a model with interfirm cost differences, which also yields an equilibrium with firms of unequal size (Stigler, 1968).
7. In the case of identical firms ($n = 0$) the concentration ratio $CR_{(k} = 1)$ reduces to $1/m$.

8. In this case where we simultaneously vary the total number of firms as well as the share of small and large firms respectively, the relationship between τ and *CR* remains positive as long as the share of small firms is below
$$\frac{1+2m}{1+3m}.$$
This critical level clearly depends on *m* and is equal to 3/4 in the case of *m* = *1* and approaches 2/3 as *m* increases.
9. A non-linear impact of concentration has also been suggested by Bain (1950) and Qualls (1979) by considering the extent of interdependencies between oligopolists. This interdependecy does not exist for firms in competitive industries and for a monopolist or very tighly knit oligopolies where conjectural uncertainties can easily be resolved through collusion. "Moderate concentration ... should tend to give rise to imperfect collusion (and) kinked demand curve conformations ... whereas high concentration should provide an environment conductive to effective collusion or its equivalent" (Bain, 1950, p. 43).
10. The results of the Augmented-Dickey-Fuller Test are reported in Weiss (1993).
11. Since the data have been transformed to first differences, the intercept picks up the effect of any time trend in the original data. Negative values reflect a downward trend in output prices, possibly as a result of technical progress (Domberger, 1979). However, the low statistical significance of the constant term in most industries does not provide evidence for either inflationary or deflationary biases.
12. Gordon (1990) provides a more intuitive explanation of the same issue: "Firms raise price in response to an upward shift in the marginal cost schedule not just because it is optimal in the textbook model, but because they will go bankrupt if cost rises sufficiently in relation to price. There is no such economic necessity of raising price in response to an increase in demand when cost is fixed ..." (p. 1150).
13. For a recent survey of econometric work on industrial pricing see Hay and Morris (1991).
14. Furthermore, the application of the usual formula to calculate sampling variances may well involve an understatement of the true sampling variance. Therefore, the t-ratios in Table III are calculated by using White's (1980) heteroscedastic-consistent covariance matrix estimation to correct the estimates for an unknown form of heteroskedasticity. The Breusch-Pagan-Godfrey test does not reject the null-hypothesis of homoscedasticity at a 90% level of significance in both equations.
15. This corresponds to Ghosal (1989) who finds a non-linear relationship between concentration and price-cost margins.
16. This suggests, that the impact of foreign competition on pricing behaviour will primarily be reflected in exports (cf. Neumann, Böbel, and Haid, 1979).

References

Aiginger, K. (1990) 'Investitionsverhalten und Marktstruktur; Empirische Ergebnisse für Österreich', in B. Gahlen, ed, *Marktstruktur und Gesamtwirtschaftliche Entwicklung*. Berlin *et al.* Springer Verlag.

Allen, F. (1988) 'A Theory of Price Rigidities When Quality is Unobservable', *Review of Economic Studies*, **55**, 139–151.

Amemiya, T. (1978) 'A Note on a Random Coefficient Model', *International Economic Review*, **19**, 793–796.

Andrews, M.S., and G.C. Rausser (1986) 'Some Political Economic Aspects of Macroeconomic Linkages with Agriculture', *American Journal of Agricultural Economics*, **68**, 413–417.

Bain, J.S. (1950) 'Workable Competition in Oligopoly', *The American Economic Review*, **40**, 35–47.

Blinder, A.S. (1982) 'Inventories and Sticky Prices: More on the Microfoundations of Macroeconomics', *The American Economic Review*, **72**, 334–348.

Bradburd, R.M., and R.E. Caves (1987) 'Transaction-Cost Influences on the Adjustment of Industries' Prices and Outputs', *The Review of Economics and Statistics*, **69**, 575–583.

Buse, A. (1973) 'Goodness of Fit in Generalised Least Squares Estimation', *American Statistician*, **27**, 106–108.

Carlton, D.W. (1989) 'The Theory and the Facts of how Markets Clear: Is Industrial Organisation Valuable for Understanding Macroeconomics?', in R. Schmalensee, and R.D. Willig, eds, *Handbook of Industrial Organisation*, Vol 1. Amsterdam, Elsevier Science Publishers B.V.

Daughety, A. (1990) 'Beneficial Concentration', *The American Economic Review*, **80**, 1231–1237.

DePodwin, H., and R.T. Selden (1963) 'Business Pricing Policies and Inflation', *Journal of Political Economy*, **71**, 116–127.

Domberger, S. (1979) 'Price Adjustment and Market Structure', *Economic Journal*, **89**, 96–108.

Encaoua, D., and P. Geroski (1986) 'Price Dynamics and Competition in Five OECD Countries', *OECD Economic Papers*, **6**, 47–76.

Ghosal, V. (1989) 'Market Structure, Price-Cost Margins, and Unionism: An Empirical Note' *Economics Letters*, **29**, 179–182.

Godley, W., and W. Nordhaus (1972) 'Pricing in the Trade Cycle', *Economic Journal*, **82**, 853–882.

Gordon, R.J. (1990) 'What is New-Keynesian Economics', *Journal of Economic Literature*, **28**, 1115–1171.

Hahn, F. (1990) 'Kapitalproduktivität in der Österreichischen Industrie', *WIFO-Working Paper*, Vienna.

Hay, D.A., and D.J. Morris (1991) *Industrial Economics and Organisation, Theory and Evidence*. Oxford, Oxford University Press.

Jones, J.C.H., and L. Laudadio (1990) 'Price Rigidity, Inflation and Market Concentration: Some Canadian Evidence from the 1970s', *Applied Economics*, **22**, 1625–1634.

Kelton, Ch.M.L., and L.W. Weiss (1989) 'Change in Concentration, Change in Cost, Change in Demand, and Change in Price', in L.W. Weiss, ed, *Concentration and Price*. Cambridge, MA, London, England: The MIT Press.

Kmenta, J. (1986) '*Elements of Econometrics*', Second Edition. New York, London: Macmillan Publishing Company.

Means, G.C. (1935) *Industrial Prices and their Relative Inflexibility*, US Senate Document 13, 74th Congress, 1st Session, Washington.

Mills, D.E., and L. Schumann (1985) 'Industry Structure with Fluctuating Demand', *The American Economic Review*, **75**, 758–767.

Neumann, M., I. Böbel, and A. Haid (1979) 'Profitability, Risk, and Market Structure in West German Industries', *Journal of Industrial Economics*, **27**, 227–242.

Phlips, L. (1971) *Effects of Industrial Concentration: A Cross-Section Analysis for the Common Market*. Amsterdam: North-Holland.

Phlips, L. (1973) 'Illusions in Testing for Administered Prices: A Reply', *Journal of Industrial Economics*, **21**, 196–199.

Phlips, L. (1980) 'Intertemporal Price Discrimination and Sticky Prices', *The Quarterly Journal of Economics*, **95**, 525–542.

Qualls, D. (1979) 'Market Structure and the Cyclical Flexibility of Price-Cost Margins', *Journal of Business*, **52**, 305–325.

Saxonhouse, G.R. (1977) 'Regressions from Samples Having Different Characteristics', *The Review of Economics and Statistics*, **59**, 234–237.

Stigler, G.J. (1968) *The Organisation of Industry*. Chicago and London: The University of Chicago Press.

Weiss, C.R. (1993) *Preisrigidität und Marktstruktur: eine Theoretische und Empirische Analyse*, Europäische Hochschulschriften. Frankfurt am Main: Peter Lang.

Weiss, L.W. (1966) 'Business Pricing Policies and Inflation Reconsidered', *Journal of Political Economy*, **74**, 177–187.

Weston, J.F., and S.H. Lustgarten (1974) 'Concentration and Wage-Price Changes', in H.J. Goldschmid, M.H. Mann, and F.J. Weston, eds, *Industrial Concentration: The New Learning*. Boston: Little, Brown.

White, H. (1980) 'A Heteroskedastic-consistent Covariance Matrix Estimator and Direct Test for Heteroskedasticity', *Econometrica*, **48**, 817–838.

K. Aiginger and J. Finsinger (eds.), Applied Industrial Organization, 205–217.

Portfolio Choice, Transactions Costs and Monopoly Power*

MANFRED NEUMANN
Volkswirtschaftliches Institut, Universität Erlangen-Nürnberg, Germany

Abstract. By using optimal stochastic control, where risk can be reduced by appropriate efforts, monopoly power is shown to engender reduced efforts to lower risk. It therefore gives rise to a relatively high ratio of liquid assets to net wealth. Furthermore, a decline in demand is shown to generally elicit increased efforts to reduce risk and thus yields an augmented share of risk bearing assets in the portfolio. These predictions are corroborated by invoking empirical evidence that pertains to West German industries. It thus appears that a capitalist economy is characterized by a built-in-mechanism stabilizing macroeconomic activity. This mechanism, however, is attenuated by monopoly power. That provides an additional rationale for competition policy.

JEL codes: G11, L10.

Key words: Portfolio choice, market structure, firm strategy, market performance.

1. Introduction

This paper was inspired by two observations. First, over the past decades large firms have been criticized for holding excessive hoards of liquid assets or being insufficiently leveraged or both. Second, J.M. Keynes (1936, p. 185) suggested that liquidity preference might prevent the rate of interest from falling such that savings and investments are equalized at the full employment level. These two observations give rise to the question to what extent market power affects portfolio choice and consequently the level of macroeconomic activity.

Since the seminal paper by Tobin (1958) and the Capital Asset Pricing Model portfolio choice has been explained by invoking expected returns and risk, as depicted by the mean and the variance of the portfolio return, respectively. In these models risk has been treated as being exogenous. In a second line of literature risk has been considered to be endogenously determined. On one hand it has been argued that a monopoly, due to its ability to control prices and other terms of contract, is subject to less risk than a firm operating under competitive conditions. On the other hand, as suggested by Caves and Yamey (1971), periodic breakdowns of collusive agreements among oligopolists may raise the variability of returns and

* Helpful comments on previous drafts by Armin Frisch, Rainer Klump, Doris Neuberger, Karl W. Roskamp, and F.A. Schmid are gratefully acknowledged. Jürgen Weigand provided excellent research assistance. Remaining errors are due to the author.

thus give rise to higher risk. The empirical evidence is mixed. Whereas Hurdle (1974) and Sullivan (1978) found support for an inverse relationship between horizontal concentration and risk, Winn (1977) found evidence supporting the Caves/Yamey hypothesis.

A low risk firm can be expected to find it more easy to borrow funds. This 'risk debt hypothesis' suggests a positive association between concentration and the debt/equity ratio in the respective industries if monopoly power entails a lower risk. Actually, just the opposite has been repeatedly observed (Hurdle, 1974; Sullivan, 1974). That is a puzzle unless one accepts the Caves/Yamey hypothesis. As an alternative solution it has been suggested that firms with monopolistic market power might underutilize their borrowing capacity to maintain a high degree of liquidity as a war chest serving as a threat to potential entrants (Neuberger, 1989, p. 185) or as a safeguard for survival (Chamberlain and Gordon 1991). Without denying the possible merit of these arguments, in the present paper an alternative explanation will be submitted which appears to be preferable because it allows for a larger set of testable hypotheses.

The apparent conundrum can be solved, without invoking strategic considerations, by an analysis of a capitalist-entrepreneur maximizing expected utility of consumption who is able to affect risk by incurring transaction costs. Risk can be reduced in particular by gathering information, advertising, negotiating and writing contracts which specify mutual obligations in such a way that little uncertainty is left, and by diversifying business activities which gives rise to increased coordination efforts. Endogeneity of risk thus is an implication of maximizing behavior.

It will be shown, first that monopoly power engenders reduced efforts to lower risk and will thus give rise to a relatively high share of liquid assets and less debt per unit of net wealth in the capitalist's portfolio. Second, a decline in demand is shown to generally elicit increased efforts to reduce risk and thus yields an augmented share of risk bearing assets in the portfolio. This built-in stabilizing mechanism, however, is attenuated by monopoly power. These tendencies will be derived theoretically and subsequently are shown to be borne out by empirical evidence.

The rest of the paper is organized as follows. The model is set out in Section 2. In Sections 3–5 comparative static results are given regarding the determination of transaction costs and the ensuing level of risk, the composition of the portfolio and its changes upon shifts of demand. In Section 6 some empirical evidence is given supporting the theory advanced in the paper.

2. The Model

Consider a representative capitalist-entrepreneur who expects an annual return R from which c is consumed. The net wealth $b = k + m$ is composed of capital k, the return to which is subject to risk, and riskless assets m, the value of which may be positive or negative. Hence, in principle, the capitalist under consideration may be a creditor or a debtor, respectively. As entrepreneur he will ordinarily be a debtor. Let $k = \lambda b$, where $\lambda \geq 0$. If $\lambda > 1$ the capitalist-entrepreneur incurs debt and thus offers a riskless asset to other people who are more risk averse but disregard the risk of bankruptcy. Ordinarily the capitalist pays interest on his borrowings or receives interest if $\lambda < 1$. Simplifying, the interest rate on risk-free assets is subsequently assumed to be zero.

The expected annual return depends on capital invested such that $R(k)$ is strictly concave with

$$\beta := \frac{kR'(k)}{R(k)} < 1$$

where β depends, first, on decreasing returns, and, second, on the elasticity of demand with respect to the price of the commodity sold. Ceteris paribus, a small price elasticity and, for that matter, a small coefficient β signifies a high degree of monopoly power and vice versa. In order to quantify the impact of monopoly power β shall be treated as an exogenous variable. For the case of a constant price elasticity of demand the relationship between that elasticity and β is illustrated by an example in Appendix A.

The capitalist-entrepreneur is assumed to be a Cournot oligopolist. The price elasticity, as seen by the individual seller, is $e = \eta / H$ where H is the Herfindahl index of horizontal concentration, and η is the price elasticity of market demand. Hence β is affected by both H and η.

Wealth accumulation shall be depicted by a stochastic differential equation

$$\mathrm{d}b = [(1-\tau)\,R(\lambda b) - c)]\,\mathrm{d}t + \sigma(\tau)\,\lambda b\,\mathrm{d}z \qquad (1)$$

The first term on the right hand side is the expected increase in wealth where expectations are predicated on current informations. In the second term, which depicts the effect of uncertainty, $z(t)$ is a Wiener process, and $\sigma(\tau)$ is the standard deviation of the rate of change of $b(t)$.[1]

The standard deviation, which is a convenient measure of risk can be affected by efforts which give rise to transaction costs. Transaction costs will be depicted as a fraction $\tau := T/R$ of the expected portfolio return. Let $\sigma(\tau)$ be an inverse function of τ with $\sigma'(\tau) < 0$ and $\sigma''(\tau) > 0$. Furthermore define the elasticity $\gamma := -\tau\sigma'(\tau)/\sigma(\tau)$. If no efforts would be made to reduce risk $\sigma(0) = \sigma_0$ is a positive constant. Although, in principle, σ may depend also on β, as explained in the introduction, in view of the inconclusive evidence regarding the influence of market power on risk, σ shall be assumed to depend solely on τ.

The capitalist-entrepreneur is assumed to maximize expected utility by selecting time paths of consumption $c(t)$, the ratio of risk-bearing capital to net wealth. $\lambda(t) := k(t)/b(t)$, and the ratio of transaction costs to expected returns, $\tau(t)$. We thus have to solve

$$\max_{\{c(t),\lambda(t),\tau(t)\}} E_0 \int_0^\infty u(c)\,\exp(-rt)\,\mathrm{d}t$$

subject to the stochastic differential equation (1).

The instantaneous utility function is assumed to obey

$$u(c) = \frac{1}{1-\varepsilon}\, c^{1-\varepsilon}$$

with $u'(c) > 0$ and $u''(c) < 0$, the coefficient ε being a measure of relative risk aversion.

The problem can be solved by using the stochastic Maximum Principle (see Appendix B). At a steady state of expected values of the state variable b and the controls c, λ, and τ the following equations hold,

$$c = (1-\tau)\, R(\lambda b) \tag{2}$$

$$\lambda = \frac{(1-\tau)\, R(\lambda b)/(\lambda b)}{\varepsilon \sigma^2} \tag{3}$$

$$\frac{1-\tau}{\tau} = \frac{1}{\beta\gamma} \tag{4}$$

$$r = \frac{1}{2}\,\frac{\varepsilon+1}{\varepsilon}\left[\frac{(1-\tau)\, R'(\lambda b)}{\sigma}\right]^2 \tag{5}$$

Among these equations, (3) corresponds to the well-known relationship (Kamien and Schwartz, 1981) originally developed by Merton (1969) for a case where the expected rate of return on risk-bearing capital is constant and thus average and marginal rates of return are identical.[2] As usual, according to equation (3), the ratio of risky capital to net wealth decreases with the level of risk, as depicted by σ, and the coefficient of risk aversion, ε.

Equation (5) says that upon a rise of the rate of interest which is used to discount future utility the expected marginal return to the risky asset is raised. That engenders a reduction of $k = \lambda b$, due to the strict concavity of $R(k)$.

3. Transaction Costs and Monopoly Power

According to equation (4) the ratio of transaction costs to the expected return, τ, depends solely on β. Differentiation yields

$$\frac{\beta}{\tau}\,\frac{\mathrm{d}\tau}{\mathrm{d}\beta} = \frac{1}{\frac{\tau}{\gamma}\left(\beta - \frac{\mathrm{d}\gamma}{\mathrm{d}\tau}\right)}\,.$$

Hence, $\mathrm{d}\tau/\mathrm{d}\beta > 0$, if $\beta > \mathrm{d}\gamma/\mathrm{d}\tau$, where $\mathrm{d}\gamma/\mathrm{d}\tau \leq 0$ is a sufficient condition. Thus if γ, i.e., the elasticity of σ with respect to τ, is constant or decreases with increasing transaction costs the ratio τ is positively associated with β, and, for that matter, with the price elasticity of demand. The assumption $\mathrm{d}\gamma/\mathrm{d}\tau \leq 0$ appears to be reasonable since in this case increasing transaction costs exert a non-increasing effect on risk. That is in line with the assumption that the efforts to reduce risk are subject to the law of diminishing returns.

Since the price elasticity of demand is inversely related to the degree of monopoly power, and $\gamma > 0$ we arrive at

Proposition 1: Under the given assumptions, in particular if $\beta > \mathrm{d}\gamma/\mathrm{d}\tau$, increasing monopoly power yields a lower ratio of transaction costs to expected return and hence a higher level of risk.

4. Investment and Liquidity

Combining equation (3) and (5) yields

$$\lambda = \frac{A}{\varepsilon\sigma(\tau)\beta}, \quad A := \left(\frac{2r\varepsilon}{\varepsilon+1}\right)^{1/2} \tag{3'}$$

and, consequently

$$\frac{\partial\lambda}{\partial\beta} = -\frac{A}{\varepsilon\sigma\beta^2}\left(1 - \gamma\frac{\beta}{\tau}\frac{\mathrm{d}\tau}{\mathrm{d}\beta}\right) \tag{6}$$

Notice that if no efforts are undertaken to reduce risk $\sigma(0) = \sigma_0$ is exogenous. In that case λ is inversely related to β, monopoly power causing a relatively high share of risk bearing assets and a low share of liquid assets in the portfolio. Hence, efforts to reduce risk are crucial for the influence of β and λ. If the efforts to reduce risk are sufficiently strong such that

$$\gamma\frac{\beta}{\tau}\frac{\mathrm{d}\tau}{\mathrm{d}\beta} > 1$$

it follows that $\partial\lambda/\partial\beta > 0$. That yields

Proposition 2: If efforts to reduce risk by incurring transaction costs are sufficiently strong an increase in competition, i.e., less monopoly power, gives rise to a higher share of risk bearing assets in the portfolio.

Whether the effects which enhance investments in risk-bearing assets are sufficiently strong can ultimately be assessed only by empirical investigations.

5. Changes in Demand

Shifts of the demand curve may change the price elasticity of demand at a given price level. In particular, if the demand schedule shifts to the left price elasticity of demand may increase, as can be seen by looking at Figure 1. In the depicted case of a linear demand curve price elasticity of demand at p_0 increases from PB/AP to QD/CQ.

In the case of a Cournot oligopoly, which has been assumed to prevail, price elasticity as seen by the seller is $e = \eta/H$ where η is the price elasticity of market demand and H is the Herfindahl index of horizontal concentration. Therefore, a shift of the demand curve to the left which raises η, translates into a change of e which is larger the smaller the Herfindahl index of concentration. That lead up to

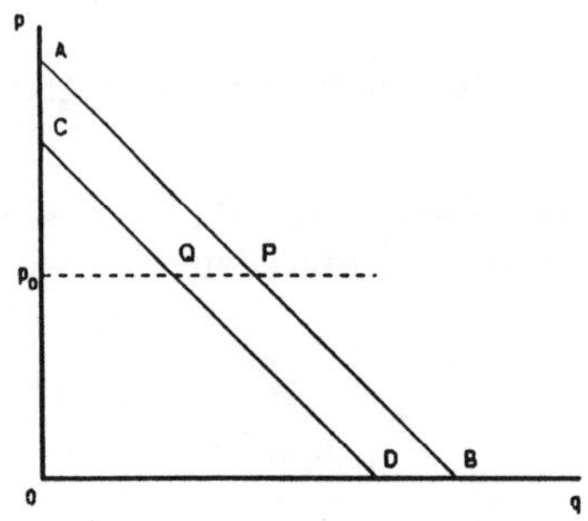

Fig. 1.

Proposition 3: Assuming that $\partial\lambda/\partial\beta > 0$, upon a shift of the demand schedule to the left, a low Herfindahl index of concentration yields a comparatively large increase of e, and for that matter also an increase of β. Hence λ increases more than at a higher degree of concentration.

Therefore, any increase in liquidity holdings which in a recession may occur because risks may generally be considered to be higher, is dampened by changes in β. The dampening is the stronger the less monopoly power prevails.

According to Proposition 3 a competitive economy is characterized by a built-in stabilizing mechanism. If demand decreases in a recession the share of risk-bearing assets in the portfolios of capitalist-entrepreneurs tends to increase which gives a boost to investment. This stabilizing mechanism is weakened, however, by monopolistic market power and may even degenerate into a destabilizing process if efforts to reduce risk are too weak or even absent.

6. Empirical Evidence

Whether more competition actually yields a higher ratio of risk-bearing assets to net wealth will be checked by looking at data for 16 German manufacturing industries, as regularly published by the Deutsche Bundesbank. The industries are listed in Appendix C.

The ratio of risk bearing assets to net wealth, λ, is depicted by the ratio of non-financial assets (Sachanlagen) to net wealth (Eigenmittel). In 1989, for all but one industry this ratio turned out to exceed one. To capture market structure the Herfindahl index H and the cumulative market share of the three largest firms, $C3$, have been used for 1989. For the whole period before 1989 for which data are available, i.e., 1976–1988, $C6$ had to be used since neither the Herfindahl index nor $C3$ is available for every year. Horizontal concentration, as depicted by these coefficients, is assumed to convey monopolistic market power.[3]

It is furthermore assumed that the comparative static results derived from the simplified model of a representative capitalist-entrepreneur come sufficiently near

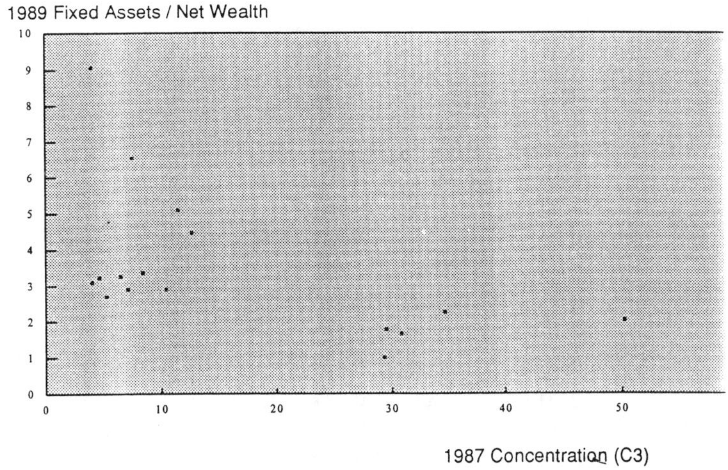

Fig. 2.

TABLE I. Logarithm of the ratio of non-financial assets to net wealth in 1989 as dependent on the logarithm of H and $C3$ in 1987 for 16 industries (t-ratios in parentheses).

Constant	log H	log $C3$	R^2
3.95	−0.49	–	0.326
(3.55)	(2.58)	–	
2.28	–	−0.48	0.631
(8.67)		(4.65)	

to relationships arising in the real world under far more complex conditions. In particular it is assumed that despite the separation of ownership and control in modern corporations the interests of owners are heeded by the respective management.

Portfolio Choice

To give a first impression of the portfolio choice observed the ratio λ of non-financial assets to net wealth of the individual industries of 1989 is regressed on the Herfindahl index and $C3$ of 1987 for the respective industries.[4] As suggested by the above scatter diagram (Figure 2) the relationship between λ and $C3$ appears to be a double logarithmic one. The regression analysis yielded results summarized in Table I.

In accordance with theoretical predictions derived above for both measures of concentration, the ratio of non-financial assets to net wealth is inversely related to

TABLE II. Ratio of the logarithm of non-financial assets to net wealth, as dependent on the logarithm of $C6$, 1976–1988.

Year	Coefficient	t-ratio	R^2
1976	−0.18	3.34	0.50
77	−0.20	3.69	0.553
78	−0.20	3.48	0.524
79	−0.22	2.66	0.391
80	−0.23	4.10	0.546
81	−0.20	3.37	0.447
82	−0.20	3.22	0.425
83	−0.20	2.88	0.371
84	−0.23	3.28	0.435
85	−0.24	3.06	0.400
86	−0.42	3.04	0.398
87	−0.42	3.12	0.409
88	−0.44	3.37	0.448
Pooled ($N = 196$)	−0.26	10.49	0.362*

concentration.

The corresponding results for the period 1976–1988, using $C6$, are given in Table II.

Again, we find a significantly inverse relationship between concentration and the ratio of non-financial assets to net wealth. This relationship implies that indebtedness, i.e., the ratio of net debt to net wealth, decreases with increasing concentration. Here, again, is the puzzle alluded to above. It can be solved by reference to the advanced theory which allows for a negative impact of concentration on the share of risk bearing capital in the portfolio.

Liquidity Preference under Changing Demand

If, upon a shift of the demand curve to the right, price elasticity of demand declines both output and price increase. If the output of an individual industry has risen relatively to the industry average a relative decline in the price elasticity of demand and thus of the ratio of fixed assets to net wealth should be expected. Conversely, decreasing relative output should be accompanied with an increasing ratio of fixed assets to net wealth. This effect should be expected to decrease with increasing monopoly power.

The first check of these implications of the theory was undertaken by regressing the logarithm of fixed assets to net wealth on the logarithm of the ratio of net output of the individual industry to the net output of all manufacturing industries in Germany, $Q_{\mathrm{it}}/\bar{Q}_{\mathrm{t}}$. The impact of monopolistic market power can then be captured

TABLE III. Relative Output as determining the ratio of non-financial assets to net wealth, 1976–1988, $N = 196$, (t-ratios in parentheses).

Constant	$\log Q_{it}/\bar{Q}_t$	$\log Q_{it}/\bar{Q}_t \times \log C6$	R^2	DW
0.88	−1.07	–	0.206	1.869
(13.39)	(6.91)			
0.89	–	−0.37	0.207	1.859
(13.81)		(6.94)		

by an interaction variable $\log Q_{it}/\bar{Q}_t \times \log C6$. The results are given in Table III.[5]

As $\partial \log \lambda / \partial \log (Q_{it}/\bar{Q}_t) < 0$ increasing demand yields a lower λ. Since $\partial^2 \log \lambda / \partial \log (Q_{it}/\bar{Q}_t)\, \partial \log C6 < 0$ the absolute rate of decline is larger if concentration is higher. Conversely, if demand decreases the ensuing increase of λ becomes weaker if horizontal concentration is higher. The theoretical predictions arc thus fully borne out by the evidence.[6]

An alternative test runs as follows. Starting from the price-cost margin $(p - c)/p = 1/e =: m$ and assuming that marginal costs are identical with average variable costs one obtains the ratio of revenue over variable costs $pq/cq =: S/C = 1/1 - m$. Differentiating with respect to time yields

$$\frac{\dot{S}}{S} - \frac{\dot{C}}{C} = -\frac{\dot{e}}{e} \frac{1}{e - 1}$$

Hence $\dot{S}/S - \dot{C}/C \geq 0$ as $\dot{e} \leq 0$. Whether the price elasticity of demand has decreased or increased can thus be assessed by looking at the difference of the rates of changes of revenues and variable costs. Then, in accordance with the advanced theory one expects the ratio of fixed assets to net wealth to decrease if $\dot{S}/S - \dot{C}/C > 0$ and vice versa. Again, this effect will bc rcinforced to decrease if $\dot{S}/S - \dot{C}/C > 0$ and vice versa. Again, this effect will be reinfored or weakened, respectively, by monopoly power. For the test, variable costs have been identified with the sum of wages and expenditures for intermediate input. The results are given in Table IV, which confirms the results of the regression shown in Table III.[7] The theory thus appears to stand up quite well to empirical testing.

7. Conclusion

It has been shown, first, that in accordance with theoretical predictions derived from a model of stochastic optimization, in West German manufacturing industries from 1976 to 1989, the ratio of risk bearing assets to net wealth, and consequently leverage, was inversely related to horizontal concentration. Second, upon an increase in demand in a particular industry the ratio of risky assets to net wealth decreased, and it increased if demand declined. Hence, the economy was character-

TABLE IV. Changes of the price elasticity of demand in the ratio of non-financial assets to net wealth, 1976–1988, (t-ratios in parentheses), $N = 196$.

Constant	G	$G \times \log C6$	R^2
-0.13×10^{-4}	-0.82	-	0.048
(0.003)	(3.12)		
-0.78×10^{-4}		-0.22	0.042
(0.018)		(2.92)	

$G := \Delta \log S - \Delta \log C$

ized by a built-in-mechanism stabilizing macroeconomic activity. This mechanism, however, is shown to be attenuated by monopoly power.

Finally it may be suggested that the analysis of factors determining the ratio of physical assets to net wealth should be expected to apply as well to the ratio of intangible capital, as created by research and development, to net wealth.

Appendix A

Let $R = pq - wl$, where

$p = q^{-1/e}$ is the inverse demand schedule, as seen by the seller ($e > 1$)

$q = k^{\alpha} l^{1-\alpha}$ is output, depending on capital k and labor l

w is the exogenous wage rate.

A profit maximizing choice of labor input implies

$$\left(1 - \frac{1}{e}\right) (1 - \alpha)\, p(k/l)^{\alpha} = w$$

hence

$$l = \left[\frac{(1 - 1/e)(1 - \alpha)\, p}{w}\right]^{\frac{1}{\alpha}} k$$

and

$$R = \left\{\frac{\frac{1}{e} + \alpha\left(1 - \frac{1}{e}\right)}{\left(1 - \frac{1}{e}\right)(1 - \alpha)}\right\} w \left\{\frac{\left(1 - \frac{1}{e}\right)(1 - \alpha)\, p}{w}\right\}^{\frac{1}{\alpha}} k\,. \tag{i}$$

From $p = q^{-1/e}$ and $q = k^{\alpha} l^{1-\alpha}$ one obtains

$$p = \left\{ k^{-\frac{1}{e}} \left[\frac{\left(1-\frac{1}{e}\right)(1-\alpha)}{w} \right]^{-\frac{1-\alpha}{\alpha}\frac{1}{e}} \right\}^{\frac{1}{1+\frac{1-\alpha}{\alpha}\frac{1}{e}}}$$

Substitute into (i) to get

$$R = Dk^{\beta} \tag{ii}$$

where

$$D := \left\{ \frac{1}{e} + \alpha \left(1 - \frac{1}{e}\right) \right\} \left[\frac{\left(1-\frac{1}{e}\right)(1-\alpha)}{w} \right]^{\frac{1-\alpha}{\alpha}\beta}$$

$$\beta := 1 - \frac{1}{\alpha e + (1-\alpha)} = 1 - \frac{1}{1-\alpha(1-e)} < 1$$

Thus $\beta(e)$ with $\beta'(e) > 0$.

Appendix B

The current value Hamiltonian is (Malliaris and Brock, 1982; Neumann, 1989)

$$H = u(c) + y[(1-\tau)\, R(\lambda b) - c] + \tfrac{1}{2}\, \frac{\partial y}{\partial b}\, [\sigma(\tau)\, \lambda b]^2 .$$

Necessary conditions for maximizing H with respect to the controls are

$$\frac{\partial H}{\partial c} = u'(c) - y = 0 \tag{i}$$

$$\frac{\partial H}{\partial \lambda} = y(1-\tau)\, R' b + \frac{\partial y}{\partial b}\, (\sigma b)^2\, \lambda = 0 \tag{ii}$$

$$\frac{\partial H}{\partial \tau} = -yR + \frac{\partial y}{\partial b}\, (\lambda b)^2\, \sigma\sigma' = 0 \tag{iii}$$

Second order conditions are satisfied by assumption.

Optimality requires furthermore

$$(1/\mathrm{d}t)\, E_0\, \mathrm{d}y = ry - \partial H/\partial b = y \left[r - (1-\tau)\, R' - \frac{b}{y}\, \frac{\partial y}{\partial b}\, (\sigma\lambda)^2 \right] \tag{iv}$$

Equations (ii) and (iii) yield (3) and (4), respectively.

From (i) one obtains $\mathrm{d}y = \mathrm{d}[u'(c)] = u''\, \mathrm{d}c + (1/2)\, u'''(\mathrm{d}c)^2$ by a Taylor expansion. Since the optimal c depends on b we have $c(b)$, and, again by a Taylor expansion, $\mathrm{d}c = c'\, \mathrm{d}b + (1/2)\, c''(\mathrm{d}b)^2$. Using Ito's lemma to calculate $(\mathrm{d}c)^2$ and $(\mathrm{d}b)^2$ yields

$$dy = u'' \, dc + (1/2) \, u'''[c'\sigma\lambda b]^2 \, dt \, .$$

Insert into (iv) to find that at a steady state, i.e., at $E_0 \, dc/dt = 0$,

$$r - (1-\tau) \, R'\lambda - \frac{b}{y} \frac{\partial y}{\partial b} (\sigma\lambda)^2 - (1/2) \, (u'''/u') \, [c'\sigma\lambda b]^2 = 0 \, .$$

At a steady state, $c = (1-\tau) \, R(\lambda b)$ and (i). Hence,

$$\frac{b}{y} \frac{\partial y}{\partial b} = \frac{cu''}{u'} \frac{b}{c} \frac{\partial c}{\partial b} = -\varepsilon \frac{(\lambda b) \, R'}{R} = -\varepsilon\beta \, .$$

Substituting into (v) and using $u'(c) = c^{-\varepsilon}$, $u''(c) = -\varepsilon c^{-(\varepsilon+1)}$, and $u'''(c) = \varepsilon(\varepsilon+1) \, c^{-(\varepsilon+2)}$ yields equation (5).

Appendix C

Chemie
Herstellung von Kunststoffwaren
Gewinnung und Verarbeitung von Steinen und Erden
Eisenschaffende Industrie
Nichteisen-Metall-Industrie Stahl- und Leichtmetallbau
Maschinenbau
Straßenfahrzeugbau
Elektrotechnische Industrie
Herstellung von Eisen-, Blech- und Metallwaren
Holzbearbeitung
Holzverarbeitung
Papier und Pappe verarbeitende Industrie
Textilgewerbe
Bekleidungsgewerbe
Ernährungsgewerbe

Notes

1. Employing a geometric Wiener process implies that returns are assumed to be lognormally distributed. The underlying presumption that uncertainty can be depicted by a probability distribution has been questioned by Knight (1921) who distinguished risk from genuine uncertainty. Investment decisions are generally subject to genuine uncertainty. According to this view, to which Keynes (1937, pp. 213–14) emphatically subscribed, each individual may be holding differing views about the future, some being very optimistic, others less so or even pessimistic. Yet, presumably these different individual states of confidence are normally distributed within the population. This distribution can then be captured by invoking the heuristic figure of a representative capitalist.
2. It will be noticed that in the case of the present paper the Separation Theorem of financial economics, according to which the composition of the portfolio is independent of the level of wealth, does no longer hold. As the average return to capital decreases with an increasing level of wealth the ratio λ decreases as well, given the risk and some risk aversion.

3. This assumption appears to be well founded in view of previous studies; Neumann, Böbel, Haid, (1979, 1985).
4. All equations have been estimated by OLS.
5. In the second equation log $Q_{it}/\bar{Q}_t$ has been deleted because his variable is almost perfectly correlated (+0.97) with log $Q_{it}/\bar{Q}_t \times$ log $C6$. Thus reliable estimates are not feasible.
6. Since pooling cross-section and time series data may engender auto-correlation of residuals the results have been double-checked by using the maximum likelihood procedure suggested by Beach and McKinnon (1978). The coefficients associated with the explanatory variables remained statistically significant and turned up with the same signs and in the same order of magnitude as with OLS.
7. Again, since G and $G \times$ log $C6$ are highly correlated (+0.98), G has been deleted from the second equation.

References

Beach, C. and J. McKinnon (1978), 'A Maximum Likelihood Procedure for Regression with Autocorrelated Errors', *Econometrica* **46**, 51–58.

Caves, R.E. and B.S. Yamey (1971), 'Risk and Corporate Rates of Return: Comment', *Quarterly Journal of Economics* **85**, 513–17.

Chamberlain, T.W. und M.J. Gordon (1991), 'The Financial Consequences of Monopoly Power', *The Manchester School* **59**, 244–256.

Deutsche Bundesbank (1979), *Monatsberichte der Deutschen Bundesbank*, November 1979 ff., Frankfurt a.M.

Hurdle, G. (1974), 'Leverage, Risk, Market Structure and Profitability', *Review of Economics and Statistics* **56**, 478–85.

Kamien, M.I. and N.L. Schwartz (1981), *Dynamic Optimization*, New York: Elsevier (North Holland).

Keynes, J.M. (1936), *The General Theory of Employment, Interest, and Money*, London: Macmillan.

Keynes, J.M. (1937), 'The General Theory of Employment', *Quarterly Journal of Economics* **51**, 209–23.

Knight, F. (1921), *Risk, Uncertainty and Profit*, Boston and New York: Houghton Mifflin.

Malliaris, A.G. and W.A. Brock (1982), *Stochastic Methods in Economics and Finance*, Amsterdam: North Holland.

Merton, R.C. (1969), 'Lifetime Portfolio Selection under Uncertainty: The Continuous-Time Case', *Review of Economics and Statistics* **51**, 247–57.

Neuberger, D. (1989), *Finanzstruktur, Wettbewerb und Kapitalakkumulation*, Frankfurt a.M. und New York: Campus Verlag.

Neumann, M. (1989), 'Market Size, Monopoly Power and Innovations under Uncertainty', in D.B. Audretsch, L. Sleuwaegen, and H. Yamawaki (eds.), *The Convergence of International and Domestic Markets*, Amsterdam: Elsevier (North Holland).

Neumann, M., I. Böbel, and A. Haid (1979), 'Profitability, Risk, and Market Structure in West German Industries', *Journal of Industrial Economics* **27**, 227–42.

Neumann, M., I. Böbel, and A. Haid (1985), 'Domestic Concentration, Foreign Trade and Economic Performance', *International Journal of Industrial Organization* **3**, 1–19.

Statistisches Bundesamt (1979), *Statistisches Jahrbuch für die Bundesrepublik Deutschland*, various issues, Stuttgart-Mainz: Verlag Kohlhammer.

Sullivan, T.G. (1974), 'Market Power, Profitability and Financial Leverage', *Journal of Finance* **29**, 1407–14.

Sullivan, T.G. (1978), 'The Cost of Capital and the Market Power of Firms', *Review of Economics and Statistics* **60**, 209–17.

Tobin, J. (1985), 'Liquidity Preference as a Behaviour Towards Risk', *Review of Economic Studies* **25**, 165–86.

Winn, D.N. (1977), 'On the Relation Between Rates of Return, Risk and Market Structure', *Quarterly Journal of Economics* **91**, 1157–63.

K. Aiginger and J. Finsinger (eds.), Applied Industrial Organization, 219–238.

Private and Public Sector Regulation of Competitively Tendered Contracts

SIMON DOMBERGER and DAVID HENSHER*
Graduate School of Business, University of Sydney, Australia

Abstract. This paper addresses two contractual issues using a sample of competitively tendered contracts for cleaning services. First, the paper considers the characteristics that distinguish private from public sector organisations in their methods of selection and regulation of contractors. Secondly, the paper examines the perceived effectiveness of such regulatory mechanisms in terms of compliance with contract specifications and overall assessment of quality. Econometric analysis reveals that private sector organisations differ from their public sector counterparts in the selection procedures of contractors. Moreover, significant differences emerge in the apparent efficacy of a range of regulatory instruments in assuring contractual performance.

Key words: competitive tendering, contracts, outsourcing

JEL-Codes: L33, L50, L84

Introduction

The last decade has witnessed widespread reforms of the economic activities undertaken by the public sector in many industrialised countries and, particularly, in Australia, the UK and the USA (see for example Savas, 1987). Underlying these reforms, which include privatisation and deregulation, is the belief that improved public sector performance requires a commercial outlook and a managerial culture. Private sector modes of operation are increasingly being viewed as a reference or benchmark for their public sector counterparts. This is no less true of the policy of competitive tendering and contracting out.

The policy involves putting out to competitive tender activities and services previously performed exclusively in-house by the relevant public sector agency. It has been singularly successful in reducing the costs of provision, with financial savings typically in the region of 20–25%, and sometimes even greater (see Domberger *et al.*, 1986 and Hensher, 1989). Although some concerns have been expressed over the quality of service delivery under private modes of provision, the evidence on this issue is by no means clear cut. But it is evident that public sector agencies are having to behave more commercially, to optimise with respect to contractor selection, performance monitoring, and contract enforcement. In this respect they are having to take an increasingly strategic approach to the fundamental "make or buy" decision, in effect to mimic private sector behaviour.

In this paper we compare the approach taken by private and public sector organisations to competitive tendering and contracting. Specifically, we examine the characteristics that distinguish contracts let by the private sector from those let by public sector organisations. We then analyse, by means of an econometric analysis, the effectiveness of various instruments that are used to regulate contracts and safeguard performance. The paper is organised as follows. Sections I and II outline, respectively, the theoretical and empirical framework of the analysis. Section III discusses the data and econometric methods used for estimation and section IV reports the estimation results. Finally section V concludes with a discussion and assessment of our findings.

I. Theoretical Analysis of Competitively Tendered Contracts

Contracting out the supply of goods and services involves a two-step decision process. The first is whether to "make or buy"; the second is how to structure the contract so that performance will be sustained over its lifetime. The former decision involves a straightforward comparison of costs; the latter is more subtle and requires consideration of four essential elements. First, specifications of the service or product will need to be determined, together with the design of the competitive tendering mechanism that will be used to identify potential operators.[1]

The second element, the selection of the winning bid, turns out to be a more complicated decision than would appear at first sight. For example, selecting the lowest bidder in a sealed tender auction can sometimes result in serious performance problems after the contract is awarded. This appeared to be the case with some early hospital cleaning contracts in the UK (see Domberger *et al.*, 1987, for further discussion).

Third, to ensure contract compliance the supplier will have to be monitored during the contract term. This requires collecting *and* interpreting information which can be used to determine whether the specified goods/services are being delivered. Finally, to correct deviations of actual from desired performance the contract will have to be enforced. Enforcement will be based on incentives and penalties that will be applied when such deviations are observed. We now briefly consider the likely influences on performance of contractor selection monitoring and enforcement.

CONTRACTOR SELECTION UNDER UNCERTAINTY

The uncertainty associated with contractor selection arises from two sources. The contract specifications will need to be precise, but it may nevertheless be difficult if not impossible to encompass all the required performance characteristics in them. Hence, the contracting authority will need to ascertain that the selected operator can meet certain implicit requirements. The other source of uncertainty, which is potentially more troublesome, is that the output or service contracted for is not observable at the time of "purchase". Hence, the "quality" of the prospective contractors is essentially unknown and the contracting authority has to rely on past performance as a proxy, that is, on reputation.[2]

In these circumstances contracting authorities resort to screening devices, the most important and ubiquitous of which are prequalification restrictions – a preliminary vetting process of potential contractors. Prequalification allows the contracting authority to sort potential operators into those of high and low expected quality before the tendering takes place. Such separation is important because if low and high quality contractors bid simultaneously, difficulties will arise in distinguishing low bids that are due to cost efficiency from those that involve reduced quality of service. Moreover, the trade-off between price and expected quality is not one that can easily be made explicit; it is therefore preferable to establish the minimum level of quality expected from the contractor, identify those contractors that are deemed to satisfy those requirements and only then invite this group to submit a tender. This two stage process ensures that tendered prices are strictly comparable and do not reflect unwarranted variations in likely performance. The competitive element that is retained will also ensure that the cost of provision does not stray far from the minimum consistent with the required quality standard.[3]

Another potential problem which can be addressed at the prequalification stage is known as the "winner's curse". This occurs in "common-value" auctions where bidders have to estimate the value of the object that is bid for. In the context of publicly contracted services, a serious underestimate of the costs of provision could lead to serious deterioration in performance after the contract is let. Pre-tender screening allows the contracting authority to select those contractors whose previous performance record makes such outcomes unlikely.

CONTRACT MONITORING AND ENFORCEMENT

The problems faced by a public sector organisation in its efforts to secure contract compliance fall into the classic principal/agent mould. The principal is the contracting authority (the contractee) and the agent is the contractor hired to perform a predetermined level of service. The agent can have an incentive to reduce the degree of input/effort, particularly where a highly competitive bid has resulted in slim profits. Asymmetric information – the principal's difficulty in observing the agent's actual activities – serves to exacerbate the incentive problem. Some variations in the agent's contractual performance may be beyond its control due to random factors. As a result, the principal will not always be able to disentangle the impact of the agent's efforts from the consequence of random factors. Rewarding or penalising contractors according to service performance under these circumstances becomes a serious issue of effective contract enforcement.[4]

To mitigate information asymmetries and adverse incentives, specific monitoring mechanisms are written into contracts. The most common are regular inspections, the use of performance indicators and certification of contract compliance prior to payment. To further align incentives with respect to specifications some contracts include renewal clauses that are conditional on satisfactory performance over the contract term. The econometric model will incorporate variables that identify the type of monitoring device used and the incentives/penalties applicable to specific contracts.

II. Empirical Analysis: The Determinants of Contractual Performance

Our empirical analysis involves specifying and estimating an econometric model that links contractual performance to specific characteristics associated with individual contracts. The measure of performance used and a discussion of the relevant contract characteristics will be given below. But first we describe the estimation procedure that takes into account the fact that our sample comprises both private and public sector contracting authorities (contractees). That is, some of the buyers of the services provided under contract are public sector organisations and others are privately owned companies.

The allocation of contracts between private and public sector organisations creates the potential for endogeneity bias. Since the supplier typically chooses which contract to bid for, the decision to operate for public or private sector client is essentially endogenous. In other words the population of potential bidders from which the sample is drawn "chooses" whether to bid for a private or public sector contract. Moreover, our inability to observe each contractor's performance in both the private and public domain means that we have potential sample selectivity bias (due to self-selection). Because we have a sub-sample of private contract awards and a sub-sample of public contract awards we can combine the two samples and use the endogenous dummy variable contractee status (private or public) together with an auxiliary regressor to test for the effect of any likely selectivity bias due to the absence of such information. If the publicly awarded contracts have characteristics similar to privately awarded contracts which influence their propensity to perform after allowing for sources of influence on the choice between private and public contracts, then we would expect to reject the hypothesis of selectivity bias.

Formally, we begin by assuming that the sample of publicly awarded and privately awarded contracts are drawn from a single population of *successful* bidders. For the ith contract ($i = 1, \ldots, c, \ldots, C$), let y_i be the measure of performance; z_i the contractee status variable (1 = private, 0 = public); ω_i the unobserved effects; x_{1i} the exogenous vector of k background variables (including the constant); x_{2i} the exogenous vector of m background variables, where x_{1i} is a subset of x_{2i}; and z^* is the unobserved continuous variable determining contractee status. The model system which recognises the relationships between these elements is:

$$y_i = \omega_i + \alpha z_i + \varepsilon_{0i} \tag{1}$$

$$\omega_i = x'_{1i}\beta_1 + \varepsilon_{1i} \tag{2}$$

$$z_i = x'_{2i}\beta_2 + u_{2i} \tag{3}$$

$$z_i = 1 \text{ if } z_i^* > 0 \tag{4}$$

$$z_i = 0 \text{ if } z_i^* \leq 0$$

Substituting Equation (2) into (1) gives Equation (5)

$$y_i = x'_{1i}\beta_1 + \alpha z_i + u_{1i} \tag{5}$$

where $u_{1i} = \varepsilon_{0i} + \varepsilon_{1i}$.

It is assumed that u_{2i} is normally distributed and $E(u_{1i}|u_{2i})$ is a linear function of u_{2i} such that: $E(u_{1i}) = E(u_{2i}) = 0$,

$$\begin{aligned}&\text{Var}(u_{1i}) = \sigma_1^2\\&\text{Var}(u_{2i}) = 1\\&\text{cov}(u_{1i}, u_{2i}) = \rho\sigma_1 \text{ and}\\&\text{cov}(u_{1i}, u_{1j}) = \text{cov}(u_{1i}, u_{2j}) = \text{cov}(u_{2i}, u_{2j}) = 0 \text{ if } i \neq j\end{aligned}$$

u_{2i} is constrained to have unit variance without loss of generality. Let us now define $\theta_i = -x'_{2i}\beta_2$, Barnow *et al.* (1981) have shown that:

$$E(u_{2i}|\theta, z_i) = z_i f(\theta_i)/(1 - F(\theta_i)) - (1 - z_i)\, f(\theta_i)/F(\theta_i) \tag{6}$$

$$= h_i(\theta_i, z_i) \text{ or } h_i$$

where $f(\ .\ )$ and $F(\ .\ )$ define the standard normal density and the cumulative distribution functions. It follows that:

$$E(u_{1i}|\theta_i, z_i) = \rho\sigma_1 h_i. \tag{7}$$

The application of OLS to Equation (5) with 'h_i' added as an independent variable, will produce unbiased estimates of α and β only if $\rho\sigma_1 = 0$. This condition can be satisfied if one or more of the following requirements are met:

a. Equation (3) predicts contractee status without error ($u_{2i} = 0$ for all observations)
b. Contracts are randomly assigned to private and public organisations (i.e., $\text{var}(u_{1i}) \neq 0$, $\text{var}(u_{2i}) \neq 0$, $\text{cov}(\omega_i, z_i) = 0$ and thus $\text{cov}(u_{1i}, u_{2i}) = 0$)
c. Although inferences on performance and contractee status are correlated in the population $[\text{cov}(\omega_i, z_i) \neq 0]$, there is no correlation between performance and contractee choice after conditioning on observed $x_2[\text{cov}(\omega_i, z_i^*|x_2) = \text{cov}(u_{1i}, u_{2i})] = 0$ for all the population.

Requirement (a) is unlikely to be met. Requirements (b) and (c) need to be tested. We cannot impose the assumption that (b) or (c) is satisfied. Given the single-population assumption, if we can assume that the values of β_1 are independent of contractee status choice, then consistent estimates of parameters can be derived as follows:

Implement an agency choice model of the binary probit form using the maximum likelihood method to obtain parameter estimates for β_2:

$$\Pr[z_i = 1] = F(x'_{2i}\beta_2). \tag{8}$$

Given the estimator $\hat{\beta}_2$ calculate a parameter index

$$\hat{\theta}_i = -x'_{2i}\hat{\beta}_2 \tag{9}$$

and define the auxiliary or selectivity regressor:

$$\hat{h}_i = z_i\, f(\hat{\theta}_i)/(1 - F(\hat{\theta}_i)) - (1 - z_i)\, f(\hat{\theta}_i)/F(\hat{\theta}_i). \tag{10}$$

Then include the selectivity term in equation (5), denoting the unknown scaling or parameter of $\rho\sigma_1$ as c, to obtain the selectivity regression:

$$y_i = x'_{1i}\beta_1 + \alpha z_i + c\hat{h}_i + \eta_i. \tag{11}$$

The parameter estimates in (11) are consistent when OLS is used; however a correction is required to allow for heteroscedastic errors ω_i and η_i unless $\rho = 0$. The correction is implemented in this study to ensure that the standard errors of the OLS model are correct (Greene, 1981).

The version of Equation (11) used for estimation is given as follows:

$$R_i = \beta_{0i} + \beta'_{i1}X_{i1} + \beta'_{i2}X_{i2} + \beta'_{i3}X_{i3} + \beta'_{i4}X_{i4} + c\hat{h}_i + \eta_i \tag{12}$$

where R_i denotes a measure of performance for contract i and X_1, X_2, X_3 and X_4 are respectively vectors of bid selection, contract type and size, monitoring and contract enforcement variables. $\beta_1, \beta_2, \beta_3$ and β_4 represent the corresponding parameter vectors, which were estimated separately for private and public sector contracts.[5]

Bid selection variables, X_1, identify the criteria used in determining which contractor is awarded the contract. The simplest approach is to assume that the lowest tender (bid) will be selected in all circumstances. However, as the theoretical discussion indicated, under certain conditions this may be an inappropriate decision rule. The model therefore discriminates between contracts awarded to the lowest bidder and those that were not. Also included is a variable identifying contracts in which prequalification restrictions were applied.

Contract type/size variables, X_2, categorise contracts by dollar value and by type; i.e., those that are fixed-price versus those subject to cost escalation clauses (incentive contracts). Another variable included in this group is the type of tender document used in the bidding process; many public sector organisations use standard tender documents whereas others rely on their own.

Monitoring variables, X_3, identify the kind of information that the principal (the contractee) uses to monitor and enforce the contract. The better informed is the principal, the easier it is to enforce contractual obligations and hence these variables relate to the method and type of information collected.

Enforcement variables, X_4, identify the use of penalty clauses and informal conflict resolution mechanisms as a way of managing relations with the contractor. Also included is a variable that indicates whether renewal clauses conditional on satisfactory performance are incorporated in the contract.

The individual explanatory variables within each vector are described in Table I. With the exception of the size of contract, all variables are dichotomous – taking the value of zero or one depending on the particular type of contract feature under consideration. The model was therefore specified in simple linear form. The dependent variable (R_1) is a contract compliance rating measured on a ten point scale rising from 1 to 10. This rating is recorded by each contracting authority participating in the survey. Two additional performance measures were used in the econometric analysis: public perception of quality of service (R_2) and a weighted performance index (R_3). The latter was constructed, using varimax factor analysis, as a linear combination of seven additional performance attributes. These are attention to detail, information provided to contractee, access to contractor, on-time performance, courtesy of employees, adherence to safety standards and incidence of complaints. Each of these was also rated on a 1–10 scale and reported in the questionnaire. In this way we were able to test the sensitivity of the estimated models to the use of three alternative qualitative performance variables. For a discussion of the use of rating scales in economic analysis see Beggs and Cardell (1982) and Hensher (1981).

To collect information on individual contracts we developed a self-administered questionnaire which was sent to every public sector organisation in New South Wales (Australia) – 309 in total. The survey was carried out in October 1989, and all completed returns were received by May 1990. The public sector organisations involved were broken down as follows: 89 (state) government departments, 42 county councils and 178 local authorities. Each organisation was asked to complete the questionnaire for a single contract of its choice. In addition, a similar number of private sector organisations in the manufacturing and services industries were surveyed with an identical instrument. However, at around 8%, the private sector response rate was significantly lower than that obtained from the public sector.

Respondents were asked to select a contract which had been in operation for at least six months at the time of reporting so that a valid assessment of its performance could be made. Letting respondents choose the particular contract on which to report could induce some sample selection bias. Its effect could be to increase the incidence of successful contracts which would be reflected in relatively high

TABLE I. Explanatory variables in the contract performance model

Variable	Definition	Type
LBID	Identifies contracts awarded to the lowest bidder. Equals 1 when observation relates to such a contract, 0 otherwise.	Dichotomous
PREQUAL	Takes the value of 1 when the contractor was selected from an existing or newly created prequalifying list.	Dichotomous
CREP	Takes the value of 1 when the contractor's good reputation was used as the dominant criterion in the selection process.	Dichotomous
CCRED	Takes the value of 1 when the contractor's credit rating was used as the dominant criterion in the selection process.	Dichotomous
FPCON	Takes the value of 1 when the contract is fixed-price, with or without inflation adjustment. Variable equals 0 for any other contract type.	Dichotomous
INDAD	Takes the value of 1 when the contract document is compiled by the contractee. Equals 0 when SCCB or other standard documents are used.	Dichotomous
BIDPRICE	Variable measuring the annual dollar value of the contract, as a proxy for contract size.	Continuous
FTCON	Takes the value of 1 when the contract is for a fixed term. Open ended contracts take the value of 0.	Dichotomous
INSP	Takes the value of 1 with the following forms of inspection: certification prior to payment; announced or unannounced inspections. Equals zero if no formal inspections are undertaken.	Dichotomous
INDICAT	Takes the value of 1 if performance indicators are used to monitor the contractor.	Dichotomous
DELEG	Takes the value of 1 if management of the contract is delegated, 0 if the contract manager is directly involved.	Dichotomous
NOFP	Takes the value of 1 when no financial penalties are used in the contract.	Dichotomous
INCENT	Takes the value of 1 if the contract includes a renewal and/or price renegotiation option after a year's satisfactory performance.	Dichotomous
NEG	Takes the value of 1 when dispute resolution is always preceded by negotiation and consultation.	Dichotomous
CONEVER	Takes the value of 1 if the present contractor has previously held a contract with the contractee.	Dichotomous

TABLE II. Descriptive statistics of variables

	PUB	(SD)	PRIV	(SD)
CONYEARS	2.38	(1.32)	0.95	(0.94)
FIRSTCON (1,0)	0.26		0.05	
NUMBIDS	9.1	(8.73)	3.25	(1.94)
LBID (1,0)	0.46		0.65	
PREQUAL (1,0)	0.206		0.75	
CREP (1,0)	0.42		0.35	
CCRED (1,0)	0.02		0.00	
PPCON (1,0)	0.66		0.60	
INDAD (1,0)	0.66		0.00	
BIDPRICE (A$)'000	9.84	(26.16)	12.634	(14.541)
FTCON (1,0)	0.94		0.65	
INSP (1,0)	0.94		1.00	
INDICAT (1,0)	0.18		0.10	
DELEG (1,0)	0.56		0.45	
NOFP (1,0)	0.72		0.85	
NEC (1,0)	0.76		0.85	
INCENT (1,0)	0.42		0.60	
CONEVER (1,0)	0.36		0.50	
RATESPEC (R_1)	7.94	(1.77)	7.75	(1.83)
RATEPERC (R_2)	7.42	(2.17)	7.55	(1.39)
RATEIX (R_3)	7.74	(1.59)	8.17	(0.95)
SAMPLE SIZE	46		18	

performance ratings. Respondents were also asked to report the number of contracts which they held concurrently within a specific category. Over 50% of organisations had only one such contract at the time of the survey thus limiting the potential for selection bias.

III. Data and Econometric Methods

The econometric analysis was based on a sample of 64 cleaning contracts, 46 of which involved supplying services to public sector organisations and the remainder to private sector purchasers. The sample size used for estimation is somewhat smaller than the total number of returns because of missing observations and incomplete questionnaires.

It is interesting to note the differences in characteristics of contracts held by public and private sector organisations. The means and standard deviations of the relevant variables are reported in Table II. It can be seen that some of these values diverge substantially. For example, the average number of bids received by private sector buyers is only 3.25. By contrast the number of bids received by public sector counterparts is 9.1. This observation immediately suggests that private sector organisations restrict the number of contractors that are eligible to bid. The figures on the prequalification variable confirm the suggestion. Among private sector organisations 75% used a prequalification list containing those contractors whose bids would be considered. The corresponding number in the public sector was 20% – a much lower figure which suggests that more open tendering procedures were being used.

Another noticeable difference is that contract duration varied substantially between the agency type: average length is approximately one year in the private and almost two and a half years in the public sector. In addition, the proportion of cases that involve first time contracts between the parties is also much lower in the private than in the public sector. This finding is not surprising in the light of the fact that the public organisations are increasingly putting services such as cleaning out to tender for the very first time.

As for contract size, measured by the mean dollar value, the differences between the agency types appear to be small. However the standard deviation in the size of public sector contracts is A$26,160 whilst the corresponding figure for private sector organisations is A$14,500. Further investigation reveals significant differences in the range of contract value: from A$2600 to A$1,800000 in the public sector and A$3,750 to A$460,000 in the private sector.

Turning to the dependent variables R_1, R_2 and R_3 it is noteworthy that the mean ratings turn out to be of similar magnitude across type of contracting organisation. There is a somewhat greater divergence in the standard deviations as highlighted by examining Figures 1 to 3 in which the frequency distributions of the ratings are depicted for each variable by contractee type. It is immediately observable that the distributions tend to have a much lower spread in the case of private sector contracts. For R_2 and R_3 the difference in spread is striking; for R_1 there is a far lesser incidence of low rated, poorly performing contracts. This could mean either that private sector organisations are less willing to report significant contract failures, or more plausibly that the public sector is still relatively new to this activity and therefore more likely to experience serious problems of implementation.

In line with the discussion of Section II, estimation proceeded in two steps. The first was the estimation of a binary probit equation that identifies the characteristics that distinguish private from public sector contracting organisations. The equation, which is estimated by maximum likelihood methods, defined the contractee status as equal to 1 if the contract is with a private sector organisation and 0 if it is in the public sector. The variables in the vector z, already discussed, are reported in Table III.

The second step involves estimating Equation (12) which relates perceived performance to the regulatory instruments discussed above. This equation includes two separate sets of variables, one for private and the other for public sector

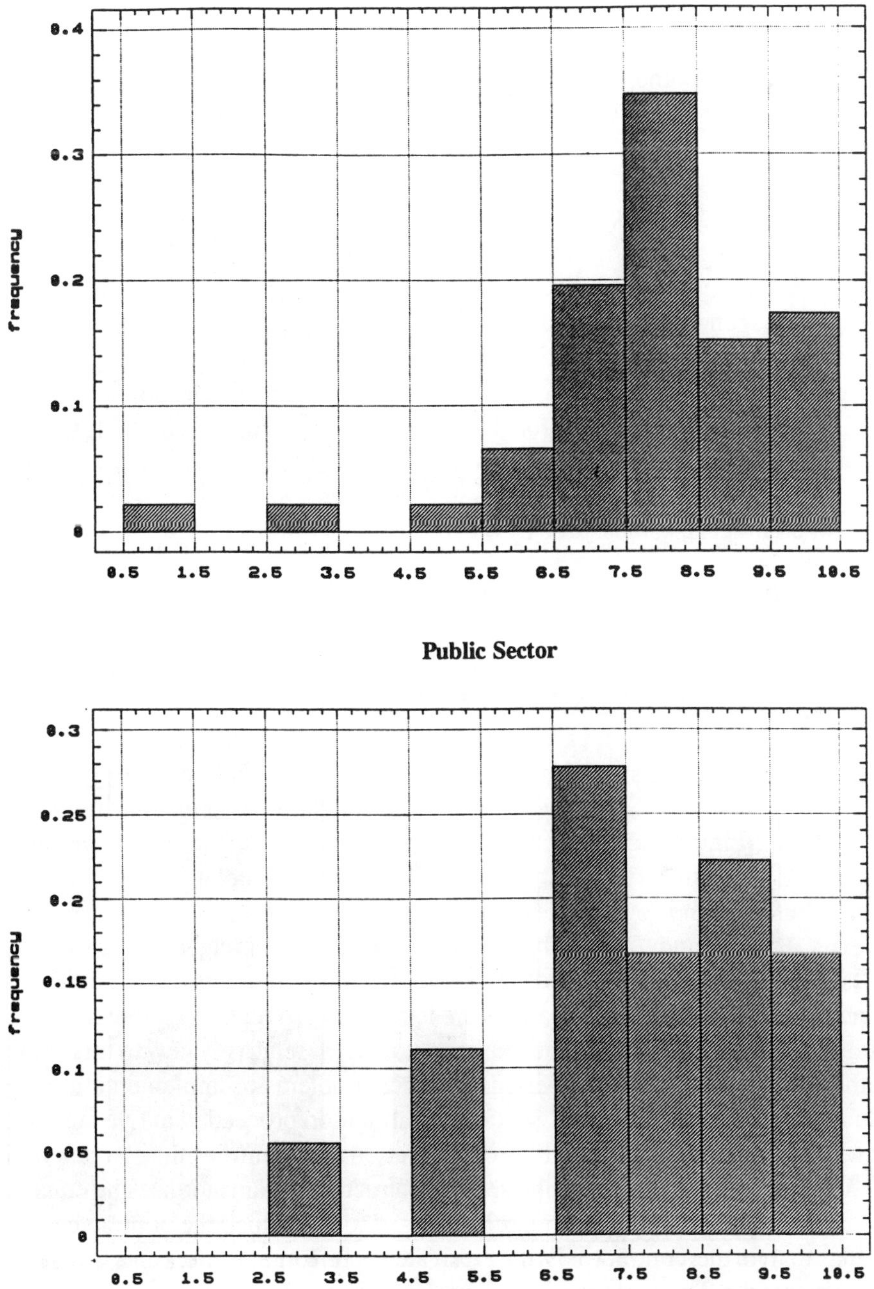

Fig. 1. Distribution of Dep. Var. R_1.

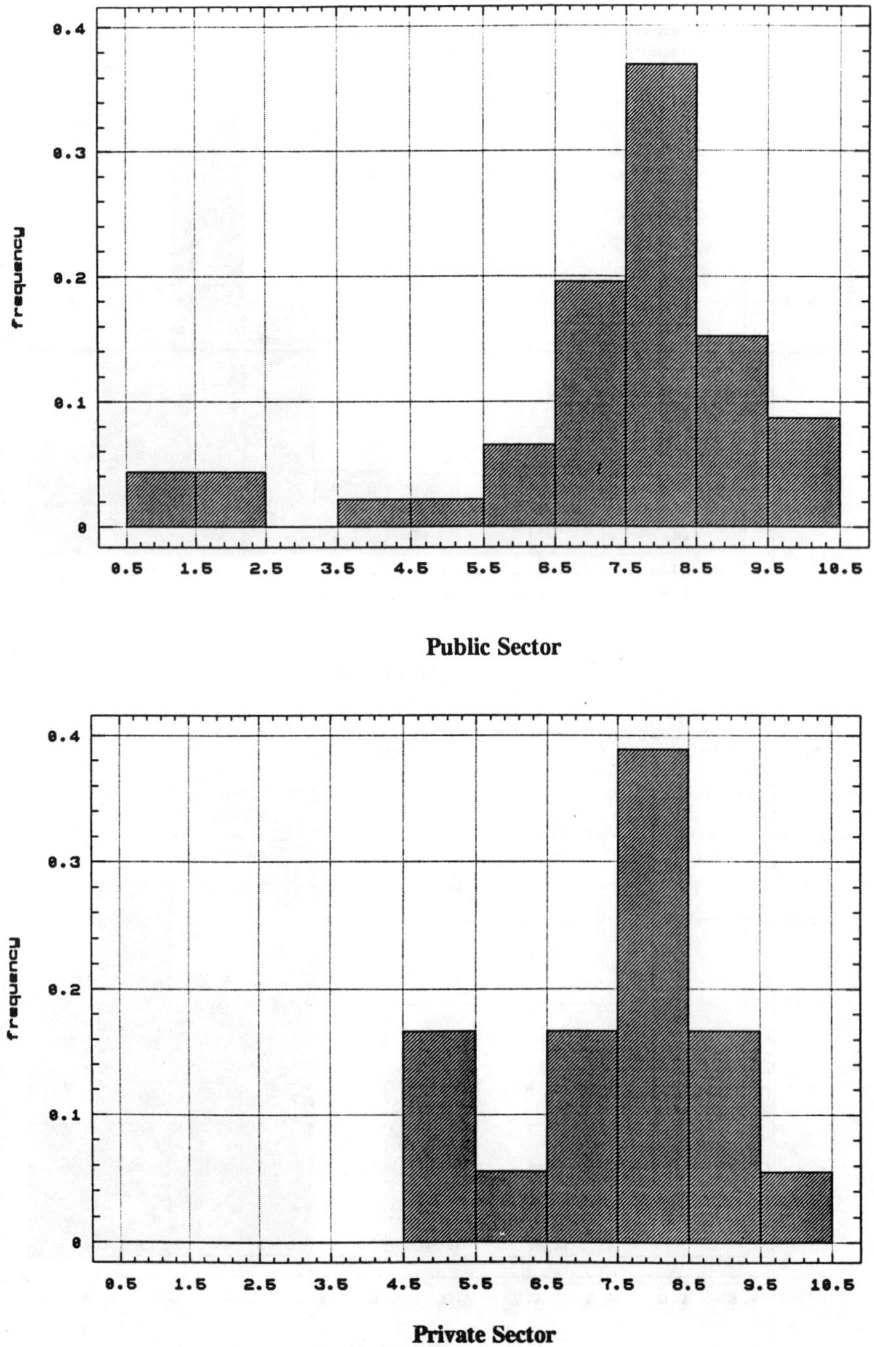

Fig. 2. Distribution of Dep. Var. R_2.

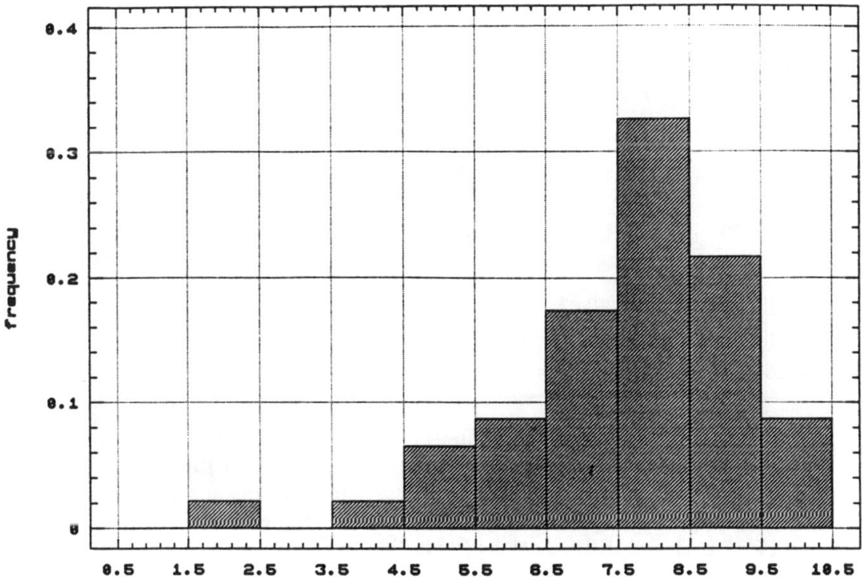

Public Sector

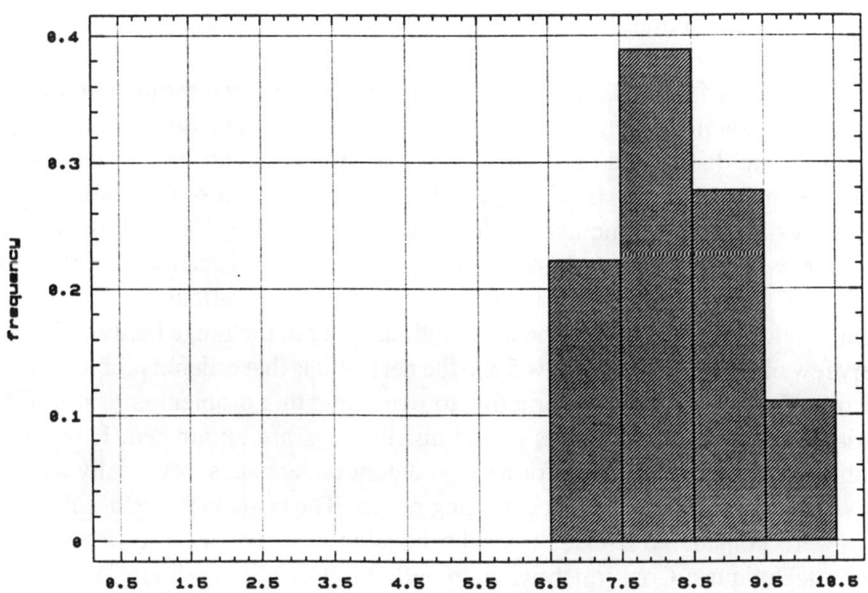

Private Sector

Fig. 3. Distribution of Dep. Var. R_3.

TABLE III. Binomial probit regression. Dependent variable: prob. (private sector)

Variable	Coefficient	t-ratio
Constant	1.5443	2.078
CONYEARS	–0.63676	–2.592
FIRSTCON	–1.7844	–1.931
NUMBIDS	–0.28323	–1.741
PREQUAL	1.7642	2.687
DELEG	–1.0576	–1.646

Log-likelihood (0) = –38.02
Log-likelihood at convergence = –16.59
Pseudo – $R^2 = 0.564$

Note: CONYEARS is the length of contract in years.
FIRSTCON is a dummy variable which takes the value of 1 if the present contractor is new to the authority and 0 otherwise.
NUMBIDS is the number of bids received for the present contract
PREQUAL and DELEG are defined in Table I.

organisations. A dummy variable approach was eschewed because of the very real danger of multicollinearity. Hence we split the variable by organisational status and estimated each effect independently.

One aspect of our data has important implications for the estimation procedure employed. When a dependent variable is discrete as in the case of R_1 and R_2 and its values are distributed on a scale with fixed intervals, Ordinary Least Squares (OLS) estimation is not strictly appropriate. In these circumstances ordered probit or logit estimation techniques should be used (see Greene, 1990). However, these techniques could not be implemented in the present study because the distributions of R_1 and R_2 were effectively truncated, with zero observations on some levels of rating scale and with most of the observations lying in the range between 7 and 10. Very few observations lay below 5 and the net result is that ordered probit estimation becomes impossible. One alternative to overcome this problem is to re-scale the variable so that discontinuities of the distributions are eliminated. However, re-scaling means reducing the information content of the data substantially due to the inevitable aggregation of adjacent rating points. The costs in terms of information loss were considered greater than the benefits of being able to apply ordered probit techniques. Consequently, we reverted to OLS but it should be noted that differences in results between ordered probit/logit and OLS appear to be negligible (see Hensher, 1991, for evidence on this point).

Lagrange multiplier tests (Breusch and Pagan, 1980) indicated that the OLS regression estimates were affected by heteroscedasticity. This is not unusual for cross-section data of this kind and our response to this was to apply two types of correction for heteroscedasticity. White-corrected standard errors have been calculated as well as Generalised Least Squares estimates. The latter are based on weights that were calculated as the reciprocals of the disturbance variances and derived from the OLS results.

IV. Estimation Results

Table III reports the estimated binomial probit equation. The results confirm the remarks made in the previous section regarding the characteristics that distinguish private from public sector contracting authorities. The probability of the contracting party being in the private sector is negatively related to contract duration, to the incidence of first time contracts, to the number of bids solicited and to the contract management/administration being delegated. By contrast, it is most strongly and positively related to the incidence of a prequalifying stage in the contracting process. In other words, if the contract was subject to prequalification restrictions, it is more likely to be in the private sector. McFadden's pseudo – R^2 of 0.56 indicates an exceptional goodness of fit for this model.

Turning to the performance rating regressions based on R_1 and reported in Table IV, the following points are worth noting. First, in all but a couple of cases the explanatory variables do not suggest a uniform and significant influence for both types of agency. For example, the variable LBID identifying the contractor as the lowest bidder, has no influence on perceived performance when public sector contracts are involved, but a positive and significant influence in private sector contracts. Second, the variables which have a closely matching effect on performance are PREQUAL and NEG – prequalification and negotiation respectively. The coefficients on these variables indicate that their effect on performance is positive and highly significant. They suggest that prequalification restrictions and reliance on a managerial rather than legalistic approach to contracting yield significantly better results, as perceived by the contracting authorities.

The third feature of these results that merits mention is that not all the estimated coefficients conform with our a priori expectations. For example, in private sector contracts the use of performance indicators suggests that performance is significantly worse than when they are not applied. The proper interpretation of this odd result is not difficult: the estimated coefficient is picking up the measurement effect: in the rare cases where performance indicators are used, they reveal lapses by the contractors that would otherwise go undetected and unrecorded. Turning to another variable, INCT it is perplexing to find that incentive contracts are generally associated with better performance in public sector agencies, but worse when the private sector is involved. Both effects are statistically significant.

The results on the dependent variables R_2 and R_3 are not markedly different from the ones just considered. They are reported in Tables V and VI respectively. Once again the coefficients on PREQUAL are positive, of similar size and statistically significant. Other variables that are significant for one contractee type but

TABLE IV. The influence of regulatory variables on performance. Dependent variable: R_1

Variable	WSE Coefficient	WSE t-ratio	GLS Coefficient	GLS t-ratio
CONSTANT	5.65	6.20	4.83	4.05
PUBLBID	0.87×10^{-1}	0.23	0.11	0.19
PRVLBID	2.68	7.82	2.95	2.67
PUBPRQ	1.51	2.79	1.49	1.65
PRVPRQ	2.54	6.23	2.81	1.97
PRVCREP	−3.23	−5.44	−2.65	−1.13
PUBCREP	1.18	2.87	1.31	2.12
PUBFPCON	−0.48	−1.15	−0.58	−1.04
PRVFPCON	−2.20	−5.41	−2.09	−1.39
PUBBPRC	-0.79×10^{-5}	−0.00	0.23×10^{-2}	0.20
PRVBPRC	0.20×10^{-1}	1.69	0.23×10^{-1}	0.57
PUBFTCON	−0.23	−0.39	−0.26	−0.26
PRVFTCON	−2.47	−5.48	−2.32	−2.25
PUBINDIC	0.21	0.42	0.28	0.44
PRVINDIC	−6.02	−11.38	−5.56	−2.43
PUBDELEG	0.72×10^{-1}	0.22	-0.53×10^{-2}	−0.01
PRVDELEG	0.52	2.46	0.21	0.17
PUBNOFP	0.20	0.38	0.64	1.17
PRVNOFP	2.83	5.99	2.80	2.00
PRVNEG	2.41	6.84	2.34	1.32
PUBNEG	1.59	2.53	2.08	3.44
PUBINCT	1.03	2.18	1.58	2.43
PRVINCT	−1.71	−3.61	−1.25	−0.65
PUBCONEV	−0.26	−0.49	−0.35	−0.62
PRVCONEV	−1.97	−6.99	−1.85	−1.54
SCVAR	−0.37	−0.74	−0.47	−0.56
$\bar{R}^2$	0.35	–	0.58	–

Note: WSE stands for OLS parameter estimates where correction for heteroscedasticity has been applied through White Standard Errors. The B–P statistic with 25 degrees of freedom was 61.11. GLS stands for Generalised Least Squares as outlined in the text.

not another are CREP, FTCON, INDIC, NEG, and INCT. R_2 generally performs better than R_3 which is the composite rating indicator. These results therefore suggest that the underlying relationships are better identified using a single, clearly defined indicator of performance. But it should be remembered that the dependent variables identify different dimensions of performance. It is not entirely surprising, therefore, if the influence of the regulatory instruments (independent variables) is not uniform across the three models.

TABLE V. The influence of regulatory variables on performance. Dependent variable: R_2.

Variable	WSE Coefficient	WSE t-ratio	GLS Coefficient	GLS t-ratio
CONSTANT	5.44	4.18	4.71	3.10
PUBLBID	–0.75	–1.3	–0.90	–1.12
PRVLBID	2.75	4.41	3.08	2.10
PUBPRQ	2.71	3.28	3.47	2.86
PRVPRQ	2.86	2.85	3.69	1.84
PRVCREP	–0.15	–0.13	0.70×10^{-2}	0.00
PUBCREP	1.56	3.00	1.87	2.26
PUBFPCON	–0.54	–1.04	–0.74	–1.01
PRVFPCON	–1.07	–1.32	–1.46	–0.68
PUBBPRC	-0.25×10^{-2}	–0.37	-0.46×10^{-2}	–0.31
PRVBPRC	0.37×10^{-2}	0.15	-0.26×10^{-3}	–0.01
PUBFTCON	–0.39	–0.35	0.23	–0.18
PRVFTCON	–1.50	–2.26	–1.78	–1.19
PUBINDIC	-0.33×10^{-1}	–0.05	–0.16	–0.21
PRVINDIC	–1.69	–1.45	–1.22	–0.38
PUBDELEG	0.77	1.57	1.13	1.54
PRVDELEG	–0.69	–1.62	–0.92	–0.58
PUBNOFP	–0.39	–0.75	–0.25	–0.35
PRVNOFP	0.97	1.10	1.00	0.51
PRVNEG	–0.33	–0.51	–0.29	–0.11
PUBNEG	1.53	2.73	1.91	2.37
PUBINCT	1.52	2.71	2.05	2.33
PRVINCT	–0.56	–0.59	–0.50	–0.19
PUBCONEV	–0.48	–0.95	–0.85	–1.17
PRVCONEV	–0.41	–0.57	–0.31	–0.19
SCVAR	0.36	0.42	0.96	0.92
$\bar{R}^2$	0.15	–	0.24	–

Note. WSE stands for OLS parameter estimates where correction for heteroscedasticity has been applied through White Standard Errors. The B–P statistic with 25 degrees of freedom was 61.11. GLS stands for Generalised Least Squares as outlined in the text.

V. Discussion and Conclusions

One result that has not yet been discussed is the selectivity correction, as captured by the coefficient on the variable SCVAR. This parameter turns out to be insignificant in every regression equation and its interpretation is clear. There is no statistically significant correlation between the unobserved influences of contractee status and each of the three measures of performance identified by our dependent variables. This in turn means that such status does not have any effect on perceived

TABLE VI. The influence of regulatory variables on performance. Dependent variable: R_3

Variable	WSE Coefficient	WSE t-ratio	GLS Coefficient	GLS t-ratio
CONSTANT	7.15	10.53	6.90	6.23
PUBLBID	0.32	0.86	0.27	0.50
PRVLBID	1.34	3.42	1.46	1.43
PUBPRQ	1.05	1.65	1.27	1.61
PRVPRQ	1.11	1.55	1.23	0.87
PRVCREP	0.16	0.19	0.28	0.13
PUBCREP	0.71	1.87	0.72	1.30
PUBFPCON	–0.60	–1.77	–0.81	–1.60
PRVFPCON	-0.51×10^{-2}	–0.01	0.37×10^{-2}	0.00
PUBBPRC	-0.48×10^{-2}	–0.77	-0.24×10^{-2}	–0.26
PRVBPRC	0.17×10^{-1}	1.06	0.22×10^{-1}	0.58
PUBFTCON	–0.85	–1.58	–1.04	–1.07
PRVFTCON	–0.49	–0.95	–0.40	–0.39
PUBINDIC	–0.52	–0.87	–0.80	–1.49
PRVINDIC	–1.85	–2.26	–1.88	–0.81
PUBDELEG	–0.40	–1.18	–0.31	–0.59
PRVDELEG	–0.90	–2.57	–0.96	–0.88
PUBNOFP	-0.78×10^{-1}	–0.17	0.84×10^{-1}	0.17
PRVNOFP	0.53	0.90	0.54	0.38
PRVNEG	–0.18	–0.34	-0.91×10^{-1}	–0.05
PUBNEG	1.31	2.55	1.61	2.94
PUBINCT	0.99	2.37	1.28	2.23
PRVINCT	–0.13	–0.18	-0.76×10^{-1}	–0.04
PUBCONEV	-0.25×10^{-1}	–0.05	0.70×10^{-1}	0.14
PRVCONEV	–0.18	–0.33	–0.26	–0.23
SCVAR	–0.30	–0.51	–0.48	–0.65
$\bar{R}^2$	0.16	–	0.32	–

Note: WSE stands for OLS parameter estimates where correction for heteroscedasticity has been applied through White Standard Errors. The B–P statistic with 25 degrees of freedom was 61.11. GLS stands for Generalised Least Squares as outlined in the text.

performance once account is taken of the other sources of influence which vary across organisations.

By way of summary it is worth noting that while the average perceived level of performance was very similar, the influence of regulatory instruments was by no means uniform across private and public sector contracts. However, the following general observations can be made. First, selecting the lowest bidding contractor does not have an adverse influence on performance, neither in public nor in private sector contracts. Problems associated with the winner's curse are not present in these contracts. Second, the one factor that does appear to have a strong positive influence on performance is the use of prequalification restrictions. This effect is present in private and public sector contracts and in all three dependent variables. It implies that screening potential contractors prior to bidding succeeds in weeding out poor performers. Third, there is a tendency, particularly in the private sector, for fixed term and fixed price contracts to do less well than their unrestricted counterparts. Finally, there is some evidence, again from the private sector sub-sample, that where performance indicators have been used perceived outcomes are significantly worse. This is counter intuitive but could be interpreted to mean that the introduction of rigourous performance evaluation leads to a more critical appraisal of contractors.

Our empirical evidence also has some implications for the application of benchmarks. There is nothing in these results that suggests that private sector contracts are administered or regulated in a manner superior to that of the public sector. It therefore places a question mark over the tendency to use private sector contractual methods as a preferred benchmark for the specification of public sector contracts.

In conclusion, we would point out that to our knowledge this is the first empirical study of its kind. The purpose of the study was to focus on contractual performance and the factors that help sustain it. The vast majority of empirical literature in this field concerns itself with the question of costs of provision when activities such as cleaning are put out to competitive bidding. The issue of service quality or performance is equally important but much more difficult to research because of the absence of any publicly available data. For this reason we have had to generate our own data which is both costly and time consuming. Yet we are conscious of the limitations of using a performance measure that is essentially a one-off assessment of the contractor. Future studies may be able to take a time-series as well as a cross section approach to performance evaluation thus reducing further our state of ignorance in this field.

Notes

* We are grateful to Jörg Finsinger and participants at the Industrial Organization Conference in Vienna (1992) for helpful comments. The usual disclaimer applies.

1. The theoretical implications of using different bidding schemes are comprehensively surveyed in McAfee and McMillan (1987). See also Waterson (1988).
2. The use of reputation proxies for goods and services whose characteristics are difficult to ascertain at the time of purchase is a widespread phenomenon. For a theoretical discussion see e.g. Klein and Leffler (1981) and Shapiro (1983).
3. Where tendering occurs frequently because contracts are short lived, there will be economies in using an existing prequalification list. Moreover, the costs of bidding incurred by potential contractors are sunk: they cannot be recovered if the bid is unsuccessful. Hence, by screening out contractors who are unlikely to be selected irrespective of their bid price, total sunk costs can be significantly reduced.
4. This incentive problem present in such contracts is the familiar "moral hazard" effect. McAfee and McMillan (1988) discuss the role of perverse incentives in long-term government projects.

In the context of public sector service contracts "moral hazard" threatens the quality of service provided.

5. In this way αz_i from Equation (11) is incorporated in Equation (12).

References

Barnow, B., Cain, G., and Goldberger, A. (1981) 'Issues in the Analysis of Selectivity Bias', in Stromsdorfer, E. and Farkas, G. (eds.), *Evaluation Studies Review Annual* **5**, Beverly Hills, Calif.: Sage.

Beggs, S. and Cardell, S. (1982) 'Assessing the Potential Demand for Electric Cars', *Journal of Econometrics* **17**, 1–19.

Breusch, T.S. and Pagan, A.R. (1980) 'The Lagrange Multiplier Test and Its Applications to Model Specification in Econometrics', *Review of Economic Studies* **47**, 239–254.

Domberger, S., Meadowcroft, S.A., and Thompson, D.J. (1986) 'Competitive Tendering and Efficiency: The Case of Refuse Collection', *Fiscal Studies* **7(4)**, 69–87.

Domberger, S., Meadowcroft, S.A., and Thompson, D.J. (1987) 'The Impact of Competitive Tendering on the Costs of Hospital Domestic Services', *Fiscal Studies* **8(4)**, 39–51.

Greene, W.H. (1990) *Econometric Analysis*, New York: Macmillan Publishing Company.

Hensher, D.A. (1981) 'Towards a Design of Consumer Durables', *Journal of Economic Psychology* **1(2)**, 135–164.

Hensher, D.A. (1989) 'Competitive Tendering in the Transportation Sector', *Economic Papers* **8(1)**, 1–11.

Hensher, D.A. (1991) 'Hierarchical Stated Response Designs and Estimation', *Transportation and Logistics Review* **26(4)**.

Klein, B. and Leffler, K.B. (1981) 'The Role of Market Forces in Assuring Contractual Performance', *Journal of Political Economy* **89(4)**, 615–41.

McAfee, R.P. and MacMillan, J. (1987) 'Auctions and Bidding', *Journal of Economic Literature* **25**, 699–738.

McAfee, R.P. and MacMillan, J. (1988) *Incentives in Government Contracts*, Toronto: University Press.

Savas, E.S. (1987) *Privatisation: The Key to Better Government*, Chatham, NJ: Chatham House.

Shapiro, C. (1983) 'Premium for High Quality Products as Returns to Reputation', *Quarterly Journal of Economics*, November, 659–79.

Waterson (1988) *Regulation of the Firm and Natural Monopoly*, Oxford: Basil Blackwell.

K. Aiginger and J. Finsinger (eds.), Applied Industrial Organization, 239–250.

On the Scope of Indirect Regulation of Monopolies in the Presence of Large Entry Cost

MICHAEL DRÖTTBOOM
Fernuniversität Hagen, Germany

and

WOLFGANG LEININGER
*Universität Dortmund and Boston University**

Abstract. This paper reexamines the ingenious regulation scheme put forward by Burnovsky and Zang (1991), that features a regulator who promises to subsidize entry into a market, which exhibits properties of a "natural monopoly". If the subsidy promise is sufficiently high, the monopolist is led to increase output and lower price at no cost of regulation. The assumption that the monopolist always honors his pre-entry commitment has been shown to be crucial for the results obtained. This motivated our inquiry into the scope of "costless" indirect regulation in situations in which the incumbent's commitment cannot be inforced. It then turns out that no commitment on behalf of the incumbent can be credible that deters entry by choosing an output (capacity) at a level in excess of the monopoly output after successful entry deterrence. This represents an additional constraint for the regulator's behavior.

Key words: Monopoly, entry-deterrence, regulation.

JEL codes: D42, L12, L51.

In a recent very stimulating paper Burnovsky and Zang (1991) present an indirect regulation mechanism which blends elements and insights of both the theory of strategic entry deterrence and the theory of contestable markets. This is a welcome departure from previous discussions of these theories, which seemed to apply an unduly dichotomous view due to the presence resp. absence of sunk costs in those theories. Moreover, Burnovsky and Zang derive very interesting results; e.g. it is shown that under some circumstances a 'natural monopolist' can be led to supply the competitive output level (at marginal cost prices) through indirect regulation *at no cost*. The regulation scheme achieving this consists of a promise to subsidize entry, making the market effectively 'contestable', and the strategic exploitation of the monopolist's optimal strategic response to this promise by the regulator. The latter consists in letting the monopolist *deter* entry (in order to save the inefficient expense of the entry subsidy) thereby forcing it to forfeit monopoly power (in the traditional sense). It is the purpose of this note to comment on this mechanism and to point out some of its limitations. It appears that the results reported in Burnovsky and Zang (1991) represent an extreme, yet – for precisely this reason – very useful upper benchmark for the scope of this regulatory scheme. We show, that, while it is possible to implement the first-best outcome under some circumstances, it is also possible that social surplus after regulation falls even short of the unregulated (natural) monopoly outcome under less ideal circumstances.

Section 1 gives a brief description and discussion of Burnovsky and Zang's (1991) indirect regulation scheme and points to some strong underlying assumptions. Section 2 discusses the impact of a weakening of those assumptions with the help of a detailed example. In Section 3 we assess the scope of 'costless' indirect regulation under weaker (and more realistic) assumptions in some generality. Section 4 offers concluding comments.

1. 'Costless' Indirect Regulation

This term was coined by Burnovsky and Zang (1991) to describe a four-stage regulation scheme, that is applied to the economic environment of a so called 'natural' monopoly. We give a brief description. Consider the market for a homogeneous good, in which demand is given by the (inverse) demand function $P(x)$. $P(x)$ is assumed to be downward sloping and concave, i.e. $P'(x) < 0$ and $P''(x) \leq 0$. The good in question can be produced with a (to all potentially active firms common) technology, that gives rise to the following cost function:

$$c(x) = e + \bar{c}(x)$$

where x denotes the quantity produced and e refers to a fixed and sunk (entry) cost; $\bar{c}(x)$ is a standard variable cost function satisfying $\bar{c}'(x) > 0$, $\bar{c}''(x) \geq 0$ and $\bar{c}(0) = 0$. This is the only technology available to produce the good and it has already been adopted by one firm, which is serving the market. This firm enjoys a monopoly as the size of e is – by assumption – such that one firm can profitably serve the market, but not two (or more); i.e. in technical terms $P(0) > \bar{c}'(0)$ and $\pi_d^* < e < \pi_m^*$, where π_d^* resp. π_m^* denote profits per firm in duopoly and monopoly. In fact, for all quantities that can be sold above marginal cost a subadditivity property of the cost function $c(x)$ is assumed to hold:

$$c(x_1 + x_2) \leq c(x_1) + c(x_2)$$

(which is not to be confused wiht subadditivity of variable cost $\bar{c}(x)$) since it only implies that $\bar{c}(x_1 + x_2) \leq \bar{c}(x_1) + \bar{c}(x_2) + e$).

Moreover, the potential market is finite in the sense that demand $P^{-1}(\bar{p}) < \infty$ for $\bar{p} = \bar{c}'(0)$ and there is $x > 0$ such that $P(x) < \bar{c}'(x)$.

Suppose now there exists a sufficiently large pool of potential entrants, who all seek access to the technology given by $c(\cdot)$, but are blockaded from entry by the sunk cost e. A regulatory agency G can now implement the following four-stage-mechanism: The agency G announces a (lump-sum) subsidy of size S,

$0 \leq S \leq e$, to each potential entrant conditional on actual entry. This forms stage 1. Thereafter, at stage 2, the incumbent monopolist commits to a production output of $x_m(S)$ (stage 2). Observing $x_m(S)$ and knowing the size of S the potential entrants decide whether to enter or not (stage 3). Finally, at stage 4, the actual entrants decide on their supplies by engaging in Cournot competition for residual demand $D(p) - x_m(S)$. Assuming strictly non-cooperative behavior this set-up can formally be analyzed as a game in which the participating players have the following pay-off functions:

Let $x = \sum_{i=1}^{n} x_i + x_m(S)$ denote total supply at stage 4, given subsidy S and n entrants. The entrants treat $x_m(S)$ as given and thus maximize $\pi_i = x_i \cdot P(x) - \bar{c}(x_i) - (e - S)$ whereas the monopolist (at stage 2) – knowing S – maximizes $x_m \cdot P(x) - \bar{c}(x_m)$.

Finally, the regulator attempts to maximize social surplus generated by the good, i.e. his pay-off function is

$$\pi_G = \int_0^x P(x)\,dx - \sum_{i=1}^{n} \bar{c}(x_i) - \bar{c}(x_m) - n \cdot e\,.$$

Note that this game is one of perfect information: when deciding on entry (at stage 3) the potential entrants' know their pay-off functions, in particular the size of S and x_m, at stage 4. Hence they enter if and only if their profits (net of entry cost and subsidy) are at least $(e - S)$. This optimal behavior on the part of entrants can be foreseen by the incumbent, who can influence the entry decisions by committing to a production level x_m (at stage 2), which in turn will depend on the size of the subsidy offered to potential entrants', S.

The monopolist might wish to deter entry or keep the number of entrants at a desired level, whatever is more profitable for him. The regulator anticipates incumbents' and entrants' optimal behavior when choosing the size of S. He seeks the optimal level of S according to his social surplus maximization goal.

Burnovsky and Zang (1991) established the following two theorems:

Theorem 1: With linear demand and constant marginal cost the unique subgame-perfect equilibrium has the following features: the regulator promises full subsidization of entry ($S = e$), the monopolist commits to the competitive output level, and no entry takes place.

Theorem 2: Equilibrium in general is unique. Its path never exhibits entry and the monopolist always sells output at marginal cost prices. Maximal industry-wide surplus is obtained.

Note, that the offered entry subsidy is never actually paid! In deciding on its optimal size the regulator strikes a delicate balance between encouraging entry (high value of S) and letting maintain the incumbent the capacity to deter entry (low value of S). In the original situation of natural monopoly entry-deterrence is costless (entry costs are prohibitive). The "right" size of S makes entry-deterrence costly (but not prohibitively costly) and entry (almost) costless. The beauty of this scheme is that not only are entry-deterrence costs "paid" to the consumers, they also generate further surplus for them: consumers not only recoup the monopoly rent but also the deadweight-loss (at least in the linear case of Theorem 1). In general, as Theorem 2 shows, it is always possible to realize the surplus maximizing outcome and force the monopolist to marginal cost pricing.

These remarkable results rest on a number of important assumptions. Firstly, as the proofs of the theorems reveal, it is necessary to postulate the existence of a potentially infinite number of potential entrants. This vast pool of entrants creates sufficient "pressure" to reduce the former price-making monopolist to a price-taker *in case of entry*! That price depends on the cost function and the subsidy but *not* the monopolist's output. While this assumption is perfectly in line with the spirit of contestable markets theory, it creates a problem for the credibility of the subsidy announcement by the regulator, who cannot possibly support arbitrariliy many entrants. One may consider this a minor point, but one should be aware of the fact, that a promise of only subsidizing n entrants, $n \in N$, would lead to a rather different game (and outcome). Secondly, and more importantly, the mechanism postulates a very special form of competition among firms at stage 4. Entrants treat the incumbent's output not only as given but-practically-also as *sold* (at whatever price will result from their actions) and therefore only compete for residual demand among each other. This expectation formation facilitates entry deterrence. A probably better (and more realistic) description of competition at stage 4 is represented by an asymmetric Cournot game between incumbent and entrant. In this game all entrants would have (post entry) cost function $\bar{c}(x)$ and the incumbent would have cost function

$$\tilde{c}(x) = \begin{cases} 0 & \text{if } x \leq x_m(S) \\ \bar{c}(x - x_m(S)) & \text{if } x > x_m(S) \end{cases}$$

where $x_m(S)$ denotes output produced or committed to at stage 2. Now we could think of stage 4 as a 'production stage' for all firms, whereas stage 2 behavior allows the incumbent to commit to a cost function. Note that in this formulation the incumbent could supply more or *less* than $x_m(S)$ to the market at stage 4. This, in particular, raises the question whether the incumbent in Burnovsky and Zang's formulation really *wants* to supply his entire entry-deterring output or is merely forced to do so *by assumption*.

2. Commitment, Credibility and Welfare

Burnovsky and Zang (1991) are perfectly aware of the nature of their commitment assumption, which they describe as enforceable through court monitoring and the right to damage claims by misled entrants under tort law (see page 19 op. cit.). While this justification is acceptable in many applied contexts, it does appear weak as a general defense. From a methodological point of view this strong commitment assumption appears odd, since it is certainly in conflict with the spirit of

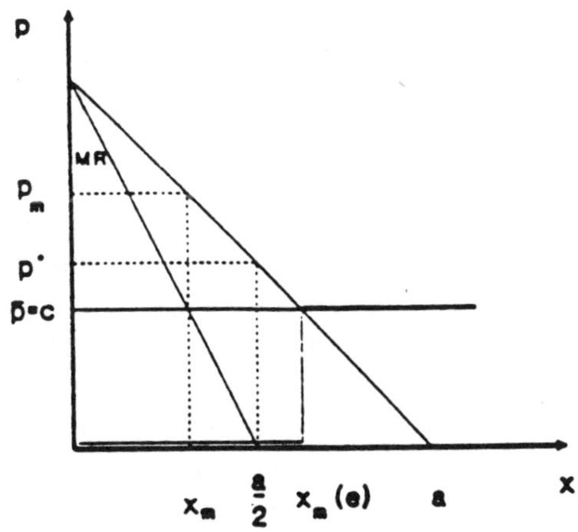

Fig. 1.

subgame-perfect (i.e. strategic non-cooperative) behavior that otherwise underlies the behavioral rules of the four-stage set-up of the regulation scheme.

The following example shows that the incumbent indeed may not have an incentive to supply the entry-deterring amount of output (at stage 4). The reader will doubtless recognize the analogy to the 'perfection' – problem which sparked off a debate on Spence's (1977) analysis of strategic entry-deterrence with the help of building excess capacity. Dixit (1980) rejected the analysis, it was later partly vindicated by Bulow, Geneakoplos and Klemperer (1985). Due to the complicating regulation stage the impact of correcting a seeming 'imperfection' is here quite different.[1]

Consider the linear case (Theorem 1) of Burnovsky and Zang.

$$P(x) = a - x \text{ and } \bar{c}(x) = c \cdot x.$$

Theorem 1 states that in equilibrium the monopolist will supply the competitive output $x_m = a - c$ in response to the regulator's promise to pay subsidy $S = e$ to any actual entrant; i.e. $x_m(S) = x_m(e) = a - c$. Imagine the monopolist's situation at the beginning of stage 4, when he observes that all potential competitors have decided to stay out. Let us assume he already *has* produced the amount of $(a - c)$ units of the good. Would he want to supply it after having incurred its cost of production? The answer is negative, instead he would supply an amount of $\frac{a}{2}$ $(< a - c)$ as is shown in Figure 1.

(p_m, x_m) denotes the (unregulated) monopoly solution; $(\bar{p}, x_m(e)) = (c, a - c)$ denotes the (competitive) outcome of the regulation game. We claim, that the monopolist has an incentive to deviate from the latter: at the last stage the monopolist-knowing he will go unchallenged-faces the cost function

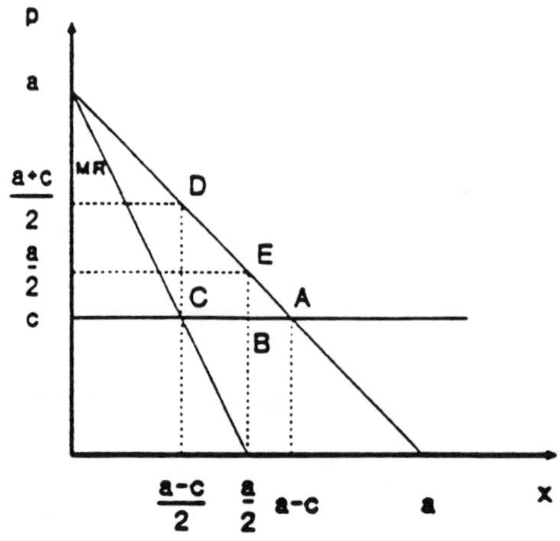

Fig. 2.

$$\tilde{c}(x) = \begin{cases} 0 & \text{if } x \leq a - c \\ c \cdot (x - (a - c)) & \text{if } x > a - c \end{cases}$$

and the profit function (excluding the cost sunk at stage 2)

$$\pi_m = x \cdot P(x) - \tilde{c}(x) \, .$$

Note that the cost of producing $(a - c)$, $c \cdot (a - c)$, is already sunk!

Equating marginal cost and marginal revenue now leads to the optimal supply of $x^* = \frac{a}{2}$ (the dotted line in Figure 1 represents $\tilde{c}'(x)$), which is sold at price $p^* = \frac{a}{2}$. As a consequence the monopolist makes a positive profit (by just maximizing revenue)

$$\pi^* = x \cdot P_m(x) - \tilde{c}(x) = \frac{a}{2} \cdot \frac{a}{2} - 0 = \frac{a^2}{4} > c \cdot (a - c)$$

since $a > 2c$ (as $\frac{a}{2} < a - c$). The overall payoff reads $(\frac{a}{2} - c)^2$. This profit is less than the (unregulated) monopoly profit $\pi_m = (\frac{a}{2} - \frac{c}{2})^2$.

However, this reduction in monopoly rent comes at the cost of considerable "waste": the monopolist produces an amount of $x_m(e) - \frac{a}{2} = \frac{a}{2} - c$ for the sole reason to deter entry as only an amount of $\frac{a}{2} = (a - c) - (\frac{a}{2} - c)$ is supplied to the market. Unfortunately, this results in an overall welfare loss compared to the unregulated monopoly solution! Consider Figure 2, which shows gains and losses due to regulation and subsequent deviation by the incumbent.

If the monopolist is not regulated profits measure at $\pi_m = (\frac{a+c}{2})$ DCc. If regulated (and no deviation is considered) they are zero. But if the monopolist deviates to a supply of $\frac{a}{2}$, then he incurs a cost of $AB(\frac{a}{2})\,(a - c)$ in order to gain profits of $BE(\frac{a}{2})\,(c)$. As shown above the latter exceeds the former constituting an *incentive* to deviate. Welfare (in case of a deviation) is then measured by

$$W_d = aEBc - BA(a-c)\left(\frac{a}{2}\right)$$

while welfare under unregulated monopoly is given by

$$W_m = aDCc.$$

Hence

$$\begin{aligned} W_d - W_m &= DEBC - BA(a-c)\left(\frac{a}{2}\right) \\ &= \left[\frac{c}{2}\left(\frac{a}{2}-c\right) + \frac{1}{2}\cdot\frac{c}{2}\cdot\frac{c}{2}\right] - \left(\frac{a}{2}-c\right)\cdot c \\ &= \frac{5}{8}c^2 - \frac{1}{4}a\cdot c < 0 \text{ iff } a > \frac{5}{2}c. \end{aligned}$$

This shows that a welfare *loss* will result from regulation, if the incumbent's commitment cannot perfectly be enforced! The commitment assumption is thus seen to be crucial and strong. There are worse market structures than monopoly: in this case it is a regulated monopoly! The regulation scheme should never 'push' the incumbent to deter entry with an output (or, for that matter, *capacity*) commitment in excess of its monopoly output *after* successful entry deterrence. Note, that the monopoly output *ex post* (i.e. after having deterred entry) is *endogeneous* to the mechanism since the commitment at stage 2 determines the cost function at stage 4. The regulator should take account of this fact when deciding on the subsidy. This point also highlights the role of the assumption regarding the existence of sufficiently many potential entrants. With just one potential entrant the incumbent could never be led to deter entry with an output commitment beyond its subsequent monopoly output (under the circumstances of Theorems 1 and 2). I.e. with just one entrant – as the received theory of strategic entry deterrence demonstrates (see e.g. Dixit, 1980) – there is no excess capacity resp. 'perfection' problem. Entry could always be deterred x with an expost optimal outpout level of less than $\frac{a}{2}$ (in response to only partial subsidization of entry).

We believe our point has some force even in the case described by Burnovsky and Zang; i.e. when the monopolist is subjected to court survaillance. Suppose an entrant-by mistake or clever anticipation of the incumbent's (monitored) incentive to deviate in case of no entry enters at stage 3. Then at the beginning of stage 4 his entry cost is sunk (and paid for by the regulator). Moreover, the entrant knows that he can share producer rent with the former monopolist if the former reduces its supply. The monopolist, in turn, has an incentive to do so, if faced with a positive supply of the entrant. It is hardly conceivable, that in this situation the regulator could "punish" the entrant for entry by taking the monopolist to court! In fact, if the entrant's supply is sufficiently high, he has no incentive to do so from his surplus maximizing point of view! Thus, a "witty" entrant could easily upset the costless indirect regulation equilibrium.

3. Perfect Indirect Regulation

The findings of the previous section suggest to explore the scope of the costless indirect regulation mechanism without *any* commitments enforced by agents who are outsiders to the game. To this extent we now allow the incumbent to decide on his *supply* at stage 4 along with the entrants, while he still can commit to a *production level*, $x_m(S)$, at stage 2. In order to stay as close as possible to the original formulation we assume, that the incumbent is *constrained* in his supply decision at stage 4 by $x_m < x_m(S)$; i.e. he cannot supply *more* than what he decided to produce at stage 2, alas, he can supply less.

3.1. THE LINEAR CASE

Obviously, the first-best outcome is now not achievable. However, as in the original analysis, it is still not desirable, neither from the incumbent's nor from the regulator's point of view, to admit entry. In order to avoid wasteful entry deterrence by the incumbent, the regulator must choose a subsidy level to which the incumbent *optimally* replies by deterring entry *and* supplying the entire entry-deterring output to the market at stage 4. Such a level of subsidy can indeed be found: from Figure 2 we infer that the incumbent will always supply less than the entry-deterring output level, x_m^d, if $MR(x_m^d) < 0$. If, on the other hand, $MR(x_m^d) \geq 0$ it is optimal to supply x_m^d (as the monopolist simply has to maximize revenue under the constraint $x_m \leq x_m^d$). Indeed, under the circumstances given, if $MR(x_m^d) > 0, x_m(S) = x_m^d$ is the monopoly output after entry deterrence. The monopoly output is x^* (determined by $MR(x^*) = 0$), if $MR(x_m^d) < 0$. It is thus socially optimal to have the entry-deterring level $x_m^d = x_m(S)$ satisfy $MR(x_m(S)) = 0$; i.e. the incumbent should be led to produce (at stage 2) and supply (at stage 4) $x_m(S) = \frac{a}{2}$.

This can be accomplished by choosing a lower subsidy S. From the analysis of Burnovsky and Zang (1991) it follows that

$$x_m(S) = a - c - 2\sqrt{e - S}$$

(e.g. in Theorem 1 $S = e$ holds). We now in addition require that

$$x_m(S) \leq \frac{a}{2}$$

and hence at the social optimum

$$S = e - \left(\frac{a}{4} - \frac{c}{2}\right)^2$$

must hold. The gain in social surplus obtainable through perfect indirect regulation is limited to $DEBC = \frac{c}{4}\left(a - \frac{3}{2}c\right)$ as can be seen from Figure 2. *Yet it is still realized at no cost*! Entry would only partially be subsidized ($S < e$). We summarize this in

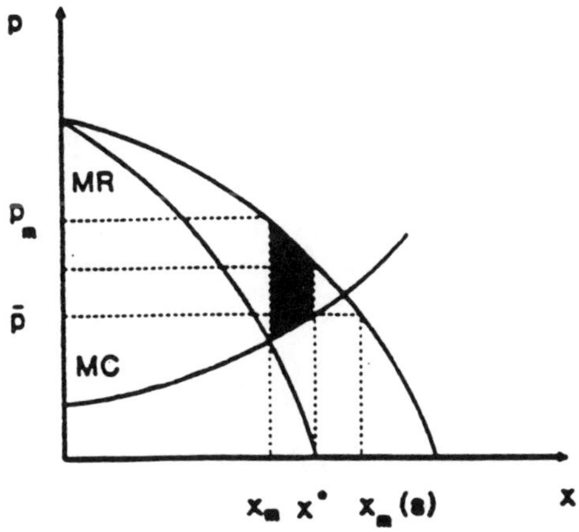

Fig. 3.

Theorem 1': With linear demand and constant marginal cost the unique subgame-perfect equilibrium has the following features: the regulator promises only partial entry subsidization ($S < e$), the monopolist commits to the minimal entry-deterring output level, which is sold at a price above marginal cost. No entry takes place.

3.2. CONVEX COST, CONCAVE DEMAND

Since the linear case treated in 3.1 might be viewed as a limiting case of the present one, it is clear that for only 'slightly' convex cost curves and only 'slightly' concave demand functions the previous arguments remain valid. Figure 3 illustrates this.

$(\bar{p}, x_m(S))$ is the solution of indirect regulation (with the commitment assumption) according to Theorem 2 which now also implies that $S < e$. However, $x^* < x_m(S)$ is the monopoly output level after successful entry deterrence. Again, the promised subsidy must be lowered in order to have $x_m^d = x_m(S) = x^*$. (It is not difficult, but tedious to show that such an S exists). The perfect indirect regulation gain in surplus is then shown as the dark area in Figure 3.

In contrast, consider the cost and demand structure of Figure 4:

The solution according to Theorem 2 is $(\bar{p}, x_m(S))$ and $x_m(S) < x^*$. The incumbent has *no* incentive to deviate as $MR(x_m(S)) > 0$. In other words, the commitment assumption is *not binding*. The monopolist can deter entry with the monopoly output level applying after entry deterrence. It is instructive to graph the latter as a function of S in a separate diagram (Figure 5).

As before, x_m and x^* denote the (unregulated) monopoly supply and the supply at which marginal revenue are zero. The dotted line in Figure 5 refers to the entry-deterring output level $x_m(S)$ as a function of S, which becomes non-existent for

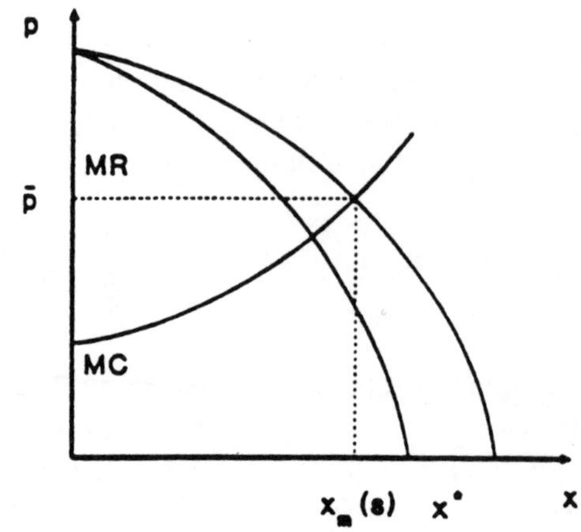

Fig. 4.

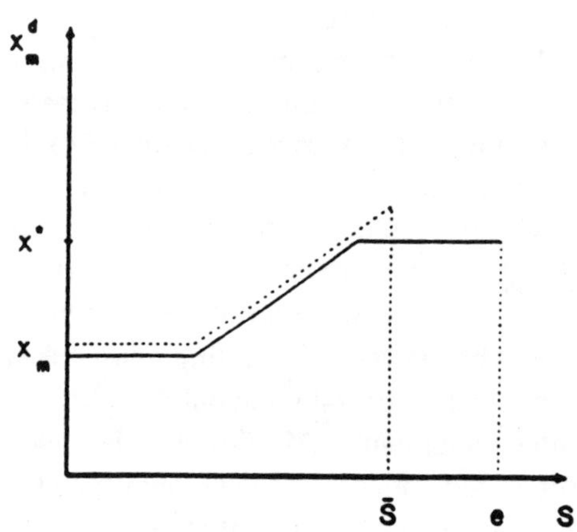

Fig. 5.

$x > \bar{S}$.

Remark: The diagrams of Figure 3 and 4 can easily be generated from demand functions of the type $P = A - x^t, t > 1$ and cost functions of the type $\bar{c}(x) = B \cdot x^2$ by suitable choice of t, A and B.

Theorem 2': With convex costs and concave demand equilibrium is unique. The monopolist makes a positive profit by producing either at or above marginal cost (depending on the elasticities of cost and demand function). Entry never takes place.

An unfortunate consequence of Theorems 1' and 2' is that the informational advantages of the original scheme are lost. Theorem 3 in Burnovsky and Zang

(1991) states that the equilibrium in case of constant marginal cost can be implemented by the regulator without knowledge of demand and cost function. He only needs to know e as $S = e$ constitutes his optimal policy. This is no longer true without the commitment assumption: for perfect indirect regulation the regulator must know the demand function (resp. the monopolist's marginal revenue curve) at least locally in order to calculate S^* leading to the 'target' output $x_m(S^*) = x^*$ (see Figure 3).

4. Concluding Comments

We have reexamined the ingenious regulation scheme put forward by Burnovsky and Zang (1991). This scheme features a regulator who promises to subsidize entry into a market, which exhibits properties of a 'natural monopoly'. If the subsidy promise is sufficiently high, entry becomes profitable (although it would be socially inefficient) and the incumbent realizes his interest in preventing entry. He therefore commits to an increased output (or capacity) level, which benefits consumers. The regulator counts on this reaction and chooses the size of the subsidy in such a way that it is never profitable for the incumbent to let entry happen. This saves him payment of the subsidy. Consequently, the monopolist is led to increase output and lower price at no cost of regulation! This argument uses the assumption that the monopolist always honors his pre-entry commitment (or is forced to do so by outside agencies). This assumption has been shown to be crucial for the results obtained, since the incumbent may have a strong incentive to deviate from his announcement. If deviation occurs the result of indirect regulation (in welfare terms) can be *worse* than the unregulated 'natural' monopoly outcome! These observations motivated our inquiry into the scope of 'costless' indirect regulation in situations in which the incumbent's commitment cannot be enforced. It then turns out that no commitment on behalf of the incumbent can be credible that deters entry by choosing an output (capacity) at a level in excess of the monopoly output *after* successful entry deterrence. The latter output level is endogenously determined through the actions of regulator and incumbent. It thus represents – as shown – an *additional constraint* for the regulator's behavior. Since he *wants* the incumbent to deter entry, he must realize that while he can drive the incumbent to commit to (and produce) surplus maximizing output levels in order to deter entry, he cannot drive him to supply those to the market. The incumbent will choose to supply the monopoly output level that applies after having successfully deterred entry. Hence the regulator is restricted to low subsidy levels, which do not 'push' the incumbent beyond this level in his effort to deter entry. Only in cases, in which the potential gains from regulation are small *a priori* (e.g. with steeply rising marginal cost) is it true, that the commitment assumption of Burnovsky and Zang is not binding. In those cases the incumbent cannot be pushed to high output levels in order to deter entry for cost reasons: steeply increasing marginal cost make it unprofitable to deter (highly subsidized entry). However, entry is not in the interest of the regulator.

Finally, note that we addressed the problem of regulating an already *existent* 'natural' monopoly, which presumes that the incumbent did not or could not foresee the subsequent perfect indirect regulation policy. If e.g. one would add a further stage at the beginning, in which the incumbent's seat is auctioned off, one could only attract bids with the incumbent's profits (after being subjected to perfect indirect regulation) being in excess of the entry cost e. This would further constrain the regulator's actions. Several topics suggest themselves for future research: the case of convex demand functions should be considered and the model should be extended in the direction of a more dynamic formulation of the competition stage. If incumbent and entrants' interact repeatedly in the market after entry the possibility of output *storage* should be considered. The approach of making a market environment *more competitive* by promising to subsidize potential entrants may then become prone to the so-called 'topsy-turvy' principle (Shapiro, 1988): any measure that makes things more competitive in a *static sense*, may make them less competitive in a *dynamic sense*, since it increases the potential to punish competitors. In the present context this could well mean, that high entry-deterring output levels by the incumbent can *induce* entrants to enter, which read them as a signal for subsequent collusive behavior (see e.g. Benoit and Krishna, 1991). The emergence of this type of equilibria can only be avoided by setting a sufficiently low level of subsidy, which in turn makes entry deterrence feasible at a relatively low production commitment.

Notes

* I like to thank Deutsche Forschungsgemeinschaft and the Economics Department at Boston University for generous support.

1. Strictly speaking, equilibria in Burnovsky and Zang (1991) are not 'imperfect'; rather, they are subgame-perfect in the presence of a very strong commitment assumption restricting the strategy set of a player.

References

Benoit, J.P. and V. Krishna (1991) 'Entry Deterrence and Dynamic Competition', *International Journal of Industrial Organization* **9**, 477–495.

Bulow, J., Geneakoplos, J., and P. Klemperer (1985) 'Holding Idle Capacity to Deter Entry', *Economic Journal* **95**, 178–182.

Burnovsky, M. and I. Zang (1991) "Costless' Indirect Regulation of Monopolies with Substantial Entry Cost', Tel Aviv University, Discussion Paper.

Dixit, A. (1980) 'The Role of Investment in Entry Deterrence', *The Economic Journal* **90**, 95–106.

Shapiro, G. (1988) 'The Theory of Oligopoly', *Handbook of Industrial Organization*.